John Jacobs' Impact on Golf

By the same author

Five Up: A Chronicle of Five Lives
The Sport of Prince's: The Reflections of a Golfer
Flying Colours: The Epic Story of Douglas Bader
Wings of War: Airmen of all nations tell their stories 1939–1945
Out of the Blue: The Role of Luck in Air Warfare 1917–1966

John Jacobs' Impact on Golf

The Man and His Methods

Laddie Lucas

Stanley Paul
London Melbourne Auckland Johannesburg

Stanley Paul & Co. Ltd
An imprint of Century Hutchinson Ltd
62–65 Chandos Place, Covent Garden, London WC2N 4NW

Century Hutchinson Australia (Pty) Ltd
16–22 Church Street, Hawthorn, Melbourne, Victoria 3122

Century Hutchinson New Zealand Limited
32–34 View Road, PO Box 40–086, Glenfield, Auckland 10

Century Hutchinson South Africa (Pty) Ltd,
PO Box 337 Bergvlei 2021, South Africa

First published 1987
Copyright © Laddie Lucas 1987

Set in Linotron Sabon by
Wyvern Typesetting Limited, Bristol

Printed and bound in Great Britain by Anchor Brendon Ltd, Tiptree, Essex

British Library Cataloguing in Publication Data
Lucas, Laddie
John Jacobs' impact on golf: the man
and his methods.
1. Jacobs, John   2. Golfers——Great
Britain——Biography
I. Title
796.352′092′4   GV964.J3/
ISBN 0-09-171450-8

Contents

Acknowledgements

I wish to express collective thanks for the help I have received from all those in the United Kingdom and Europe who have contributed so willingly to this work. By giving me their first-hand impressions of John Jacobs, and the impact he has made upon the game, they have added greatly to the authority and interest of the narrative. I am much in their debt.

One of the prime purposes in telling this story has been to expose the measure of Jacobs's teaching achievement in the United States and his influence upon American thinking. Little is known of it, yet the accomplishment is virtually without parallel in the modern British game.

To obtain the detail of Jacobs's United States work, it was necessary to lean heavily upon my American sources. I must therefore thank certain kind friends individually –

Ken Bowden, former editorial director of US *Golf Digest*, journalist, author, publisher and chronicler of Jack Nicklaus. It was he who set Jacobs on his way in the US seventeen years ago: Dick Aultman, fellow southpaw, who fastened on to the Jacobs message and now teaches golf as well as he writes about it: Shelby Futch, president and chief executive of John Jacobs Practical Golf Schools, who had the eye and the ability to exploit Jacobs's instructional genius and so build the company into the force which it is today: and two members of the US schools' teaching team – the widely experienced Bert Buehler, from Napa, California, and Donald Crawley who took the risk of leaving his native England in his early twenties to work in America, and made good. . . .

To my friend Dean Cassell, one-time vice-president of Acushnet, later president of the Dunlop Sports Company in the US and later still president of Merrill Lynch Realty's Mid-Atlantic company, I offer a special salute. Cassell has contributed much to the Anglo-American golfing cause and thereby to this story. He once matched Jacobs's teaching skills against the accuracy of a computer – and saw the human print-out win.

I also thank Doubleday & Company Inc of New York for permitting me to quote from Bobby Jones's arresting work, *Golf Is My Game* (1960). The quotations will show the reader how close is the affinity between John Jacobs's thinking about what the Americans call 'the ball-flight laws' and that of the marvel from Atlanta, Georgia, in his distinguished lifetime.

Finally, a special nod for Peter Dobereiner, *The Observer*'s golf correspondent, who has written the Preface which follows. I have an uneasy feeling my friends will say it's the best thing in the book.

Photographic Acknowledgements

For permission to reproduce copyright photographs, the author and publisher would like to thank Peter Dazeley, Bert Neale, Sport and General, the *Daily Express*, the *Evening News* and the *Sunday Standard*.

Preface
Dobereiner on Jacobs

John Jacobs once told me that it was not until he retired from competitive golf that he began really to understand the swing, adding wryly 'If only I had known then what I know now'. I am glad that he ordered his career in this back-to-front manner. The world may have lost a great player but they are ten a penny. But because John turned his intelligence and energies to teaching whilst in his prime he was able to develop into one of the most significant figures in contemporary golf as a coach. As a student of the game I was greatly influenced by his teaching. Never having been much of a performer, I took a mathematical approach, studying the dynamics of the swing and analysing what had to happen to produce a good shot. John taught me how to apply this theory. In summary his advice went like this: Start not by watching the player but the ball. The flight of the ball will tell you what the club-head was doing and that will tell you what the player was doing wrong. To conventional teachers this working back from effect to cause was also back-to-front but it surely explained why John became the most cute diagnostician in golf.

Tournament professionals are enormously bitchy about teachers. Spending much of my time in locker rooms I have heard players sounding off in blasphemous terms about Bob Toski, Henry Cotton, Jim Flick and even Ben Hogan. John has not escaped villification for what I heard described as the Jacobs shut-faced system. Having spent hours observing John at work, and having accompanied him on one of his teaching courses, I am at a loss to understand this criticism. He does not teach a system; he teaches people. He assesses a pupil's potential, decides which areas to leave well alone and concentrates on parts of the swing which will yield major improvements. His approach to the next pupil may be completely different. His method is pragmatic and individual, quite the reverse of the PGA Manual method of trying to impose a universal drill on everyone.

When he was asked to take charge of the ramshackle tournament operation he showed a rare combination of vision and sound administration, laying solid foundations for what was to become a remarkable success story. Even if he had not been the greatest teacher of his era or the father of European tournament golf I would still have admired and liked him for one reason. He is an enthusiast, a real golf person. For my money, enthusiasm washes away all sins. In John's case it is a welcome bonus on top of his achievements and doubtless in no small measure a cause of them.

PETER DOBEREINER
Golf correspondent, *The Observer*;
Associate editor, *Golf World*;
Contributing editor, US *Golf Digest*

Introduction
'Now Hit Me A Straight One'

The lesson was given on the day of Winston Churchill's funeral – 30 January 1965 – and the picture is still sharp.

John Jacobs and I had just had an early morning meeting with Mark McCormack in the American lawyer's London hotel. Then, instead of watching the former prime minister's last journey to Bladon, near Blenheim, on television with millions of others, the two of us drove out to Sandy Lodge, his old club and mine. I badly needed a cure for a golfing ill.

A searing east wind was blowing across the practice ground from left to right. For a *left hander* with a hook, the conditions were unsympathetic. 'Hit a few at that flag stick,' said Jacobs.

Three medium iron shots finished tolerably close to the target. But each ball, swinging on the wind, moved fifteen or twenty yards from left to right in the air. 'Now hit me a straight one.' I suspected the professor's tongue was in his cheek. The wind still won.

Jacobs stepped forward from behind the line of flight. Diagnosis, Explanation and Correction followed in succession, each spoken slowly and shortly in plain and positive language. He made sure the correction, and the need for it, were properly understood.

'I want you to aim forty yards to the right of the target (pointing to a spot on the horizon) keeping the ball well forward . . . Now hit it there with a firm bottom hand and forearm . . . Feel you're driving it there with a firm forearm (tapping my left forearm with his club).'

'With this wind,' I said, 'I'll hit it straight into the wood on the right.' 'Never mind,' he countered, 'just aim forty yards right and feel you're hitting it there with a firm left forearm.'

The next three shots flew straight at the stick. It was over in ten minutes.

The scenario – or something like it – must have been repeated ten thousand times in the last quarter of a century on practice grounds and golf courses in Europe, the United States and other golfing parts of the world. This is the teaching genius which has earned for Jacobs, tournament winner, Ryder Cup player and captain, the synonym, Dr Golf.

Pedigree and upbringing lie at the base of it and Lindrick, in Yorkshire, was where it all started. John Jacobs's father, Robert – Bob to all the members – was the professional at Lindrick and his mother, Vivien (no one called her anything but 'Mrs Jacobs', such was her presence and status), was the stewardess.

Bob Jacobs died prematurely when his son was nine years old, the victim of dreadful years spent in the trenches of France and Flanders in the First World War. He had been born at Brancaster just before the turn of the century, becoming assistant to 'old' Tom King, the highly respected professional at the Royal West Norfolk Club, a golf club which, like Lindrick, was shaped by the 'establishment'. Tom King had himself been apprenticed to 'old' Tom Morris at St Andrews. The lineage was unmistakable.

When Bob Jacobs died, his nephew, Jack, son of the postmaster at Brancaster, took his place. Jack Jacobs had also absorbed in boyhood the individual ethos of the Royal West Norfolk Club. He was the professional at Lindrick for more than fifty years; the members regarded him as a friend. With his humour and his natural rectitude, he became in his time an accepted influence for good in the professional game.

The early years that John Jacobs (everyone at Lindrick knew him as 'Maurice') spent under his cousin's tutelage, both on the golf course and off it, were priceless and special. Seventeen years older, cousin Jack filled the void which the boy's father had left, and set a pattern to follow.

It was a humble upbringing that Bob and Vivien Jacobs gave their family. With their son and daughter, Pam, two years older than her brother, the four lived contentedly in a tiny three-roomed flat behind the club. When the breadwinner died, and Mrs Jacobs was asked to stay on as stewardess, money was tight; pennies and shillings had to be husbanded.

The golfing start was traditional for those days. Chipping old balls off bare surfaces into sunken tin cans round the back of the caddy shed taught its rough lessons. Competition with the caddies was keen and wagers, made seriously in the currency of peg tees, had to be settled on the spot.

It is unlikely that John Jacobs's career which, in its total, composite form, is one of the most extraordinary that British golf has known, could have developed, as it has done, without the antecedents that Lindrick bestowed . . . From this beginning sprang the ambition and the drive to succeed. It is against this backcloth that the teacher has made his own way to the top, not only here in Europe, but, more remarkably now, in the United States. Yet the extent of the story is still barely known.

Jacobs attracts a fanatical loyalty among his followers. He has also drawn criticism and vehement opposition, and even at one stage enmity, to his side. Success and a strong, dogmatic personality can usually be relied on to arouse such a mixture of emotions. But no one will keep ability hidden for long.

When Colin Snape was starting his fourteen-year stint as the executive head of the Professional Golfers' Association, Jacobs, then the tournament director-general, was making his name as the architect of the modern European Tour in the face of well-marshalled opposition. The two men were openly at loggerheads.

I once asked Snape whether he thought there was another member of the PGA at the time who could have done the executive job that Jacobs then did for the tour, amid all the traumas. 'You saw it all,' I said, 'and no one could accuse you of being biased in the former director-general's favour.'

The executive director paused longer than I expected. 'No,' he said, 'there was no one.'

PART ONE

CLIMB TO THE SUMMIT

1
'French: Wastes Time'

Schooldays leave legacies which are usually retained for life. A master's example remembered . . . a trick of learning preserved . . . a habit dispensed: all are ingrained in the youthful memory for ever, and more often than not for the pupil's benefit.

With John Jacobs, the process was, in a sense, reversed. It was, paradoxically, from what he thought were certain teachers' short-comings that he gained experience for the future. As a boy, he did not learn quickly, but when once something had been properly explained – and understood – it stuck. In his initial terms at Maltby Grammar School, he found that, often, explanations given in class either lacked clarity or were rushed, or both. It made it much harder to assimilate a thesis first time; and he did not like to ask for things to be repeated. But such was his determination to get at the basics, and comprehend the principles of what he was being taught, that, as time went on, he developed the practice of going to a master after class and asking for the proposition to be explained a second (or even a third) time – slowly. He seldom had trouble memorizing the work after that.

The lesson was not forgotten. 'I'm sure this taught me the absolute necessity in my own teaching of explaining everything to do with the golf swing *slowly*,' says Jacobs. 'It isn't that one is teaching down to a pupil; rather that I want to be totally satisfied that the diagnosis, explanation and corrections are understood. And this means that one must speak clearly and very deliberately. Rush an explanation and it becomes confusing. Present it slowly and it is much easier to get across.'

One may learn much about the character and temperament of this golfing tutor by examining his progress at school. Its vicissitudes find

3

their echoes in later life.

His first school, at Woodsetts, was a mile or so from his home, just across Lindrick Common. When he started there as a new boy in January 1930, he was still a couple of months short of his fifth birthday which fell on 14 March. Yet, even at that age, he always walked with his sister, Pam, two years his senior, to and from school. How many parents nowadays would let a four year old and a six year old walk to school unattended, albeit in the country? From the beginning, young Jacobs was left to think and act independently. This was never for want of caring; rather, his parents believed that at an early age, as far as possible, their son should act on his own.

It was when he moved on to Maltby Grammar five years later, in the autumn of 1935, that the signs of the embryo man truly began to emerge. Sadly, his father had died the year before and his upbringing was then left in the able and courageous hands of his mother, and to the vigilant guidance of cousin Jack, who was then the Lindrick club's new professional.

All his life, Jacobs has felt able to handle responsibility. Some are born number ones and make poor number twos. Others slip naturally into the number two slot and never crave to be number one. They are essential to a team which is well led, yet their qualities are not those of a true leader. Given the top spot, they usually fall short of its needs. Jacobs is a good number one, but much less effective at number two, unless the leader is someone who commands his special respect. He prefers to order things his way. Conversely, his attributes are not fully employed below the summit, and interest and incentive suffer.

There was a plain hint of this as a new boy at Maltby, a seat of good basic learning. Still under eleven, and nearly a year younger than the average age of his class, Jacobs showed little inclination to pursue his studies. Frankly, he could not see the purpose of them and, anyway, his thoughts lay elsewhere. This is reflected in his initial report. In the light of what was to follow, it is instructive to pick out a few of the criticisms. Twenty-nine pupils in the form, 1B, had sat the terminal examination. Jacobs had finished an indisputable twenty-ninth. Comment was, therefore, direct:

English: Lacks effort and interest.

History and geography: Most disappointing; shows no interest.

French: Wastes time.

General science: Needs to work much harder.

His form master, Mr E. Illingworth, summed it up: 'This is a very poor report indeed. Jacobs has been at the bottom of the form throughout the term and in the examination he obtained less than one third of the total marks. Very hard work and much greater interest will be necessary next term. Conduct: unsatisfactory.'

It was the school's custom to require a parent to sign their child's report as having noted its contents. Mrs Jacobs's signature, in bold and clear handwriting, appears at the end: *Vivien Jacobs*. It is dated 8 January 1936. With school fees running at three guineas a term, which, in the values of those days, represented quite a burden for the hard-pressed family, she must have wondered about the return her son was obtaining on her investment.*

The truth was, of course, that in his first year or so at Maltby Jacobs had no concern whatever for school work. He was absorbed with other things – games, which he played naturally well, country activities and golf. He loved them all, as he did his modest home. It enabled him, years later, to declare with spontaneous feeling, 'I had a wonderful childhood. There was little money in the family, but my mother made sure that neither my sister, Pam, nor I wanted for anything. I was so happy as a boy.'

Maybe he was a bit too happy. It became a standing joke in his form that, when the headmaster, Mr G. Rush, was dealing in class with the end-of-term reports and he came to Jacobs, the following dialogue – or something like it – would invariably ensue:

HEADMASTER: How many nights a week do you play golf, Jacobs, and how many nights a week do you do your prep?
JACOBS: I play golf every evening, sir.
HEADMASTER: Obviously.

The headmaster probably knew quite well that it wasn't only golf which caused havoc with the pupil's studies. At Christmas 1938, as he approached his fourteenth birthday, the teenager was given a double-barrelled .410 shotgun – 'a beautiful little gun, the best present I ever had'. It became the light of his young life. And here the tutelage of his cousin, Jack, who had now turned thirty, was of timely and lasting worth.

Jack Jacobs, as befitted a fine shot, was a stickler for all the gun-handling disciplines. Safety, beyond all else, must come first. There

---

*Jacobs has never forgotten his mother's reaction to one criticism in this report. 'Never bring home another report with 'conduct unsatisfactory' in it,' she warned. He never did.

could not have been a stricter, or better, mentor: 'If I put half a foot wrong, Jack was down on me like a ton of bricks. He never missed a mistake.'

Cousin Jack was himself a frequent guest of the owners of some of the coveted shoots in Yorkshire and Nottinghamshire – the Dukes of Portland and Newcastle, Edward Dixon, Sir Albert Bingham, Lady Laycock 'and with every member of Lindrick who had a shoot'. Not only was he the professional at Lindrick, he was also a friend of the 'establishment' – 'Lord Lindrick' was the pseudonym the locals often gave him.

Gordon Dixon, son of Edward, who played golf for Cambridge in the 1930s, has the plainest recollection of the special relationship: 'Jack was a very great friend, with whom I enjoyed many days on the racecourse, and shooting, as well as on the golf course . . . I have a clear memory of going into his shop by the first tee one morning and Jack turning to Maurice (John), a tall, dark, good-looking lad, and saying, "Maurice, get Mr Gordon's clubs out, please . . ." There was "Mr" John and "Mr" David, as well as "Mr" and "Mrs" Dixon, in those days . . .'

Jack Jacobs was determined that his young cousin's early promise on the golf course should be matched by his mastery over a gun and a thoroughgoing knowledge of the etiquette of field and covert. He well knew that these things, learned young, are never forgotten; they become automatic and are instantly recognizable the moment a man picks up a gun. The times the two spent together, walking with their guns and dogs over the farmland surrounding Lindrick Common and the course, still make for each a treasured memory.

There was one autumn afternoon in the late 1930s which John Jacobs remembers as magical. There were, at the time, several good coveys of partridges on the neighbouring Deepcar Farm. On this day, he and his cousin had walked over the land (as they were always able to do) with their dogs and driven the birds across the boundary onto the golf course and common. With all the gorse there was about in those days, the cover was plentiful. The subsequent walk through the rough and gorse bordering the fairways brought a rich bonus: 'Jack and I knew pretty well where the coveys had settled. At the end of it, seventeen birds lay dead on the second fairway.'

For John Jacobs, that was only the start. Years later, pheasants at Tetworth, Sir Peter Crossman's estate in Bedfordshire, partridges in Pakistan with the chief of the air staff of the Pakistan air force, Air Marshal Asghan Khan, and duck by the score in the Nile delta with members of King Farouk's entourage, all became a part of Lindrick's heritage.

Apart from the shooting, there is also now no difficulty in tracing Jacobs's lifelong affair with rod and line back to his schooldays. Once again his cousin Jack played an important role: 'I'd collect John from his home behind the club at eight o'clock sharp in the morning, with his rod and the packet of sandwiches his mother had made up for him. Then we'd drive the seven or eight miles over to Welbeck Lakes, where I would leave him for the day. At seven o'clock in the evening, I'd go back and fetch him and get him home in time for supper. They were happy days for him at Welbeck, I'm sure of that, and the times we spent together in those years prepared him for the two leisure recreations of his life.'

Of the two pastimes, fishing has probably given Jacobs more genuine respite from his taxing schedule. The days he has spent at Two Lakes and on the rivers Test, Avon and Tweed, fishing with friends, totally absorbed and occupied, have provided a mental and physical release which nothing else has quite matched. Since his boyhood days at Welbeck, he has become a thoroughly able fisherman.

Richard Doyle-Davidson, who for many years has presided over the golfing affairs, first of Formby, and later of Wentworth, is well placed to judge: 'I have watched John casting a fly and can only describe his action in golfing terms as being of plus-four standard. Most people who fly fish have a pretty fair action, but his is outstanding. He can throw out the longest line and yet present the fly lightly and accurately to a fish. Like his short approach shots to the pin, he can put the fly just where he wants it – and consistently.'

Recalling Maltby Grammar, one can see that Mr Rush clearly had a point when he underscored the conflict between Jacobs's early studies at school and the attraction of his golf and his other boyhood pursuits. Scholarship was unlikely, in the initial stages, ever to win.

The change in Jacobs's fortunes at school came slowly. As he progressed to the sixth form, won his colours for cricket and football and found responsibility thrust upon him, so his attitude to school life altered: 'I think a sense of realism came into it.' He knew he must get a School Certificate. Moreover, having gained places in the cricket and football elevens, he badly wanted the teams to win; and after being made vice-captain of his house, Bart's, he recognized that a lead should be given.

He had, in a word, become interested in what he was doing. There had never been any doubt about his predilection for games and team

7

spirit, but now, for the first time, he could feel a purpose in school life itself. He responded to his new responsibilities, finding it neither difficult nor worrying to be 'put in charge'.

The contrast between the inauspicious start at Maltby and his eventual achievements can be seen from three short extracts from his final report. They were written in the spring of 1942, when he was just seventeen. First, the games master, Mr W. J. Wright: 'Jacobs's achievements on the games field have been of the highest order. With the school football and cricket teams, he has shown great skill and enthusiasm. This ability has been matched by his sportsmanship.'

Next, his housemaster, Mr F. H. Kemp, spoke of his 'outstanding worth as a member of Bart's . . .' and added, with a touch of nostalgia, 'We shall cherish happy memories of his comradeship and support.' Then the headmaster confirmed the transformation which the adolescent years had brought: 'John R. M. Jacobs . . . has spent one and a half terms in the VIth form. He [has] obtained his School Certificate, reaching credit standard in English literature and history, and passing in geography, mathematics, physics and chemistry and handicraft* . . . His work has been very satisfactory and good, steady progress has been made . . . He [has] devoted himself unselfishly to house and school activities . . . His developing powers of leadership were recognised when he was appointed a prefect of the school and, later, given sergeant's stripes in the school ATC.' The headmaster ended by thanking Jacobs for his 'loyal services'.

Two other events in the Lindrick years were to cast their shadows.

Jacobs had spent much of his early childhood on nearby Deepcar Farm, watching and, when he could, joining in the work. He enjoyed the farm days and his involvement with the animals. Then, in 1942, just after Jacobs had left Maltby, the owner of the farm, Billy Clarkson, became ill with ringworm which he had caught from one of the animals. It was an illness which could be dangerous in those pre-antibiotic days and the unfortunate Clarkson had to spend weeks in hospital. In his absence Jacobs ran the farm with a fifteen-year-old to help him: 'It was mixed farming. We grew corn, and there was a herd of sheep, and a milking herd. I did all the tractor work and the ploughing. We worked horses then and did the harvesting, building stacks, and so on. I was as strong as an ox and could carry an eighteen

* Mrs Jacobs had insisted on her son taking woodwork. His father had shown him something of the clubmaking and club repairing art at a time when wooden clubs were still made by hand. It was already clear that he could work well with his hands.

stone sack of corn. When you're chucked in at the deep end and find yourself loaded with the responsibility, you have to get on with it.'

This year's experience, and the familiarization with land, soil and grass, was later to pay dividends. From the time he joined the Athlon board in the 1960s, and began designing and constructing golf centres and courses, right up to the present, that early, practical contact with the earth stood Jacobs in good stead.

Three or four years before he ran the farm, there had been another experience which was to have a far-reaching effect upon the golfer in Jacobs. He had been taken by his mother to see the 1938 Open Championship at Sandwich. He was recovering from the effects of the first of two major abdominal operations within five years, the second being at the insistence of the Royal Air Force to enable him to obtain the A1B medical category necessary to qualify for flying duties. The days on the east Kent coast were intended not only to widen his golfing knowledge, but also to hasten his return to his normal robust health. It was, however, a year before he was fit enough to pass the service medical, which gave him the extra twelve months' experience on the farm.

1938 was the year of the great gale at St George's which Henry Longhurst, the golfing journalist and TV commentator, later captured in a few graphic phrases:*

> When I got to the course, the marquee, the biggest I've ever seen, was looking like a great eight-masted ship with tattered canvas. Seams were splitting like the tearing of gigantic calico, and the billowing canvas was heaving and straining to bring the whole contraption to the ground. The stalls of the manufacturers ... were smashed like matchwood. Steel-shafted clubs were twisted into grotesque figures of eight ... Pullovers, shirts, scarves, mittens, hats and caps were blown wildly across to Prince's nearby and thence into the sea ... Fantastic were the tales of woe ... Rounds of 90, 95 and even 100 were ... commonplace – and this among the last forty survivors, presumably the finest golfers in Great Britain.

That was the scene on the last day of the championship when Henry Cotton, the defending champion,** then at the peak of his career,

---

*It Was Good While It Lastest, J. M. Dent, London, 1941.
**He had won brilliantly at Carnoustie the previous year, beating the might of a very strong US Ryder Cup team, which included Nelson, Snead, Sarazen, Horton Smith, Dudley, Picard, Shute and others, in the process.

played the final thirty-six holes at St George's in 77 and 74 for a 151 total – two strokes better than anyone else in the field. It did not bring victory – Reggie Whitcombe prevailed by three shots – but his striking that day, through the eye of the gale, was to be remembered by all who were lucky enough to see it.

For the thirteen-year-old Jacobs, the first sight of Cotton, on the practice ground at Sandwich, had an electric effect: 'I can see Henry now, hitting balls to his caddy 150 yards or so away, with his left arm alone. The balls were dropping one after another at the caddy's feet. The impression I was left with was that the fellow never had to move to pick them up. It was marvellous for me, at my age, being able to watch someone like that. For the next umpteen years, every time I played golf I was Henry Cotton.'

Sixteen years and a world war later, Jacobs was to succumb to Cotton in the final of the Penfold 2000 Guineas Tournament at Llandudno, in Wales.

Jacobs has rarely misjudged a golfer's talents. When he saw Cotton at St George's, he knew, even then, that he was witnessing something special. He may not have known that it was his first introduction to greatness, but it certainly established an impression which the passage of half a century has done nothing to dim. Cotton had become in Jacobs's youthful mind the yardstick by which others' skills would for years thereafter be measured.

2
Hallamshire's Pluses

Like many other young men who had volunteered for flying duties with the Royal Air Force during the Second World War, John Jacobs longed for the day when he could complete his training and get into the air against the enemy. The trainee had already had a taste of flight at Lindrick. Captain Halcombe, a club member, had been a pilot with the Royal Flying Corps in the First World War. He and his wife kept a de Havilland Tiger Moth and a Moth Minor at the local airfield at Netherthorpe, three miles from the course. Halcombe knew how keen Jacobs was to become a pilot and, whenever there was a chance, he would take the boy up and put the little biplane through its paces. Once in the air, he would usually hand over the controls to the occupant of the front seat. Jacobs knew very well that not all the manoeuvres to which he was treated would be found in the *Flying Manual*: 'Captain Halcombe was a very experienced pilot and he would often come down low, run the Tiger Moth's wheels along the sixteenth fairway, the long par five, before opening the throttle fully and zooming up over the clubhouse. All the windows would fly open as people looked out to see what was happening. Then he would climb up again, come round once more and repeat the performance. It was very exciting.'

One suspects that the veteran pilot probably enjoyed it almost as much as his passenger.

Halcombe ran a gliding school at Netherthorpe and looked after the local Air Training Corps squadron. He gave the young cadets glider training. Jacobs took quickly to handling these powerless aircraft and it wasn't many days before he was going solo and qualifying for a glider pilot's licence. His tutor gave him a high rating, said he had the

11

qualities of a born leader and recommended him as officer material; then he persuaded him to stay on at the school as an instructor. All this only increased Jacobs's appetite for the real thing.

When his chance eventually came, in 1944, he was understandably disappointed to be told by the Royal Air Force that, at that late stage of the war, they had all the pilots they needed and that he would be invited to remuster and undergo training as a flight engineer. Bomber Command's great night bombing offensive, under the aggressive direction of Air Chief Marshal Sir Arthur Harris, was in its final and most lethal phase. Flight engineers and air gunners were the current requirement for the crews of the Lancasters and Halifaxes.

Although Jacobs readily accepted the switch, he made it clear that his was not a technical mind and that the intricacies of the products of Rolls-Royce and Bristol were quite foreign to him. 'I just learned the stuff off parrot-fashion,' he says now, 'enough to enable me to pass all the exams and complete my course.'

It was something of an anti-climax when Germany surrendered to the Allies just as his flight engineer's wing was pinned on his tunic. Still, he had thoroughly enjoyed his time in the service and was sorry when it was all over. The cricket and the football, and all the inter-unit games in which he had played, had appealed to him and so had the easy friendships he was able to make. He had appreciated the spirit and the comradeship.

John Jacobs's experience of war had been in merciful contrast to the appalling time his father had had to endure a quarter of a century earlier. Bob Jacobs had fought on the western front virtually throughout the First World War. He had served in the Sportsmen's Battalion of the Royal Fusiliers with three others whose names were synonymous with professional golf – James Bradbeer, Horace Fulford, and Ernest Jones, who was later to settle in the United States and earn for himself a reputation in the interwar years as one of the game's most successful teachers.

Bob Jacobs who was himself a good teacher, had played a little-known part in Ernest Jones's survival from the war. In a German attack on British positions, a hand grenade had been hurled into the trench close to where Jones was standing. The explosion caused him awful injury and resulted in the loss of a leg. However, had Jacobs and his golfing friends not been there to bring two stretcher bearers to their wounded comrade, he could never have lived to develop his world-renowned practice of 'swinging the clubhead'. With a penknife tied to the end of a pocket handkerchief, Jones would demonstrate his lifelong belief in the game's true 'secret'. 'Swing the clubhead,' he would say, 'and everything else will fall into place.'

John Jacobs's demobilization from the Royal Air Force, in 1947, coincided with the advertising of a vacancy for an assistant to Willie Wallis at the Hallamshire club, to the west of Sheffield. As Wallis was then sixty-four, and believed to be approaching retirement, the response to the advertisement was unusually strong and included established professionals as well as aspiring assistants. The lucky candidate might well expect, within a short time, to drop into his master's shoes.

Jacobs presented himself for interview by the club's popular secretary, Tom Woodward, 'a delightful character and a former chief of the Sheffield police'. The applicant was twenty-two at the time, fit, personable and good-looking. With a thatch of curly black hair running down to a pronounced V in the centre of his forehead, he cut quite a dash. His bearing, recent service discipline and clarity of speech, plus his Lindrick background, gave him the edge over his rivals.

At the end of the interview Woodward asked him whether he had a question to put.

'Yes, sir,' he replied, 'might I inquire which day I can expect to have off each week?'

'There are no days off in this job,' came the reply.

A short while later, Jacobs was required to play a few holes with Sidney Banks, the Yorkshire and England player and a member of the club. It was a blustery summer's evening, not at all easy for golf, particularly when under close scrutiny. But all went well; Jacobs's game and conduct seemed to satisfy Banks's discerning taste and within no time the club confirmed his appointment.

Long hours, no days off, no annual holiday and a maximum of ten days off a year to play in the local Sheffield and Yorkshire competitions – this, and a hard task-master. It would not have had much appeal for the modern trade unionist. But Jacobs thought nothing of the regimen. Here was a chance to get started at what, at Lindrick, with just the faintest trace of aristocratic disdain, they regarded as the 'second best club in the Sheffield area'.

Although Hallamshire was on the other side of Sheffield from Lindrick, and an hour's bus journey away, the new assistant continued to live at home with his mother in the winter months. He caught the 7.55 am bus each day, and one Christmas morning he had to leave home at 5 am to be on duty at the appointed hour. But there was always his mother's cooking to come home to at night. It was one of her prime concerns to see that her son was properly fed.

Her cooking and the food at Lindrick enjoyed an exceptional rating even by Yorkshire's culinary standards. Sir John Cradock-Hartopp remembers it well: 'We thought the food Mrs Jacobs gave us was the best to be found at any golf club in the country. Nothing ever tasted so good as the bread and the rolls and the buns she baked herself.'

Jack Jacobs has a similar recollection: 'In my early days at the club, I seemed to spend a lot of my time in the kitchen, sampling the soups and the various dishes. Auntie Viv's cooking had a reputation all over Yorkshire. I remember our game always used to be cooked in milk, with a little water added just to soften the birds. Bacon and butter covered the breast. One Christmas I recall seeing the turkey cooked that way.'

For Peter Alliss, thirty-four years have likewise done nothing to dim the memory of Vivien Jacobs's breakfast: 'It was 1953 and the Stuart Goodwin foursomes at Lindrick. John and I had driven up overnight in his enormous left-hand-drive American Ford. We woke up to a lovely autumn morning with the dew and the mist and the sun just breaking through. "Come on," said John, "I expect mother has got some breakfast for us."

'You never saw such a sight. Wartime austerity still wasn't far away, but there was a great dish on the table, big enough to take a thirty-pound turkey. There must have been ten or a dozen eggs, all neatly arranged round the outside; and inside there was the lot – kidneys, bacon, sausage, liver, mushrooms, chops, tomatoes and fried bread. And, to back it, a couple of racks of thick, hot toast and an enormous jug of coffee – not that *ersatz*, tasteless stuff we'd been drinking, but the real thing, freshly ground and steaming . . . 'Cor what a memory!'

The summer days at Hallamshire were, however, too long (8.00 am till dark) to allow the assistant to go on living at home. Instead, he lodged with a local bus driver's family near the course. Bed and breakfast cost him twenty-seven shillings and sixpence a week, which was just about all he could afford for his living out of the three pounds ten shillings a week retainer he was receiving from Wallis and the club. He had met Rita Wragg while he was still in the Royal Air Force and he had already made up his mind that she was the girl for him. He must try, he felt, to put a few pounds away if he was to be in a position to marry.

If the work was hard, there were a number of pluses at Hallamshire to set against it.

All his life, Jacobs has been fortunate with the people he has worked with. There have been exceptions, of course, but generally his connections have benefited his career. This may partly have been a matter of choice: by instinct a delegator, and exacting and firm, Jacobs tends to be able to discern similar qualities which appeal to him in others. However, luck also had something to do with it.

In the case of the Hallamshire job, he was undeniably lucky at the outset of a professional career to have come under the wing of Willie Wallis, one of the 'old school', and a strict and punctilious master. Wallis's service as assistant to the immortal J.H. Taylor at Royal Mid-Surrey, near Richmond, in Surrey, had taught him a lot of the skills, but, above all, it had taught him the value of precision, rectitude and respect in the shop. His example wasn't lost on his assistant: 'If you forgot and put a chisel down on the bench the wrong way up – not on the bevelled side – so that it dulled the blade, Willie would never let you forget it. He was a corker, but he was good for me at that time.'

Although Wallis was probably best known for his expertise as a first-class clubmaker, he had deservedly also built a reputation for himself in the Sheffield area as a good teacher. He was steeped in golf as a game, and did not regard it simply as a means of acquiring a livelihood. He thus acted as a guide and counsellor for the young man as he stood at the threshold of a golfing career.

'Willie used to talk golf to me because he was interested. If I wasn't playing well, I'd say to him, "Please, come and have a look at me, I'm not hitting it well." And he would do just that. It might only be for ten minutes, but you felt he was interested enough to do it willingly. I remember so well the advice which he gave me. "You've got to turn," he would say, "got to get the lumbar muscles working, and you've got to cock your wrists." I never thought about it at the time – I didn't then know anything about it – but I tried to do what he told me.

'I had played golf from childhood – had a club in my hand from the time I could stand up. I suppose, at fifteen or sixteen, I could get round Lindrick on occasions in under seventy, but at other times I would have to walk in from the course because I had run out of golf balls. I was gifted in the sense of being able to hit the ball because I had grown up with it and had the chance of watching fine players in the area – Arthur Lees, Frank Jowle, Johnny Fallon and, of course, my cousin, Jack. So when Willie Wallis said to me. "You must turn your body and use your lumbar muscles and you must cock the wrists," I took notice of it.

'Today, I will tell pupils they must turn the body because you have to do that to get the clubhead swinging from inside to inside, and you must cock the wrists otherwise the club will follow the body too much. What Willie was saying was similar to what I am saying today. The difference is that I explain it, whereas he didn't.'

It was, however, the clubmaking skills that Wallis instilled in Jacobs which brought lasting advantage. His products, which he both wholesaled and retailed, were fashioned and finished to a uniformly high level of workmanship. The size of this side of his business may be judged by the number of staff he employed. In the 1930s, he had eight clubmakers working for him in the shop. Jacobs comments, 'After the war, and as he neared retirement, obviously things were different, but he remained to the end a fine clubmaker and a very good teacher.'

It was in the winter that the clubmaking activity went on apace. For the assistant, there was little respite. 'From September through until April or May – and it was so cold and windy up there on those Yorkshire moors in winter – I used to make a lot of golf clubs. I'd make wood after wood, and by about February I'd have stacks and stacks of sets of woods all made up but none of them finished. In those days, you had to do all the sandpapering, staining, varnishing, french polishing and finishing yourself.

'And Willie would look at all these sets and say to me: "When are you going to finish those clubs off?" So I then had six or eight weeks of it . . . Oh! the misery of it . . . sandpapering and finishing all those flipping clubs. I'll never forget it. But Willie injected into me a lot of the art of making good wooden clubs and for this I have always been grateful.'

Despite the long hours working in the shop, the assistant also found good opportunities at the club for developing his game. Yorkshire golf is nothing if not competitive, and there were always keen, hard games to be had. Now and then, there would be the chance to play in some of the Sheffield and Yorkshire competitions which, in those days, carried a lot of local prestige.

The Yorkshire Professional Foursomes of 1947, played at North-cliffe, near Shipley, offered just such an opportunity to test himself against the best in the county. Jacobs has for long been a bull of the now sadly rare foursomes game – playing alternate shots with a partner. Twenty-two at the time, he teamed up with Alfred Sanders, the Horsforth professional, 'a lovely little man,' and the two of them, blending well together, prevailed over some formidable Yorkshire opposition. 'I might say that my partner did all the good stuff . . . but I remember afterwards travelling back to Lindrick by train very late at night and having to throw pebbles up at the window to get my mother to let me in. As she put her head out of the window to see who it was, I said: "There, would you believe it we won!" She just replied. "Your father won that competition in 1929, playing with Allan Dailey."'

Jacobs's transparent enthusiasm for the game got another lift in the following year, 1948, when he tied with Johnny Fallon for the Yorkshire Professional Championship. Fallon was to be his partner five years later in the Ryder Cup match against the USA at Palm Springs, California, when, playing top, they won Britain's only point in the 36-holes foursomes. His two-round total of 144 at Oakdale, near Harrogate, repaid some of the hard work he was then investing in his game and gave him the feeling that things were moving forward. He lost the replay, but this performance, together with the win in the Yorkshire Professional Foursomes in the previous year, convinced him that he was now capable of holding his own in good professional company.

Something else was happening at Hallamshire which was important to the twenty-four-year-old's career. The number of lessons he was giving was mounting steadily and his pupils were coming back for more. What he taught them in those days bore little resemblance to the concept which he is currently spreading around the world; but he had a compelling way with him and already he was developing a teaching style which, above all, seemed to make things simple and plain. His teaching was never convoluted or hackneyed.

Moreover, his good looks and 'macho' physique, splashed about with a flavouring of direct Yorkshire humour, gave him an appeal which was not lost on the girls. Although he had yet to think it all through, he had begun to feel a confidence in his ability to teach. More surprisingly, perhaps, he found that tuition, which was pain and grief to some, absorbed him.

It wasn't many weeks after his marriage, on 25 January 1949, and the honeymoon which had been spent in London – the first time that Jacobs had seen the capital – that the combined will and ambition of the couple began to be directed beyond the shop at Hallamshire and the boundaries of the Yorkshire moors. It was a long, hot summer that year and, given the extended hours which the breadwinner was now working and the fact that Wallis, now past his sixty-sixth birthday, showed no sign of early retirement, the desire grew for a change.

'Rita and I were both getting fed up,' Jacobs remembers. 'I was doing everything in the shop, opening it up in the morning and locking up after dark. Willie used to leave each evening at 6.40 – if he was in the middle of selling a set of clubs he'd still leave at 6.40 – to go up to the pub. Everything was left to me, including writing out the cheques for Willie to sign. He was as happy as a lark and so was the club; everyone was happy except Rita and me.'

The chance, when it came, to make a clean break, leave Yorkshire and the countryside of his upbringing for Egypt and the Middle East, was compelling. The interview in London for the professional's job at the Gezira Sporting Club in Cairo seemed to go well. Jacobs had no difficulty in putting himself across with confidence. His performance won him the offer of the post, with a six months' probationary period on either side.

The newlyweds did not agonize over the decision, as many might have done. It did not seem to them at the time to represent an unreasonable risk, nor did the prospect of a major switch in their lives make any impact. They were young, in love and had little money. They were ready for adventure. They felt, in a way, that the opportunity was 'meant'. The two, even then, shared a strong Christian faith and believed that, come what might, a Guiding Hand was never very far away.

All the same, aged twenty-four and twenty-two respectively, it was still for them a major step. It wasn't like taking a job in Europe, as a number of professional golfers had done in the past. Rita Jacobs may well have appreciated the significance of it rather more acutely than her husband: 'Without TV in those days, there were none of those nightly pictures of far-off places to make them familiar. Going to the Nile in 1949 seemed like visiting "darkest Africa".'

When, two and a half years later, the political stability of Egypt was threatened and the pair decided that the time had come to return to the UK, Jacobs had no doubt that the decision they had taken to go abroad had been right. Thirty-five years on, he is even more certain of the good sense of their original judgement: 'Of all the decisions I've made in my golfing career, the one to up sticks in September 1949, at the age of twenty-four, and go out to Gezira, was the most important and best I've ever taken. When I came back to Britain after shouldering all that responsibility, almost any normal situation seemed easy to cope with.'

From the standpoint of his own game, he missed not being able to compete regularly in the few British tournaments which were held in those times. Indeed, such was the demand in Egypt for lessons from his wealthy and cosmopolitan clientele, European and American as well as Egyptian, that his time for playing there was extremely limited. His rounds on the course were restricted to Wednesday afternoon and

Sunday, which was his day off.

For the business, diplomatic and international community in Egypt, golf had become the fashionable pursuit; its adherents and would-be participants flocked to Gezira, not only because there was now a personable and engaging young Englishman available to give them lessons, but also because it was the 'right thing' to do socially. With his wife working in the shop, and three Egyptian assistants to help him, Jacobs's time was given up almost wholly to teaching:

'I taught a tremendous amount. In my first six months at Gezira, my lesson book was full for six or nine months ahead. With that kind of thing, and with people booking up automatically so far ahead, one was bound to get pupils forgetting or not turning up. Eventually, at the end of the first six months, we scrubbed all the previous arrangements and just dealt with lessons four weeks ahead, and every one had to be booked on the first Monday in each month.

'We then got what we called the "mink coat and chauffeurs queue" on the first Mondays in the month. Chauffeurs and servants and fur-coated ladies all queued up to book. By the end of the morning every session had been taken for the following four weeks.'

Another system was then introduced. All lessons booked on the first Monday in the month had to be reserved by the pupil in person. Beyond this, no more than two half-hour lessons could be booked by the same person in any one week, and bookings would not be taken over the telephone. There were complaints, but the couple stuck it out and after the initial objections, things settled down and remained calm for the rest of their stay at Gezira.

Michael Lunt, former Amateur champion, captain of England and British Walker Cup player, is one of the few still about who saw the English professional at work on the polo ground at Gezira. On leave then from his national service in Africa, Lunt retains an impression of his first sight of the teacher for whom he was later to develop a lasting regard: 'My recollection is of seeing buckets and buckets of balls lined up under the awning, with onlookers sitting at tables in the shade, sipping cool drinks. Players of all sorts were hitting balls down the ground , with John, very much in charge, giving his attention to a not particularly promising pupil. Looking back now, I remember thinking that it was rare to see such activity on a club's practice ground. John was probably well ahead of his time.'

It would have been difficult for Jacobs's teaching technique not to have benefited from the Gezira experience. As far as his playing was concerned, he found a model. Serving with him at Gezira at the same time was the immensely talented Hassan Hassanein, who, between 1945 and 1954, won the Egyptian Desert Championship nine times, the Egyptian Open three times and the Match-Play Championship once, beating the redoubtable Australian Norman von Nida by one hole in the final.

Born half Sudanese and half Egyptian, Hassanein was winning the Italian Open at Villa d'Este, with a 72-hole total of 263, when, in the autumn of 1949, Jacobs arrived in Gezira. It was the first time he had played outside Egypt. He followed this two years later with a win in the French Open at St Cloud, bringing off another fine four-round total of 273 – 67, 70, 68 and 68. The same season, when Jacobs was on three months' home leave, Hassanein stayed with him at Lindrick and travelled with him on the British circuit. In his opening tournament at Worthing, in Sussex, he collected a 66. It brought John and Rita Jacobs personal grief when, some years after they had returned from Egypt, Hassan Hassanein died tragically and prematurely at his home. Apart from his undoubted golfing qualities, he was a man of charm and winning manners; he had become a friend.

'He was, by any standard, a great player, a super hitter', says Jacobs. 'He was a rather flat-footed and very economical golfer. As a matter of fact, he reminded me a little of the way Henry Cotton played. I was lucky to have him to play with, because to some extent, and probably unwittingly, I tended to copy his action . . .'

Such were the high-hat customs of the Sporting Club's hierarchy that the Jacobses were not allowed to become members; this attitude was no worse, let it be said, than that of many clubs in Britain. The Americans whom Jacobs taught and played with could not understand these anachronistic ways and neither could the forthright and opinionated Australian battler for the oppressed, Norman von Nida, who was disgusted by the club's plutocratic behaviour. Von Nida's chance to express, publicly, his unequivocal views came in a speech at the prize-giving ceremony following the Egyptian Professional Match-Play Championship, in which he had been beaten by Hassanein. He spent the first two minutes complimenting the winner and the organizers on the excellence of the tournament. Then he rounded on the leaders of the club, berating them for their scurvy treatment of the English professional and his wife. Von Nida sat down, after scoring strikes all over the target, to self-conscious tittering from his elegant audience. For Jacobs, it remains an indelible memory: 'It was all hugely embarrassing. Norman is such a good friend, and he was determined to do the best he could for us, but the uneasiness he caused by his speech was felt for days.'

Such talking may cause people to hop about for a while, but in the end it usually achieves its aim. The very next day, Rita Jacobs received, by the hand of an emissary, a personal note from the British Ambassador in Cairo, Sir Ralph Stevenson. His Majesty's first representative in Egypt presented his compliments; he wanted Mrs Jacobs and her husband to know that they would always be quite free to use the swimming pool at his residence and that he hoped very much they would do so whenever they felt so inclined. Norman von Nida's two-fingered salute had found a sympathetic response in what he had to confess was a welcome, but nonetheless unlikely, quarter.

Many can bear testimony to Jacobs's photographic memory for his pupils' swings. He also registers acutely the initial sight of a great player. Cotton was the first example – at Sandwich in 1938. Perhaps the next was the marvellously consistent Australian, Peter Thomson, when he and von Nida stopped off in Cairo at the start of the 1950s en route for Thomson's first visit to England.

Thomson, then barely twenty, stood at the threshold of one of the most extraordinary records in international golf. He and his compatriot played an exhibition match at Gezira with Jacobs and Hassanein. In Jacobs's mind, it might have happened no more than a couple of years ago: 'Peter and Norman had just flown in in one of the old Qantas Constellations. They had probably been sitting in the aircraft for much of two days. Both of them were very stiff, and over the first nine holes, which he covered in 36, Peter didn't hit it at all well, which was understandable. But he kept on getting it up and down. Over the second nine, he got it going very much better, holed it in 32 and there was a 68 the first time he'd seen the course. You could see then the genius and talent.'

Some thirty-five years later, with all those British Open victories intervening, Jacobs saw him again at the Vintage, in Palm Springs, playing on the US Senior tour. It was the spring of 1985 and the Australian was well on his way to amassing a total of prize money of some $400,000 – 'like walking,' as he put it, 'on a carpet of dollars'. He was two shots ahead of Arnold Palmer, who hit his second to the home hole stone dead from the rough.

'I was thrilled to see Peter again', says Jacobs. 'Nothing had changed. There was the same high left shoulder at the address, the same flatish, very compact backswing; and, for a man of his age, still the best competitive putter in the business. From the left-hand side of the fairway, he fired a 3-wood right into the heart of the green. He

walked up to the ball, just as jaunty as ever . . . Two putts for a win –
thank you very much. What a wonderful player, to have kept his game
going like that. His brain, I would say, is still the best club in his bag.'

With his return to England, and his appointment as the professional
at Sandy Lodge, Jacobs sometimes practised with Thomson. This was
in the 1950s, when the Australian was picking up one championship
after another. He once went out to Sandy Lodge specifically to get
Jacobs to look at his set-up – just that, his set-up to the ball, nothing
else. Satisfied that he was standing well to the ball, he then drove back
into the centre of London. Jacobs draws an important lesson from
this: 'Seventy per cent of all the bad shots which are hit are due to a
faulty set-up to the ball.'

The two had a lot in common and enjoyed each other's company:
'Peter had a dry humour and could be very caustic at times. We were
both keen on cricket and used to argue a lot about the game. I
remember, on one of their tours, England had won the first Test in
Australia, so I sent Peter a cable. He had won a lot in this country that
season. "Maybe we can't play golf, but we can still play cricket," I
said. For a while there was no reply. Then, after England had lost the
second Test, back came a rejoinder: "As you were saying, Peter".'

3
The Sandy Lodge Years

ACADEMY OF FLIGHT

Advance and consolidation were the watchwords of John Jacobs's career when, in December 1952, he took up his appointment as professional at Sandy Lodge, a friendly but proud club, lying some twenty miles north-west of central London. He had, by then, fulfilled his intention of playing the tournament season that year in Britain to get back into the swim after his time in Egypt. Several top-dozen or so finishes had given his game the fillip it needed. He felt ready now for the scope and challenge of the new job. The club's background, disciplines and friendliness appealed at once to him and his wife.

Opened in 1910, on a stretch of unusually sandy soil, Sandy Lodge had been founded by a dogmatic autocrat, J. Francis Markes, who had earlier returned from a rigorous and successful sheep-farming foray into Australia's outback, which no one was ever allowed to forget. In the next forty years, Mr Markes (no one ever omitted the prefix) became to Sandy Lodge what Clifford Roberts was to Augusta National in his lifetime: one among a revered line of golf's able and benevolent dictators.

Bearing in mind the money values of those days, the method Francis Markes devised for funding the enterprise bears scrutiny. The company which held all the club's assets was financed by the issue of £100 debentures, each carrying a coupon of $4\frac{1}{2}$ per cent and the right to a bonus issue of five £1 shares in the equity. Membership of the club was then free to the debenture holders for the whole twenty-one years of the original lease. Having retained for himself the largest holding, Markes then allowed a fairly tight-knit circle of his friends and acquaintances to subscribe for the balance of the debenture stock. It was hardly surprising that the issue was an instant success.

With the eventual expiry of the lease, the original company was wound up and the debenture holders, who throughout had received their 4½ per cent interest, plus 100, 150 and, in one year, 200 per cent on their £1 shares – even during the First World War – were paid in full. In addition, they received over £7 for each of the £1 shares for which they had paid nothing. All this, and free golf for twenty-one years!

For the first thirty years of its existence, up to the outbreak of the Second World War, Sandy Lodge drew its support principally from the 'establishment'. Ambassadors, Members of Parliament and the diplomatic corps, bankers, financiers, stockbrokers, members of the professions, company chairmen – if they secured the quality and status of the club in its formative years, none would claim that they contributed markedly to the raising of its playing standards. Nor did the United States' representatives in the club allow their English and Scottish counterparts to overlook that on 27 January 1919 Franklin Delano Roosevelt, then the under-secretary of the US navy, embarked upon a round of the course which a snowstorm brought to a summary halt.

Nonetheless, in its opening half-century, Sandy Lodge provided three Walker Cup captains, a spattering of internationals and a captain of the Royal and Ancient Golf Club of St Andrews. The club's credentials were undoubted. Harry Vardon had designed the course in the prime of his illustrious playing career; subsequently, at Francis Markes's invitation, he was a frequent visitor. Beyond that, of John Jacobs's seven predecessors in office, the most distinguished was Arthur Havers. Open champion at Troon in 1923, when he eased Walter Hagen and Macdonald Smith into second and third places, and six times a Ryder Cup Player, Havers went to the United States in 1924 and added fresh lustre to his record by bearing, first, Bobby Jones by two and one over 36 holes, and then Gene Sarazen by five and four over seventy-two holes in testing, set-piece challenge matches.

John and Rita Jacobs took to Sandy Lodge from the start and the membership reciprocated with a gesture which, for those inhibited days, was, to say the least, unexpected. In February 1953, within a couple of months of the Jacobses' arrival, the ladies' section wrote the professional's wife a letter. 'We do not know,' it ran, 'whether you might be thinking of joining the club, but, if you would like to apply, rest assured your application will receive the wholehearted support of the members . . .'

With this, and Jacobs himself being given the full use of the club – a significant departure from what he had been used to – things got off to a happy start. Indeed, so strongly had the relationship developed that when, a little while later, the neighbouring (and competing) Moor Park made Jacobs an attractive offer for his services, he resisted the overture. He and his wife had now bought their own home, 7 Sandy Lodge Lane. Happiness and job satisfaction counted for more in their lives than money; besides, the club had a first class practice ground, and Moor Park had none. Jacobs without a practice ground would have been like a school-teacher without a blackboard.

The daily routine at Sandy Lodge was regular and disciplined. A young, all-round club professional in the 1950s, with the help of his assistants, normally did three things. He ran his business, taught for most of the year, but primarily in the winter, and from April through to September played the tournament schedule, such as it then was. Nowadays, there are, generally, two breeds of men – the club professionals, whose activities are on the whole directed towards the club which they serve; and the tour players, who for much of the year follow the tournament trail round the world and do little else.

Jacobs's teaching days out of the tournament season (and often in it) started early and finished late. He worked on his own game – and worked was the word – before and after the lessons. The tournaments in those days usually finished on Friday, so he taught and played games with the members at the weekend. The contests were vigorous, competitive encounters which he enjoyed, and they served to engender an enthusiastic, match-play spirit in the club. He took one day off a week and was strict about its observance.

The problem he had experienced in Gezira developed at Sandy Lodge. The number of lessons escalated. There was little he could do about it. His appointments book was full for months ahead. He could tell you in September whom he would be teaching in March. Rain or shine, he would be out there on the practice ground dispensing the doctrines which were now crystallizing in his mind. Pupils kept coming back for more. He did his best to satisfy the members' needs, but as his 'outside' clientele grew – from overseas now as well as from home – so did the difficulty of putting Sandy Lodge pupils first.

There appeared to be no likelihood of the demand slackening. Nice for the revenue side of the business certainly, but no matter how great the enthusiasm or the interest, nor how easily teaching came to him, such a programme was mentally and physically gruelling. Even thirty years on, Jacobs still speaks of those times with feeling: 'When September came round, and the tournaments were over, I knew I faced the prospect of standing out there for the next six months, teaching six days a week for week after week.

'On the one hand, it was terribly satisfying to feel that I was so much wanted, and that I could help people with their games – help them to enjoy their golf more. In that kind of situation, one was making friends all the time; it was a joy to build a following of grateful pupils. But, on the other, oh! the misery of the prospect of such an unrelenting programme, running on right through the winter. It was very hard to shoulder, particularly as, all the time, I was wanting so much to be working on my own game . . .

'And then, after six in the summer evenings, when people saw me out on the practice ground with a bag of balls, hitting shots, they'd come up and say, "I see you're doing nothing, perhaps you'd be good enough just to have a look at me . . ." They didn't seem to realize – and one can understand it – that I was actually working.'

As he had done at Gezira, Jacobs decided to bump up the fees he charged for lessons sharply, to a level far above the norm for those days. He would always accommodate the members, but he wanted to keep visitors away to allow him time to practise and play. He sought the club's consent to charge four guineas an hour, an unheard-of figure in the early 1950s. John Brew, a member of the committee, remembers the reaction round the table when the professional's letter was read out. 'There was shock-horror . . . They thought John had gone off his rocker, and even that he was exploiting the market . . . Tom Waddell, the captain, took a much more relaxed view. He felt John should charge what he liked – and that we should welcome it.'

The higher charges had no effect at all. The visitors still went on booking up months ahead. Practising and playing time remained at a heavy premium.

In the face of Britain's winter weather, Jacobs had a portable, prefabricated shelter made from a strong, light-inducing plastic material. Designed by one of the club members, it could be secured with guy ropes in high winds – like an aircraft picketed down on an exposed airfield. But, as it was mounted on wheels, it was readily movable, and could be pushed to fresh ground as soon as one area had become too worn. Other clubs had had permanently fixed bays mounted at the end of a practice ground – forerunners of the covered bays to be found on the modern driving range; but none, so far as was then known, had introduced the movable principle so that balls could be hit off fresh turf in poor weather. 'I found it a wonderfully good investment,' Jacobs says now. 'It was a boon always to be able to offer pupils the chance of hitting iron shots off a decent piece of grass under cover.'

Jacobs is a physically active instructor. Standing behind the pupil and looking down the line (i.e., keeping him or her between himself and the target line), he can readily see the flight path of the ball and what the clubhead is doing to produce it. From that vantage point, the two planes of the swing – the turn of the shoulders and the movement of arms and club – are seen in clear perspective. 'Remember,' he will say, 'the shoulders go back and the arms go up.'

One might think that, with such a process, he would be glad to resort to a shooting stick or seat. But that wouldn't suit him. He is constantly moving about, watching the flight of the shot and then moving forward to help a pupil make an adjustment, tee up another ball or provide one of those simple and easily understood demonstrations. He is never still. Over long hours of instruction it can be a wearing business.

In the Sandy Lodge years, when the volume of teaching was greater than at any other period of his career, he encountered problems with varicose veins in his legs. In 1954 and again in 1958 he had to undergo operations to cure the leg pain which long stretches of standing had aggravated. Apart from this affliction, which was cleared up, and the major abdominal surgery in his teens, Jacobs has enjoyed exceptionally good health. Since his boyhood days, working on the farm at Lindrick, his health and strength have been prime assets in the balance sheet.

Quite early during his time at Sandy Lodge Jacobs started coaching national teams. Sometimes they came to him, now and then he went to them; he also went on teaching trips abroad. In this way he became acquainted with many of the outstanding amateurs of the day. With his built-in ability to 'photograph' a player, keep the picture fresh in his mind and, in a sentence or two, describe it sharply years afterwards, he can still recall vividly the swing actions of the 'names' of the 1950s and 1960s:

'I remember the first time the English Golf Union sent a lot of their top and promising players. There were so many that I got Peter Alliss and his father, Percy, both of whom knew the game so well, and Syd Scott, to come and help me. It was the first time I had seen Michael Bonallack. He was then at the start of a marvellous career in amateur golf. He was a natural competitor – in fact his competitiveness remained, throughout, the best part of his game.'

The first sight of the embryo champion was not without its blemishes. 'Michael, at that time, had no "neck posture". He tucked his neck into his shoulders and got hunched up over the ball from where he swung the club very much "up-and-under" on a straight line. He rather pecked at the ball and there wasn't much divot. Of course, that type of "up-and-under" action tends to open the club coming into the ball. If you hit it, then, as Michael did, you fade all your long shots. Gary Player, incidentally, from much the same "up-and-under" position, often hits it after his wrists have rolled – and he tends to hook the ball from the same action!

'Any golfer who, from that "up-and-under" action, tends to hit the ball, as Michael did, with the clubface open, and fades it, gives himself the best possible chance with the short shots; and Michael was a superb chipper and pitcher of the ball. He was also a great holer out. He was rather like Nicklaus on the green – hunched over, with the ball well forward. In other words, he had a view of the line as he was striking the ball.'

What, then, of the corrective therapy administered by Jacobs which contributed to Bonallack's rise?

'In trying to help Michael – and I recall he came often to Sandy Lodge and once, I think, to Sandown Park – it was a question of getting a better posture to the ball, sitting up to it, and then turning the shoulders in a flatter arc. To get this, it helped to practise with the ball above the feet. Putting the ball on the side of a slope above the player, and getting him to hit it from there, helps him to get a flatter turn of the shoulders – the opposite of the "up-and-under" action.' Then there was Michael Lunt, who had learned his golf as a child. He caught the eye of Raymond Oppenheimer, the Oxford, England and Walker Cup captain, a critical judge of a golfer, during the 1949 British Boys' Championship at St Andrews. After watching him play, Oppenheimer wrote a note to the boy's father, Stanley Lunt, like his son an English champion and an accomplished international player. In the light of what was to follow Oppenheimer's comments are worth quoting:

'I can see nothing wrong with Michael's swing ... He stands excellently [to the ball] and has first-rate hands. For a boy of fourteen he is astonishing and his only weaknesses are those of most boys of his age – he sometimes plays a shot first and then thinks afterwards ...'

Times, and swings, change. Some years later, Jacobs played Michael Lunt in an amateur versus professional match at Turnberry – 36 holes foursomes and singles, the Walker and Ryder Cup format for those days. Jacobs received what he describes as 'a tremendous drubbing' at the hands of his amateur opponent. But that has in no way clouded his objective recollection of Lunt, the golfer:

'Michael was driving for the most part with a 3-wood, dropping the ball down on the turf on those lovely, firm Turnberry tees. As to his swing, he stood still in the backswing and just picked the club straight up on too much of a steep arc and then tended to turn his shoulders in the downswing. In other words, instead of turning his shoulders in the backswing and swinging at the ball with the hands and arms from the inside, he did virtually the opposite. He picked the club up with his hands and arms in the backswing and turned through the ball from the top. This meant his angle of attack was very, very steep.

'I remember there was a divot on every tee; driving with a 3-wood with that very steep action, the ball took off ever so low, scorching the turf as it went, because Michael was tremendously powerful. Of course, the beauty of that was that the ball usually started left and cut back to the right so he wasn't as inaccurate as he might have been, although I do recall he carved a lot of tee shots that day which finished in the right-hand rough.

'There was another benefit from that action. Like Michael Bonallack, Lunt was a beautiful chipper and pitcher, and a lovely bunker player. I can see him now getting into those deep Turnberry bunkers close to the flag and chopping it out with a nice softish flight – and, of course, knocking the next one into the hole.'

Almost quarter of a century passed before Jacobs played with Lunt again. Then, in the autumn of 1985 at Deal, the two of them took part in a reunion match between former Ryder and Walker Cup players. Peter Alliss and Bruce Critchley raised the respective sides. The passage of the years had brought change: 'Michael is, of course, a far better swinger today. Like so many of us, I suppose, he learned how to swing after he had finished playing.'

There were two rather special Scots who figured in this parade of amateur talent: Charles Lawrie, a Walker Cup and Scottish captain, and Charlie Green, whose honours for Scotland and Britain are well known – few have kept their games going for as long, or at a higher competitive level, than Green. Lawrie and Green backed to the hilt the lead which Sandy Sinclair gave in changing their country's approach to coaching. It was Sinclair, another enlightened Scottish international, who brought his authority to bear on the Scottish Golf Union to appoint Jacobs as the coach for the national team and the Scots' promising juniors.

The belief had endured for years north of the border, where so many play golf instinctively well from childhood, that it was mistaken to tamper with natural talent. Leave it to the good Lord was the cry, until less rigid minds prevailed. John Jacobs saw it all at first hand: 'Coaching was a dirty word in Scotland. People said leave well alone, don't interfere. Nature would take its course. It's difficult to break down that kind of attitude.'

The change was by no means easy to achieve, and it took Jacobs's confident persuasion, plus the results which he quickly obtained, for it to gather momentum. As Jacobs now concedes, Charlie Green, by the exceptional quality of his own performance, became the bellwether of the new Scottish flock: 'It was at the Walker Cup match at Turnberry in 1963, when I had been asked to lend the British team a hand, that I first came across Charlie Green. It was his first year in the side and I could see what a potential he had, but to realize it there would have to be changes. I said to him after the match that if he would care to see what I could do to help him, I was quite sure real improvements could be made and that he could become a very good player.

'Charlie came afterwards to Largs, when I was up there teaching the Scottish juniors. Bernard Gallacher, then a sixteen-year-old, was in the class, I remember, with an excessively strong, three-and-a-half, almost four-knuckle grip with his left hand. But there was no doubt, even then, about his natural aptitude and flair for the game.' Jacobs has now been teaching the Scottish team for upwards of two decades. While Gallacher quickly resolved, after passing his eighteenth birthday, to make golf a career – a decision he can hardly have regretted – Green, from the start, became a constant attendant at the amateur sessions.

'Even now,' says Jacobs, 'when I'm seeing the present team, Charlie is always there. "As you're teaching these boys," he'll say, "perhaps you would just have a quick look at me." His enthusiasm for the game is just the same. It's all very simple with him now.

'In 1963, Charlie Green was standing thirty per cent open and, therefore, doing thirty per cent too much with the body. In this he was typical of so many people who stand open. He stood across the ball, the club cut inside too much in the backswing and it came out and over the top in the downswing. (Like Sandy Lyle, I suppose – and he's only an Open champion!) The beauty of that action, as I've said of Michael Lunt, is that very often the bad shot is a good shot in that the ball does cut back on to the fairway.

'The correction for Charlie then, as now, was very simple. Bring the ball back at the address, square up the body and, from that position, get a view of the path of the golf swing into the ball. Swing down that path with the hands and the arms and clear the left hip. In other words: stand to hit the ball from the inside and clear the left hip going through.'

Charlie Green, by his own admission, had had only 'one proper golf lesson' in his life up to the time he gained his place in Great Britain's Walker Cup team at Turnberry in 1963. Like other gifted fellow Scots, he had relied on natural talent (of which there was plenty). It wasn't until a couple of years or so after his encounter with Jacobs at Turnberry that he recognized the shortcomings of his method: 'I remember so well John's remark to me when he came up to coach the Scottish juniors at Largs one winter some while after the Turnberry match. "Ah!" he said as he had a look at me. "Now you're the man I saw at Turnberry in 1963 and have been waiting to see again ever since."' It was the beginning of a twenty-year relationship which was to set Green climbing to the summit of the national and international game, with two successive captaincies of the Walker Cup team to his credit. Green was struck by the speed and certainty of the teacher's diagnosis and the simplicity and clarity of the explanations and suggested corrections: 'As a small instance, there was a young Scottish international whom I and others had been trying to help to correct a tiny kink in an otherwise good swing. Then John, on one of his visits, saw him hit one ball – one ball only – and instantly proposed an adjustment which overcame the problem at once. And he had never set eyes on him before. That's one of the great things about his teaching. He doesn't have to work with a player for long to make things better.'

This speed factor made an impression during Jacobs's visits to the Scottish national team. According to Green, 'The work John was able to get through between about 10.00 a.m. and 5.00 p.m. on these single-day, flying visits to the driving range at Hamilton was remarkable. He would see all the side; everyone got the attention he wanted; and he would do in a day what might well have taken others a week. I'm glad to say that we now arrange for John to take the Scottish team for a week in Spain – at La Manga – during the winter, instead of getting him to fly up to Scotland for a day or so at a time. It's a much more satisfactory plan.'

The England team is now engaging in a similar winter exercise with John Stirling, another first-rate teacher, with whom Jacobs works closely in his schools at Meon Valley and abroad. In Green's view, there will be a significant international rub-off from this. It should obviate a problem which prevailed at the time of the 1983 Walker Cup match at Hoylake: 'When John was with the team, I felt that we could

31

not make as much of him as we should have been able to, had the bulk of the side already been coached by him. As it was, England weren't going to him, so I knew there were people in the team with whom he could do little with the match right on top of them. No matter what they might want, he was reluctant to risk upsetting them. He is too wary for that.

'But now that both England and Scotland are having winter coaching abroad, this should make a tremendous difference to our golf. He will have seen most of the Walker Cup team (or will know all about them from John Stirling) and this will mean that, for the majority, simple little adjustments near the time of the match will be easy to make. And, believe me, if you don't feel you're quite "on" in a Walker Cup match, that really is the time when you need a little something.'

Green stresses the enormous value of having someone of Jacobs's stature and ability on hand on the great occasion when members of the team are understandably jumpy and on edge: 'With the speed with which he can spot the tiny things – and therefore the simple adjustments that are necessary – he brings so much confidence, particularly if he knows your game. The point is he doesn't put people off.'

Green's own experience at St Andrews in 1971, the year Michael Bonallack's team scored a historic triumph over the United States, makes his case for him:

'I had been having a bad time with my driving, I hadn't been able to get it going at all, so I got John to see me the day before the match and again just before I went out on the first day. He gave me one single point to remember, and I can truthfully say I really did drive awfully well throughout the two days. Before that, I felt my driving had been in tatters.

'John just told me to grip the club rather more firmly with the right hand – the bottom hand. Hang on, he said, a bit more firmly with the right than with the left. Just that, nothing more. I had, in fact, got a bit too much wristiness into the swing and this had the effect of firming things up. It was so simple.'

Green liked the way Jacobs adapted his teaching to individual needs: 'He would teach a chap of 5ft 4in quite differently from one of 6ft 3in. In days gone by, people used to standardize teaching. I have seen, with other professionals, that the man of 5ft 4in is given much the same advice as someone, like me, of 6ft 3in. As a basic method of instruction, I just don't think that kind of thing is on.'

Talking about Jacobs's style of teaching and his intellectual approach to it, Green recalls a comment made to him at Largs, on the Ayrshire coast, by the manager of the Inverclyde Sports Centre. The manager's job had necessarily given him wide experience of coaches in all sports and games, including the famous 'names'.

'He said to me, after watching one of John's sessions with the Scottish juniors, that, in his personal judgement, John's all-round performance as a coach – as a coach of a game, not just golf alone – was the most impressive that he had himself ever seen. The diagnosis, the explanations and the corrections were made so plain and given so positively and fluently that anyone could get the message.'

To substantiate the point, Green gives another illustration of the 'instant Jacobs' brand of instruction:

'I remember going along to West Kilbride with one or two others for a round with John. It was a Sunday and we had just gone through some members in front. One of them, a man who had sliced all his life, said to John, "You ought to be teaching us, not them." "All right," he replied, "let's see what you do."

'In a moment, John had got this chap set up differently and for just about the first time in his life he hit a draw. I can still see the look of amazement on the man's face as he turned to John, who was standing, as usual, behind him. He couldn't believe that it could be so simple.'

In contrast to Green's experience at St Andrews, Jacobs cites the case of John Davies, the Sunningdale player, in the 1979 Walker Cup match at Muirfield. Davies had played in the two previous matches, but at Muirfield he was hooking the ball. So when Jacobs arrived at the club three days before the match, Rodney Foster, the British captain, asked him if he would have a look at Davies. The coach recalls it clearly: 'The treatment for him was much the same as it had been for Charlie six years before. But whereas John Davies could straighten things out on the practice ground, he couldn't reproduce it in the match. This can always be a difficulty.' After Davies's defeat in the first series of singles, Jacobs was horrified to see himself quoted in the press as having said that the British player had no guts: 'I had never said anything of the sort, nor would I, knowing the game as I do. What made it worse was that I knew John had, despite his difficulties, tried his very best . . . '

As for Charles Lawrie, a spirited golfer with a games player's flair, I recall an autumn morning in 1973, walking with him over the Duke of Bedford's Woburn estate, where he was then designing the first of the two attractive courses there. He was nearing the end of his sadly short, yet full, life. Jacobs, with another companion, was walking several paces behind, well out of earshot.

'It's rather a pity,' Lawrie said, 'we haven't got our clubs with us. John could have given us the once over – and I mean the once over. Did you ever know anyone who could put his finger on the tender spot in a swing so quickly? He has only got to see me hit half a dozen shots and he's got it in one.

'He has even now been able to persuade some of my stuffier friends in the Scottish Golf Union that there can be a life after teaching. He has done it because he has never told everyone the same thing – never suggested that people should all work on a set method. He'd tell me one thing and the next chap quite the opposite. And what's more, he did it in a sentence or two, simply spoken, so that everyone knew what he was driving at. And then he would demonstrate it himself.

'The difference with John is that he cuts a path through the jungle and you can see your way out of the undergrowth. He doesn't fiddle with the things that don't matter, and it's all done in a flash. But you have to believe in him. There are few now in Scotland who don't.'

That was Lawrie's view. And how does Jacobs recall this much-missed character? His golf game is portrayed in a few words: 'I remember Charles coming to Sandy Lodge for a lesson. He was a very good hitter. Inclined to be a little bit underneath – used the clubhead a lot – but a fine driver. I suspect he was never such a good iron player . . .'

There is a more important memory. It is, again, of the 1963 Walker Cup match at Turnberry, and Lawrie's captaincy of the British side:

'Goodness knows how many half-crowns Charles took off me in those two days as we walked about the course together watching the matches. He'd keep on betting me that one player after another would or wouldn't get down in two from wherever. Then, in the evenings there were the games of poker. Charles and Michael Bonallack, Joe Carr and I used to sit up playing every night. They took pounds off me.

'I pulled their leg at the end and said to them, "That's a fine thing. Here I am working like a slave for you fellows, there's no fee and now you skin me of all this money . . ." But it was a hugely enjoyable week for me.

'Charles asked me to the dinner for the two teams after the match. It was an unexpected privilege which very few pros could ever have enjoyed. Tables were set out in fours. I sat down with Charlie Coe, Billy Joe Patton and Joe Carr. It was an evening I will always remember.'

There is another personal memory which Jacobs retains from the

1963 match. It springs from the warm heart which stimulated many of Charles Lawrie's private acts in his short lifetime. Knowing that the professor never asked for a fee for his Walker Cup work, the British captain saw to it that his team's coach was presented afterwards with a silver cigarette case carrying the facsimile signature of each member of the home side. The gesture touched Jacobs deeply: 'It is something which means a very great deal to me.'

Two of Jacobs's dinner companions on that memorable evening at Turnberry – Joe Carr, from Ireland, and Charlie Coe, from the United States – were an exceptional pair by any test.

Carr, a keen patriot, typified the mercurial brilliance which is so often a feature of Irish sport. When he was in the mood, he would race through a championship as if he was on a prolonged 'high'. Three times Amateur Champion, twice leading amateur in the Open and ten times a Walker Cup team member, he has been for long one of the game's characters. He was a visitor to Sandy Lodge in the 1950s and often host to Jacobs at his home near Dublin when the English mentor was visiting the golf centre bearing his name in the centre of Leopardstown racecourse. He was essentially one who played his golf 'his way':

'Joe had a bit of Charlie Green in his set up,' says Jacobs. 'He used to stand tremendously open and across the ball and then turn inside. If someone stands outside the line, he has to make too much effort to get inside going back and the club then swings flat and ends up at the top of the backswing travelling backwards when it should be going upwards. Travelling backwards, of course, it starts down outside.

'I could put Joe to the inside as he stood to the ball, get him hitting it from the inside and he would actually draw the ball in practice. But as soon as he got out on to the course, the ball would go a mile forward and he'd tee it low – instead of teeing it high and standing to the inside. His way, with the ball right forward and his shoulders across it, he'd swing in and over the top and cut everything. But he cut very, very well.

'There have been a lot of good players who played like that. Harry Weetman is one who comes to mind. If you're strong enough – and Joe was hugely strong – you can, that way, become a relatively straight driver.

'Of course, although everyone used to talk about Joe's putting and about him being a bad holer out, the truth was that he was a marvellous chipper. He always said that playing a lot in the wind at Portmarnock, one tended to miss a fair number of greens. As the bunkers there aren't all that close to the putting surfaces, he made himself into a fine chipper, getting it up and down better than most . . . He was a great scrambler, was Joe.'

Jacobs adds a rider which says much about this admirable Irishman's approach to the game:

'I honestly don't think Joe took a scrap of notice of me. He just loved playing golf, and he was a fine player. Curiously, I played again with him in that match at Deal in 1985 between Peter Alliss's and Bruce Critchley's teams. He still stands there with the ball well forward and his shoulders across it. But now he hits it underneath from the outside as opposed to over the top and that gives him a fade. But at least it's a fade as opposed to an over-the-top-and-outside type of shot.'

Joe Carr's enthusiasm for the game will never be quenched. As a player in his prime, he was insatiable and Jacobs remembers the visits to him at his house overlooking the course at Sutton. He was a warm-hearted, generous host, dispensing hospitality to all comers:

'When we came down to breakfast, there would be a line of golf balls, dozens and dozens of them, all teed up by one of his retainers on the grass in front of the house, waiting for Joe to come out. He had hit the lot by the time he had to leave for the office!'

The place of honour in Jacobs's book, however, must go to Charles Coe, the American from Oklahoma City – twice US Amateur Champion and once runner-up; second in the US Masters (with other 'first amateur' finishes at Augusta besides); runner-up in the British Amateur; six times a US Walker Cup player and ever the perennial amateur. A man of charm and gentle courtesy, his talents graced a thousand fairways on both sides of the Atlantic from the forties to the sixties. Jacobs is in no doubt of his place in the game. 'Of those who have stayed amateur in my time, Charlie Coe was certainly the best I ever saw. I would have to say that. In my judgement, he was, all round, the best.'

The British coach's reflection upon Coe in the same Walker Cup match at Turnberry is instructive:

'I was particularly interested to see Charlie on the practice ground hitting balls off the turf with a driver. In the match itself, he drove mostly with a 3-wood with the ball teed low. This was sensible as he was tending to take the club back too much underneath. He was actually curling the left arm underneath and closing the clubface which, in turn, tended to make him hit up on everything with the clubface closed. He was hitting too much up from the inside.

'Charlie knew that, if you're hooking the ball, there's no better exercise (I've spent hours doing it myself) than just dropping a lot of balls down on to some good, firm turf and hitting them with a driver. It automatically makes you open the clubface up in the backswing instead of getting it too straight back and too much underneath. It avoids a player being too much in-to-out because, if you get too much to the inside coming in to the ball, there's no way that you can make contact with a driver hitting the ball off the turf. Charlie Coe understood exactly what he was doing rolling those balls out on to the grass and using his driver.'

There was one shot of Coe's in his match against Sandy Sadler in the first series of singles which Jacobs remembers in particular. He had driven into the big bunker, familiar to television viewers, down the left side of the eighteenth fairway: 'Charlie went into that deep bunker with a 6-iron, hit one of the greatest shots I've ever seen to the green and halved the match. There are very few who could have played that shot at all, let alone at such a moment.'

There are many tests of a golfer: one is the ability to keep his or her game going over the years. Examples of those who have possessed this attribute come readily to mind: Cotton, Snead, Thomson, de Vicenzo, Nicklaus, Player – and Coe.

In the late summer of 1986, Jacobs was at Castle Pines, near Denver, Colorado, to give a clinic and teach the celebrated Vickers family, whose name is synonymous with the development of the exclusive club. Six thousand feet up in the foothills of the Rockies, designed by Jack Nicklaus, and liberally funded, it bids fair to take its place in the uplands of the United States golfing hierarchy. Jacobs was there a fortnight before the Castle Pines Stableford International:

'To my surprise, I found that Charlie Coe was a member. And there he was, now well into his sixties and more than thirty-five years after winning his first US Amateur, still hitting the ball so well. It was a piece of luck for me finding him there. I was able to inject some local interest into the clinic by telling the members how I had seen Charlie all those years ago in the UK, and how I rated his ability as a golfer . . .'

CLUB AND COUNTRY

While Jacobs was now increasingly assisting the leading amateurs of the day, he was also bringing benefits to the members of his own club. Two, in particular, spring to mind: Donald Morris and John Brew.

Morris, now a retired stockbroker and one of the longest-serving members of Sandy Lodge, had been an 'instinct' golfer since childhood.

As a boy, he lived with his family in a house immediately behind the first tee. He took local instruction, first from the aforementioned Arthur Havers and, much later, from Eric Brown, a former Scottish Amateur Champion and one of the most successful singles players ever to represent Britain in the Ryder Cup against the United States. It had no noticeable effect. The relatively low single-figure handicap Morris achieved came from his own industry and the opportunities which were offered.

Let him tell his own story. It should give hope to those weekend players who have passed the mid-thirties and see little prospect of improving their games further. Morris became a participant in Jacobs's regular clinics:

'They were always well attended, and I remember the final point he used to make was that if one kept one's head still it wasn't necessary to look at the ball. He would then select one of the most attractive ladies present – usually Sally Allday – and ask her to stand facing him. He would then look her in the eye and hit the ball straight down the middle of the course!

'I recall also the Curtis Cup girls and the Walker Cup players coming to Sandy for training and I can still see most of the Walker Cup team practising from the bunkers around the third green with John saying to them, "Slow . . . Slow . . . And now even slower."

'As for me, my fault was that my swing was too long, and I let go with the last two fingers of my left hand at the top of the swing. This led to erratic shots, particularly under pressure. I remember once when I was playing with Eustace Crawley for Harrow in the deciding foursome in the final of the Halford-Hewitt* against Watsons at Deal in 1957. Bernard Darwin wrote the next day that Morris's second shot to the nineteenth "smelt of the socket".

'But my problem was that if I tried deliberately to hold on with the last two fingers of my left hand, it upset all my rhythm. John's way round this was to cut down the swing to just short of the horizontal by keeping my left thumb on top of the shaft. Putting the left thumb on top of the grip (i.e., as opposed to on the side) didn't entirely eliminate the "piccolo" grip, but it went a long way towards it. Anyway, John always reassured me by saying that Christy O'Connor had a "piccolo" grip and that he did very well with it.

'I have studied the club's competition books of around that time. I find that, when John arrived at Sandy Lodge in 1953, I was playing off

*The annual inter-school old boys' foursomes tournament. Donald Morris (after Jacobs) was in the Harrow side for ten years, captaining it in one year.

3 and returning scores of around 78 and 83. By 1961, when I was then forty-five, I was down to one and returning scores in the region of 71 to 75.

'The truth is that it wasn't until John took me in hand that I started to understand the swing. He gave me a simple, clear idea of how the swing works and how to identify errors from the divot and the shape of the shot. I am incapable of thinking of more than one remedy at a time, and John never muddled me with too many corrections. By the time he left the club, he had given me a grounding which enabled me to do it myself. On the practice ground I still work on what he used to call his "thoughts for the day".'

John Brew and his brother David, both low-handicap golfers, were playing alongside Morris in the strong Sandy Lodge team in the Jacobs years. John, a member of the London Stock Exchange, and president of the Hertfordshire Golf Union with its 1986 champion county side, and David, a doctor, were anchor men for the club. They used to play frequent tightly fought, three-ball matches with Jacobs at the weekend, the professor contesting the better ball of the two brothers. As a threesome, they tended to cover the eighteen holes in rather less time than it took the average single to play a round.

Immediately after Jacobs had beaten Cary Middlecoff on the thirty-sixth green in the singles of the 1955 Ryder Cup match at Palm Springs, to score maximum points in the series, he received a cable from the brothers. 'Congratulations,' it read, 'but apprehensive about our next match.'

John Brew is well placed to provide an assessment of what he calls 'John's rise to fame as a teacher'. He and Jacobs joined the club within a year of one another and, over the next ten years, often played together.

'It never appeared to me that there was such a thing as a Jacobs "method" or "system", although he changed my swing much more than he did my brother David's. I used to be a "tilter", with a rather ungainly dig at the ball from too upright a position. I cannot recall that he ever told me to turn more . . . More or less by stealth, he gave me a very "inside" take-away, which I still have in a less pronounced form. The point was that I could not make the backswing he gave me without doing a good turn. I have always thought, since then, that "round and then up" was a good precept.

'The other things I kept hearing were the importance of clearing the left side going through the ball, the set-up and the danger (for an amateur) of trying to go for the late hit. I have very small hands and used to use a two-handed grip. John wasn't at all keen to get me to change, but eventually I did of my own accord.

'He had two particular teaching coups that I specially remember. Richard Braddon, from Beaconsfield, came for lessons just before the Boys' Championship [at Moortown in 1958]. Had it been today, he wouldn't have got into the championship because his handicap would have been too high. He was a good cricketer and could hit hard. John told him that his only hope lay in a fundamental grip change. An ultra-strong left-hand grip had to be weakened to show no more than one-and-a-half or two knuckles. This quickly had the effect of developing a different swing and in only a couple of weeks he was a new golfer. He won the championship, and must have been the highest handicap player ever to have done so.

'The other pupil, I recall, who attracted attention was Brian Chapman, not a "natural" by a very long chalk, but there is no doubt that John made him into a very good player – good enough for a place later on in the Walker Cup team.'

Jacobs enjoyed not only helping and playing with the good golfers in the club but also taking one of the high-handicap members as a partner in a weekend game. Indeed, there was a regular foursome in which he teamed up with Nick Bowlby, a City merchant banker, a thoroughly indifferent but enthusiastic golfer, against his assistant, Alex Fox,* and another Scot, Rab Beattie, a ship's architect and a proficient player, better known as a Rugby football referee.

Bowlby, known in the club as 'the Third Man', kept a diary in which, at the end of each day, he recorded the details of any match in which he had played. There was one of these foursomes in which everything had gone unbelievably right for the merchant banker and his professional partner. As John Brew remembers it, the match was won comfortably, and with manifest jubilation, on the sixteenth green:

'Before John Jacobs walked back to drive from the seventeenth tee, he handed Nick Bowlby the ball they had been using with such success. He wanted, he said, to put down his own. When Nick remonstrated, John whispered to him that he intended to hit it out of bounds into the wood running down the left side of the fairway, which he duly did. Their unsuspecting opponents, already frustrated by the enemy's unexpectedly good play, were further incensed when "the first bad shot of the match" came after the game was over . . .'

*Sometimes it was David Talbot, the other of Jacobs's two exceptional assistants.

It is one of the more curious traits of British sport, much more than with the Americans, that when a man reaches the top it's the signal for the knocking to begin. Jacobs has had to stomach his full share of venom. No more fertile field exists than golf instruction for the critics to have their say. Well may the teaching professionals of the world unite and cry with the poet:

> . . . that we but teach
> Bloody instructions, which, being taught, return
> To plague the inventor . . .

The difficulty with golf instruction, for the pupil just as much as for the teacher, is to find a balance. Henry Cotton has been saying it since the mid-1930s: 'Good golf is played between extremes. You've got to know the extremes, and the angles, of your swing and what they give you. Then you must find a balance between them, and be able to hold it.'

Jacobs puts it another way: 'The problem with all instruction is that, without the benefit of regular supervision, most pupils will revert to the original fault: a few will go to the other extreme and overdo it . . .'

Pupils – or students as they are called in Jacobs's golf schools in America – can be divided, broadly, into two clear-cut categories. There are those – 'the reasonable guys' – who play badly after a lesson and acknowledge that corrections often take time to work through; they don't criticize the teacher. If, however, they play well and improve their games, they openly attribute the improvement to the instructor. The others – 'the wrong sort' – who go away and win put their success down to themselves. If they play badly and lose, it's the teacher who is to blame.

That is the rough path which the instructor has to tread. That and the road leading to a pupil's true understanding of what he is being taught. As a long-term Hertfordshire player, John Brew has been in as good a position as any to listen to John Jacobs's local critics from the Sandy Lodge years: 'In my time playing for the county I have run across several people who are very anti-John as a teacher. I have always been a bit surprised at this because the criticism has been that his recommended method of play did not suit the pupil, and his game was ruined as a result. My experience, as I have said, is that there never has been an obvious "system" about John's teaching. On the contrary, there is a great willingness to adapt the method to the person ... Nevertheless, there is definitely a strong "anti" element which will buy this book to burn it!'

It has been my experience that the criticisms of the 'anti-Jacobs' lobby, such as it is, have often been based on invalid concepts or on a recoil from the teacher's assertive style. There was, for instance, a dismissive remark made by one whose own playing success over the years had long since earned him a permanent place in the sun. 'Jacobs?' he queried, when asked for his opinion of the man's contemporary standing as a teacher of golf, 'Jacobs teaches a shut-face, square-to-square method. Can't be right.' When told gently that not for thirty years had Jacobs ever taught a 'method', still less one based on the 'shut-face, square-to-square' concept (ask Dick Aultman and Jim Flick!), the illustrious critic did not attempt a rejoinder. There was no evidence to sustain his contention, and the correction was allowed to lie unchallenged ... But there was no reason to think that the exchange had done anything to prevent a later repetition of the same falsehood to a more gullible audience.

ONE OFF

Every golf instructor in the national or world league has his opponents – and vehement ones at that. The nature of the game and its effect upon the mentality make this inevitable. The problem with Jacobs is to find someone who has experienced his instruction at first hand, found it to be unhelpful, and who possesses the background, authority and honesty to state a view. One who meets all these criteria is Bruce Critchley. As an amateur, he has had his share of international honours and success. Viewers of BBC television's golfing broadcasts will know him to be articulate and sensitive to the effects of the game's pressures upon the mighty.

Critchley's pedigree has a bearing upon his story. His father, Brigadier-General A. C. Critchley, the youngest brigadier in the Canadian forces in the First World War and one of the original business entrepreneurs after it ('Critch' to his friends), learned his golf after he was thirty. Fred Robson, of Addington, a master-teacher in his time and one of the game's unforgettables, helped him to achieve his diverse triumphs – the French, Dutch and Belgian Championships, medals at St Andrews, the Surrey Championship (twice) and foursomes tournaments with Dai Rees and others. These and other wins belonged to one whose volatile temperament must, at times, have made the game an almost unbearable trial or an irresistible challenge.

Bruce Critchley's mother, better known to earlier golfing generations as Diana Fishwick, played her golf from childhood in a compellingly feminine way. The early years, spent in that lovely golfing corner of East Kent, prepared her for the success which would follow. Her temperament, the antithesis of her husband's, was made for golf. When, in 1930, aged nineteen, she polished off the great American Glenna Collett (Glenna Collett Vare) by 4 and 3 in a memorable thirty-six hole final of the British ladies' championship at Formby, the press asked her for a comment. 'What a lark!' she said, and chased it with a giggle.

Her son, then, came from proven golfing stock. Living close by Wentworth and Sunningdale, he played the game as a child in the way that nature and imitation dictated. His mother, of course, held rather more than a cursory watching brief. Later it was Tom Haliburton at Wentworth and, later still, Arthur Lees at Sunningdale who lit the way.

'Tom never taught me in the true sense,' Critchley recalls. 'He talked to me about the game, discussed it and its philosophy, told me how to think my way round a golf course and put a round together. But he did not teach me in the way that pros usually do. He left such talent as there was to develop. Arthur, afterwards, went rather deeper. He would point out what he thought was wrong. He told me, for instance, that my hands took up too much room on the grip to go on holding the club with a two-handed grip – mother's grip. He got me to change to the overlapping grip. All I ever wanted with Arthur was five minutes – after that he would start telling me how *he* played golf! But mostly, up to that stage, I hadn't thought about the swing. I just played the game as it came to me.'

Critchley was picked for England at nineteen. It was 1962 and he had, by then, 'shown' in the Brabazon and the Golf Illustrated gold vase, only to fade as the pressure built up. It was understandable. As a boy at Eton, he had had little time for senior golf. He was raw and inexperienced – quite unlike the nineteen-year-olds who play the amateur circuit today.

The English Golf Union had sent its squad to Jacobs at Sandy Lodge that August, no more than a month before the internationals against Ireland, Scotland and Wales. Once there, Critchley came under the professor's microscope: 'I hit three shots with a 3-iron – super shots, as it happened – straight on one of the pylons in the distance beyond the practice ground.' The directness of Jacobs's verdict took him by surprise. The words still ring in the memory: 'You'll never hit the ball consistently with that swing.'

What, then, of the correction? The internationals, remember, were only four weeks away. 'I had then a long, sloppy, fairly attractive swing. John just told me to swing like Bernard Hunt, to try to get the idea of a rather short, compact, three-quarter swing . . .'

A short while later the student returned to Sandy Lodge with two or three of the England players, Martin Christmas among them. What, then, of the outcome?

'My rhythm went and, with it, my swing. The base of it was taken away. I had never thought about it before; I had just played with what I had been given. For two years or so my game was a disaster. I hardly ever broke 80.'

Critchley believes that Jacobs had given him the wrong treatment. He was still very young; he had grown up to play the game intuitively; he was naturally apprehensive in such an atmosphere; and he was less than a month away from his first knock for England – 'just about the most difficult form of golf that there is'. He doesn't dispute that the correction was needed, but it was proposed at the wrong time, in the wrong way, and with insufficient understanding of what he was himself hoping to get from the game.

Whatever the rights and the wrongs, Critchley's example demonstrates as well as any comparable experience the pitfalls which face the teacher; so often, in such special circumstances, he becomes 'the man in the middle'.

After two years and more in the wilderness, Critchley returned to Haliburton at Wentworth. He had, by then, embarked upon a career with the Blue Circle Cement group. He had less time for golf. He was essentially an 'amateur' earning his own living. Having already told him of his plight, he expected Haliburton to take him out onto the practice ground straightaway:

'Instead, Tom said that he would finish his cup of tea and be out to see me in about twenty minutes. Meanwhile he told me to go out, forget everything – "empty the mind" – and just swing at the ball: "You used to have a swing once and I'll be surprised if it's not still there." When, ultimately, he did come out I said to him: "Tom, that's all I want, I don't need any more. That's it for me."'

A few years later, Bruce Critchley was back in the England side and playing for Britain in the Walker Cup against the United States at

Milwaukee. A win, two halved matches and a loss in the series was a very adequate personal tally on US soil.

Two decades on, he sees his experience in rational perspective. He has the balance and intellect to assess it. He recognizes that, had he been, in 1962, totally dedicated to the game or even about to embark upon it as a career, able to go frequently to Jacobs and to practise assiduously over a period, there is little doubt he could have developed a commercial, repeating swing solid and sound enough to withstand the ravages of tournament play. But that was not the way it was. He intended always to remain an amateur and work hard for a living, which would leave him limited time to play. He reckons now that it is at least debatable whether he should have been sent to Jacobs with the England team in the first place. To be confronted with such a challenge no more than a month away from wearing an England tie for the first time was, he contends, mistaken.

These days, when fundamental coaching sessions for national teams often take place abroad, and always well away from the tournament season, Jacobs is adamant about only seeing a player who has his own familiar guru if that team member specifically asks him to do so; and then he much prefers it if the usual teacher can be present during the session.

The case of Great Britain and Ireland's Curtis Cup girls illustrates the validity of this approach. In August 1983, the Ladies' Golf Union asked Jacobs if he would go to Muirfield the following June to lend a hand with the team for the match against the United States. As he was dealing with Mrs J. V. Todd – Trish Todd, wife of John, a former president of the English Golf Union, both of whom he knew well – and with Diana Bailey, the home side's knowledgeable captain, he could be forthright without fear of being misunderstood.

No, he said, he wouldn't do that; he did not believe it would be in the best interests of the team for him to handle things that way. Nothing could be worse, he added, than for some members of the team to meet him for the first time actually at the match. Instead, he proposed that he should see the players at Meon Valley, near Southampton, that autumn and then go to Muirfield with the team the following April. This would provide both time and continuity and give a chance for him to help the girls to get to know, and play, the course on which the match would take place.

When it came to it, the girls gained the impression that the visit to Jacobs at Meon Valley was to be mandatory. For those who had their own teachers, it came as a surprise and, inevitably, led to ill-informed press comment. It was quite contrary to what the professor had intended. He only wanted to see the girls who wanted to see him; the rest should stick to their own mentors. He knew very well, for instance, that those who were already seeking Vivien Saunders's advice were in first-class hands. Miss Saunders had worked with him at Sandown Park for a period and knew the game from A to Z. Jacobs had developed a special regard for her as a teacher, rating her in the top flight of instructors, male or female.

Eventually, all was sorted out and the plan went ahead as he had proposed it. After a series of dreadfully one-sided results in recent years, only a putt on the last green separated the two sides in the Muirfield match. Later, much of the nucleus of the team, including the formidable Laura Davies, turned professional and began making their marks on the women's tour. Then, between the 1984 contest and the historic victory of Diane Bailey's side on US soil two years later, Jacobs was able to see the possibles who could enjoy the special adavantage of continuity of supervision by which he lays such store in the coaching of national teams.

It follows from this Curtis Cup example that Bruce Critchley's experience of a quarter of a century ago, when he was effectively a mandated member of the English squad, and virtually obliged to accept an English Golf Union *diktat*, would not now arise. Jacobs would never now, knowingly, see a player against his or her wish. Such, in fact, is the accepted procedure that the majority of today's aspirants to international honours are eager and well placed to accept the special opportunities which the unions – and the Royal and Ancient in the case of the Walker Cup – are prepared to offer. It is the sane approach.

In the light of all that has gone before, Critchley's current assessment of Jacobs's standing is valuable:

'John is clearly the outstanding teacher of the last twenty years. His approach is quite different from Tom Haliburton's in his time. Tom, as I knew him, was more concerned with the playing of the game and its philosophy, whereas John has studied the mechanics, thought it all through, and is completely confident of his findings. He is a pro's pro. He is the one to whom the Bernard Gallachers, the Michael Kings and others will always turn. He is ideal for today's pro and for the young amateurs who, with so much time to play, aspire to the heights and, may be, to golf as a profession. The extent of his influence behind the scenes is probably understood only by a very few.'

PRIVATE EYE

Five people lightened the load for John Jacobs in the Sandy Lodge years.

In 1955, after more than three decades, Vivien Jacobs gave up her job as stewardess at Lindrick and moved south to Northwood to be near her son and daughter-in-law and eventually to live with them at 7 Sandy Lodge Lane, opposite the club. A self-contained flat had been prepared for her in the house.

For the next eight years, until her son relinquished the pro's job to enter a new world, Mrs Jacobs ran his shop for him and much of his 'admin' as well. It removed a nagging responsibility which, hitherto, he and his assistants had had to carry. She performed the task with a rare blend of care, thoroughness and acumen. Having once been quite a golfer herself, and having had, for thirty years and more, daily contact with the golfing fraternity, she knew how to look after her customers' needs, and how to sell. Never having been called at Lindrick anything but 'Mrs Jacobs', it was strange for her to hear Sandy Lodge members addressing her as 'Mummy J', to differentiate between her and her daughter-in-law, Rita Jacobs. The appellation implied endearment as well as seniority. The club loved her for what she was, an upright, perceptive and splendidly resolute character.

Her arrival benefited others in the shop. It allowed Jacobs's two assistants, David Talbot and Alex Fox (Bryan Patterson came a little later and Grant Aitken in between), to devote more time to playing, practising and teaching. The keen ones – and these were manifestly in that category – will always want to spend all the time they can playing and hitting balls. This their employer encouraged to the hilt. But there was more to the relationship than that. Talbot and Fox were well placed to observe the example they were set, and profit from it. They could maintain a private eye on their mentor. The assistants who have served Jacobs for any appreciable time in his career have themselves mostly all done well in their own lives. Four of those who were with him at Sandy Lodge make the case.

David Talbot arrived from Sheffield at the age of sixteen, soon after leaving school and after a brief apprenticeship with Charlie Hughes, captain of the PGA in 1986, at Hallamshire. He had been a member of the junior section of the Yorkshire club at the age of twelve, when Jacobs was the assistant there after leaving the Royal Air Force. 'John used to teach me as a boy and I remember him so well then: six foot three inches tall and good looking – for a boy of my age he was an imposing figure.'

Talbot had a set of Slazenger Greensite irons at the time, which he cherished. They had brown shafts, as chrome had disappeared in the war years. But the 4-iron was missing from the set and this left a gap which the owner longed to fill. Jacobs, who has always felt that the young are there to be helped (and, after that, to help themselves),* knew where he could find the club to fill the void; Slazenger had an establishment nearby where a good selection of clubs was assured. Talbot recalls the day when he was handed the new club: 'It was a perfect, matching club, lovely head and feel. It became the favourite iron in the set and, for days, I used it all the time, even when the shot really demanded another club. I never forgot who found it for me.'

A former committee member and (very young) captain of the PGA, David Talbot is now a highly regarded member of his profession, holding one of the plum jobs in the business, at Royal Mid-Surrey, the club which lies beside the Thames and Kew Gardens, at Richmond. Within five years from now it will ring up its centenery. At Mid-Surrey Talbot presides over as strong a junior section as there is in the country. One of his recent products is the promising Robert Lee, who, in the next few years, will be bidding for high honours in the professional game. For Talbot, the start at Sandy Lodge was a bonus in his career:

'Working with John was fun. I looked forward to each day's work. He was strict, very strict, and if something was wrong, he'd tell you at once, but he never carried it on to another day. He told you, and that was expected to be enough.

'He helped me with my own game. At weekends in the winter, he would often take me into a foursome with two of the members. There aren't many bosses about who would do that with their assistant. Then in the evenings in the summer, after the day's work was done, he'd say, "Come on, we'll go out and play a few holes."

'All the teaching must have affected his game. I well remember one summer – and some will find it hard to believe today – we'd played a tournament somewhere in the south and the next one was not due for another ten to twelve days. It was next door to us at Moor Park. In the

---

*Jacobs is strongly against over-coaching the young. 'Let them see the good players and they'll imitate. That's the way to learn.' When he's with children, the message is short and simple: 'Think of sitting up on your pony at the address, then it's back to the hole, front to the hole and swing your arms up and down. Two turns and a swish ... Now, go on ... Two turns and a ...'

middle week between the two events, John actually taught for ninety hours! It meant that he wasn't able to practise at all during the week before Moor Park, yet he badly wanted to. Imagine that happening to some of the tour players today!

'In fact, the only time when I saw John get irritable, irritable with himself, was when he got lumbered with so much teaching that he couldn't get the time to work on his own game. There's no doubt that the hours he did spend at Sandy Lodge working it all out on the practice ground was when he really developed his knowledge.

'I always thought, incidentally, that in his prime John was a far better player than he has ever been given credit for. A look at his record in depth suggests that, anyway.'

Alex Fox, the Scot, profited from his six years' experience working with Jacobs in much the same way as David Talbot. After his time as an assistant (he won the Southern Assistants' Championship within a year or two of joining Jacobs), he moved up to Edinburgh to take the professional's job at Dalmahoy. Thereafter, he returned to Sandy Lodge to replace Bryan Patterson, who had himself followed Jacobs in the pro's post before transferring to Ashford Manor, in Middlesex, to take up a similar appointment.

Fox, at Sandy Lodge; Patterson, first at Ashford Manor and later Burhill, in Surrey; and Grant Aitken, of Bishops Stortford, then of Tracy Park, Bristol; all have carved out places for themselves in the top flight of teachers in the country. Each attracts a growing band of adherents. Fox describes the time that he and Talbot were working in double-harness under Jacobs:

'It was all based on teamwork; we were a team and the three of us played in it together. But there was no doubt about who was the captain. John was always decisive. He'd say, "I shall be off on Tuesday so you will both be here." If you asked for a day off and it didn't fit, he'd say so straightaway. Maybe there was a tournament that David and I wanted to play in. If it didn't suit his programme, he'd be equally firm. "You can't both play, you can't both be away together. Spin a coin or sort it out between you. Whoever stays can play next time."

'We always knew where we stood. Everything was laid down pat – the normal hours, the duties. It was very disciplined. We just worked happily to a schedule and accepted it. That was the job and you did it.

'If John thought he was right about something, there was never a discussion, never an argument. What he thought went, and that was that.

'We had a coconut mat outside the shop. Whenever one of us was doing nothing for fifteen minutes, we'd be hitting balls. Between the three of us and our duties, we'd be hitting balls all day. Sometimes, in the breaks, all three of us would be hitting. John encouraged it and we enjoyed it. He passed his enthusiasm on to us. We were *all* mad keen.

'I so well remember the way John experimented. He was always trying something new. He'd tell you to take all the grips off his clubs and make them thicker. Then he'd want them off again and a piece of leather run down the back of the shaft. He'd try that for a few days, and then it would be the lies of his short irons. "Flatten them a shade," he'd say.

'It was the same with his practising. At the end of the day we'd go out and hit balls. One evening he'd be moving them left to right; the next, it would be the other way. He was always moving the ball about. He had wonderful hands for working the ball, flighting it. He could make it talk. It fascinated him to see what he could do with it. He was great to practise with.

'I've always thought he built up a problem for himself with all that experimenting. I remember a tournament at Moor Park. The night before it started we were on the practice ground at Sandy Lodge and he said, "Now, we're on the High Course tomorrow, I think I'll be drawing the ball." He maybe took 76. That evening we'd be out again at Sandy Lodge, hitting balls. "It's the West Course tomorrow. I feel I should be fading it." And he'd do 66.

'That was John's way. He was always doing something with the flight of the ball. With him, we learned to move it about. Sometimes I used to think to myself: why doesn't he just stand up like he can and hit it, nothing fancy? He could do it, but it never seemed to appeal to him just to knock it down the middle. The ball had to be worked.'

How much did Jacobs's assistants retain for their own teaching? Again, Alex Fox is quite definite:

'After thirty years, I'd say that sixty per cent, maybe seventy per cent, of my way of teaching is John's. The point is that John never taught by the manual. He would never follow a pattern. Nowadays, if a would-be assistant is asked a question about teaching, he has to answer it by reference to the manual. That's what he's taught to do. The manual is his bible. That was never John's way, and still isn't.

'Like John, I've never taught a method – laying clubs down on the turf, measuring off and all that, making people follow a set-piece. I just work with a pupil, get him or her to hit the ball down the fairway, and enjoy the game. My aim is always to get a pupil playing better with what he's got. Around here, in Hertfordshire, they call me "Mr Repair

Man". I look to make the best of what a player has got already, then get him working well with his present mechanism. Everyone is different. I don't teach golf. I work with my pupils and their individuality. And that's the way it has been ever since I started with John at Sandy Lodge in 1953.'

Fox emphasizes another point which is sometimes forgotten:

'Henry Cotton, in his time, lifted up the status of the British golf professional. He improved his lot. He said to members of clubs: "This is your pro, this is the fellow you should be building up and supporting. He's there to help you. He's looking after your interests."

'John Jacobs has done much the same with teaching. He started charging fees in those days – £4, £5, £6, £8, whatever it was per hour – which most pros had never dreamed of. But John's pupils still came back for more. He gave the lead, set a level he knew the market would wear, and so raised the whole concept of teaching to what he believed it was worth.'

Alex Fox's final shot goes to the heart of it:

'John's life is different now. He teaches here in the UK, in Europe, in the USA. He's on the move most of the time, but he would never want to go back to the daily grind that he knew at Sandy Lodge. All the same, he will always want to be active, to be involved. John has to be in charge.

'If he happened to turn up here at Sandy Lodge one day and found me giving a clinic, he wouldn't just stand there and listen. He'd grab a club and take over . . . And finish off the session!'

It was not long before Jacobs was asked to contribute instructional articles to one of the golfing magazines. John Stobbs, then the editor of the periodical *Golfing*, and the golf correspondent of *The Observer*, was the first to give him a run. Stobbs knew a golfer when he saw one. As an undergraduate at Oxford just after the Second World War, he and his partner, David Houlding, had enjoyed the bizarre distinction of winning their 36-hole foursome in the 1947 University Match against Cambridge at Sandwich by the unfriendly margin of 14 up and 12 to play, after being nine up at lunch. Subsequently, he had become a Hertfordshire county player and knew all about the impact which Jacobs was making at Sandy Lodge, both as a teacher and as a Ryder Cup player.

The initial exchange between editor and contributor was unconventional, as Jacobs recalls: 'John Stobbs asked me what fee I would charge for each story. I said I would do it for nothing, provided I could write the copy myself. In the end, I think we agreed a fee of three guineas for each article at late 1950s' prices.'

The literary combination of Jacobs and Stobbs bore fruit. Written golf instruction, unless it is very well done, is difficult for the ordinary mortal to understand, let alone digest. He can quickly lose his way in the undergrowth. In this case, however, because the editor was a player and Jacobs, with his uncluttered golfing mind, has always been a writer of clear, straightforward prose, the contributions at once attracted attention – including, as will later be seen, that of one important competing interest.

The articles were useful in another way. Jacobs, in collaboration with Stobbs, based his first book* on them. First published in 1963, right at the end of his Sandy Lodge time, it exposed much of the wisdom which had accrued in the period. It went through several impressions before being overtaken by its author's later works. But there was much more to the publication than its commercial success.

A quarter of a century is a long time in golf. Theories and doctrines change and go out of fashion. Indeed, there is small doubt that a few of the instructional books written in the 1950s and 1960s, and some even later, would now gladly be disowned by their eminent authors. But not so Jacobs's first publication.

One day in the winter of 1986, Jacobs was due to play an early afternoon round with his close friend Bernard Gallacher at Wentworth. Gallacher, a fine professional golfer and character, and an acute student of the playing art, had been speaking at a dinner in his native Scotland the previous evening. He had flown down to Heathrow that morning to be ready for the game.

'I don't know how I'll play,' he said, as the two walked onto the first tee. 'I got very little sleep last night. I found a copy of your first book on the table beside my bed in the house where I was staying. I read it straight through before I put out the light.' There was a pause. 'I see it was published nearly twenty-five years ago. But isn't that still what you're saying today?'

If golf tends to be the subject of Bernard Gallacher's bedside reading, cricket has long been John Jacobs's preferred choice. For years his old favourite, *For Yorkshire and England* by Herbert Sutcliffe, hero of his Lindrick childhood, has lain on the table beside his bed.

Cricket – and Yorkshire cricket in particular – have a high place among his lifetime's interests. It is understandable. As a batsman at

* *Golf*, Stanley Paul, London, 1963.

school and in his service days he showed promise well above the general run of his contemporaries. The natural eye for a half-volley was always there. It emerged again unexpectedly and incongruously at St Andrews years later. Peter Alliss tells the story.

The two were playing a practice round with a couple of others on the Old Course before the 1955 Open championship. They were on the fifth green which, with the adjoining thirteenth, makes one vast double-putting area. Jacobs had just run down a long steal and was turning to walk to the sixth tee.

'Coming up,' shouted Alliss, as he picked the ball out of the cup and bowled it, overarm, back to the striker – a well-pitched-up half-volley. Jacobs, taking a couple of paces to get to the pitch of it, swung his putter in a mock stroke at the ball. The result is fixed indelibly in Alliss's mind:

'Instead of missing it, John caught it right on the meat of his putter. The ball flashed back past my ear, going at a rate of knots, and spreadeagled the players and their caddies, putting out on the thirteenth green behind. A chorus of outraged shouts left us in no doubt . . .'

Jacobs was reported and hauled up before the secretary of the Royal and Ancient. 'Playing cricket on the Old Course at St Andrews, indeed,' he said, a trace loftily.

'Fortunately for me,' recalls Jacobs, 'Brigadier Brickman was a fisherman . . . We had some lovely talks together!'

SOWING THE SEED-CORN

To have come through the tournament fire increases a teacher's authority with his pupils. Such a man has experienced at first hand what intense pressure can do to a player's mind and thus to his game.

Jacobs was well served in this respect by his tournament stint in the 1950s and early 1960s. He did not, in his Sandy Lodge years, match the records of the most successful among his generation of fellow-countrymen: Bernard Hunt, Peter Alliss, Christy O'Connor, Eric Brown, Harry Weetman, and others. But he was seldom far behind.

Jacobs tended to be more successful abroad than at home.* There was a really notable win on the thirty-fifth green of his match against

*Abroad, he could practise without interruption. At home, he had only to walk out on the practice ground to work on his game and a member would come up to him. 'I wonder if you'd just have a quick look at me, I'm . . .?'

Gary Player in the final of the 1957 South African match-play championship played at Houghton, Johannesburg. He had seen off Harold Henning, victor in four previous tournaments on the trot, in the semi-final. Jacobs followed this with victory in the Dutch Open in the same year, a 72-hole total of 284 at Hilversum leaving him clear of his rivals. Two years before, there had been his dual success for Britain in the 36-holes foursomes and singles in the Ryder Cup at Palm Springs. And this, in turn, had followed his tie with Ugo Grappasonni on 272 in the 1954 Italian Open at Villa d'Este. He was beaten next day in the play-off; that same year, Henry Cotton similarly closed him out in the final of the Penfold 2000 Guineas tournament at Llandudno.

There had been another second – with his partner, Trevor Allen – in the 1953 Goodwin foursomes tournament at Lindrick, when they were beaten in the final by Bernard Hunt and Jack Hargreaves, a formidable pair in those days; 1953 had also brought a semi-final defeat by the winner, Max Faulkner, in the *News of the World* PGA match-play Championship at Ganton in Yorkshire. He tasted second place again, eight years later, when Bernard Hunt, with a low, four-round total of 272, beat him by three shots in the 1961 German Open at Krefeld, near Dusseldorf.

During this period, there were 'top twenty' finishes in the British Open – fourteenth in 1953 at Carnoustie, Hogan's year; twentieth at Birkdale in 1954; twelfth at St Andrews in 1955; sixteenth at Hoylake in 1956; and twentieth at Birkdale again in 1961. It was a time, too, when he was never out of the first twenty in the Order of Merit table. He was twice invited (in 1956 and 1957) to play in the US Masters at Augusta – invitations which, because of his heavy teaching schedule at Sandy Lodge, he was compelled to decline. He would have played at Augusta in 1957 had not he and Bernard Hunt, then professional at nearby Hartsbourne Manor, in Hertfordshire, just spent three profitable months at the start of the year in South Africa, one of only two winter tours that Jacobs felt able to undertake abroad during all his Sandy Lodge years.

Apart from the victory over Player in the match-play championship, the South African trip had other important features. Hunt and Jacobs, close friends and playing partners, had engaged in a number of fiercely contested matches in England in the previous season with the 'pocket colossus' from Johannesburg and his compatriot, Trevor Wilkes. Player put the suggestion directly to them: 'If you fellows will come out to South Africa in your next British winter, plenty of people will be found to play you for any money you like to name.' Dunlop and

Slazenger arranged the itinerary and the matches for them.

Hunt was then approaching the zenith of a consistently successful playing career. He agreed with Jacobs that he would make the trip, subject to one proviso: that, throughout the weeks they were there, his Sandy Lodge companion would draw the ball 'and do nothing else'. Hunt had a reason for making the stipulation:

'John was a natural hooker, but whenever he got onto a golf course, he'd see a shot in terms of a fade or a draw, a cut-up ball or one floated in high, and so on; he would always see the "difficult" shot, the one which appealed to his fancy. He wouldn't stop mixing it up. In a way, he knew too much about the golf swing. He was for ever putting into practice what he had learnt about flighting the ball, moving it about and what he was teaching his pupils. I felt that he could have been a better player if he had been prepared to play more naturally and stuck to his natural shape.

'But, make no mistake, it was the knowledge he had built up of flighting the ball, moving it about and what was necessary in a swing to produce these results that made him such a good teacher.

'Anyway, that's certainly what I said to him: "Hook the ball all the time and I'll come with you".'

Bernard Hunt, an adept clinic-giver in his own right, has long believed that the really good and consistent scorers all tend, generally, to play golf to a set pattern. 'With Bobby Locke, every shot was a hook. With Hogan, every one was a fade. With Player it is a draw. Of course, the good ones can all do what they want with the ball at will. Look at Henry Cotton and Christy O'Connor ("Himself"). No two people had a wider range of "worked" shots than they did. They both had wonderful hands to work the ball with. But they, and the other outstanding scorers, developed a pattern and they went on repeating it.'

Jacobs says that Hunt's golf on their South African journey was of a quite exceptional quality.

'I know John is good enough to say that', comments Hunt. 'but so did he play very well himself. I'm sure it was because he kept his promise and stuck to his right-to-left pattern. We were playing all over the country, finishing up in Rhodesia, and there were games against different people all the time. But he didn't vary his game, that's my point.

'What few people know is that John is a very good player *when he is playing matches for his own money*. I played so many matches with him, in South Africa and elsewhere, and I have never doubted that he was a better player in those games than he ever was in medal tournaments. He really got stuck into them.'

The tour of the Springbok country was a scintillating success. The two of them played five tournaments and thirty-two exhibition games against any two amateurs whom the various clubs pitted against them. It was all-in on strange courses which they had mostly never seen before. They were never beaten in the head-to-head contests. And in an international match which they and their two compatriots, Dai Rees and Ken Bousfield, who were out there for some part of the same time, played against Player and Locke, Harold Henning and Wilkes, Hunt and Jacobs cleaned up the first two in what the latter has called 'the hell of a foursomes match'. Locke was then 'a consistently great player', as his fourth and last win in the British Open at St Andrews later that year confirmed. The next day Jacobs beat Wilkes, who had won the Daks tournament the previous year at Wentworth with a highly creditable total of 276.

Jacobs is quite positive about his assessment of Hunt's playing during their weeks together in southern Africa: 'I really do think that through the whole of that trip Bernard was the best iron player I have ever seen. I said it then and I still say it now. Whether it was a 2-iron or a wedge, he just knocked it straight at the pin. He wasn't thinking about the green, it was the stick that he was after. Over and over again, he was putting for birdies. His iron play was relentless in its accuracy.'

Within a couple of weeks of the pair's return, the British tournament season was due to open. They had agreed, as they flew home, that they would play a practice round together before the first event at Llandudno. 'I got to the club,' said Hunt, 'and asked one or two of the lads if they'd seen John. Yes, they said, he's on the practice ground. I walked over and there he was, hitting balls one after another at his caddie, right down the course. Every one was a fade.'

By the time he and Jacobs came together Bernard Hunt's swing was established. Set against Bruce Critchley's experience (see pages 42–46), the process by which he reached this happy state makes an instructive comparison. There was no more successful tournament player in Britain in the 1950s and 1960s than the future Ryder Cup captain.

Sitting in the clubhouse at Foxhills, near Ottershaw, in Surrey, where he now holds sway, Hunt let his mind run back over the traumas which he encountered before El Dorado was attained:

'I had started out with a very standard swing – quite a long backswing, but very normal. I then played Max Faulkner in the match-play championship at Walton Heath. After he had beaten me, he said: "You'll never play golf very well until you stop swaying." So I went home and, I suppose in my ignorance, in trying to stop the sway I unwittingly shortened the swing. The backswing was cut down by not using so much bodywork.

'A bit later, when I got to Wentworth for the Ryder Cup in 1953, my first time in the team, Henry Cotton, our captain, said to me, "You're too short and flat. You won't play golf consistently until you develop a better swing."

'So now I was betwixt and between. For two years, my father and brother worked with me trying to find what I would call a normal swing – a bit more upright and a bit longer. It didn't work at all, mainly, I think, because I had by that time become pretty set up with my short backswing. So after a very good year in 1953, I did nothing for two years in the tournaments. I then went back to what came naturally to me – my old short backswing. My hands went up to about shoulder level, no more.

'The lads used to say I was a bit short and flat, and I knew what they meant. But John Jacobs wouldn't have it. He saw it another way. "Don't change what you're doing. Keep what you've got now. That swing will work for you for a long time." And, of course, he was quite right. I was swinging like that when we were on tour in South Africa and I was certainly, by then, playing golf very well.'

The other winter trip which Jacobs undertook during the Sandy Lodge years was to the United States in 1955. Hunt was again with him and so, too, were Peter Alliss, Tony Harmon and John Pritchett. Pritchett, a promising young player (he won the Daks at Wentworth later that year), was then the assistant at Sunningdale. His life was cut poignantly short for, only a few years later, he was killed in a tragic motor accident with Philip Scrutton, the British Walker Cup player and English international.

All five in the party were sponsored – Hunt and Alliss by Slazenger, and the other three by Dunlop. But because the first two had become Ryder Cup players, they were accorded pink if not red – carpet treatment. They were flown out to the Pacific coast, while Jacobs, Harmon and Pritchett crossed the Atlantic by boat and thence by TWA, via Chicago, to Los Angeles. The Dunlop trio were each given

£350 spending money; and the duration of the tour would depend on how long the cash lasted. To help the collective finances, the three agreed to split their winnings between them.

In the event, they contrived to remain on the US circuit for three months, which was as long as they could manage anyway, if they were to be back in time for the start of the British season. This enabled them to play ten tournaments, starting in January with the LA Open and taking in, among others, the Crosby at Cypress Point, the San Diego Open and the Bob Hope Classic at Palm Springs, before moving on through Arizona and Texas and so home. Gene Littler was a three-time winner that winter, when the first prize in each tournament carried a purse of $2000.

For John Jacobs and his mates, it was a 'tremendous experience'. The going was certainly rough. There were the Monday morning qualifying battles to find a place in the subsequent tournament ... queueing up before daybreak to get starting times for practice rounds and, generally, joining the ranks of Jimmy Demaret's picturesque friends, 'the dew sweepers'.

Ed Lowery, a real Anglophile, put a Lincoln – 'the largest car you ever saw' said Jacobs – at the party's disposal while they were playing in California. Lowery, as a boy, had carried Francis Ouimet's bag at the Brookline Country Club in the 1913 US Open when the twenty-year-old amateur 'founded the American golfing empire' (Bernard Darwin's phrase) with his cataclysmic victory over Harry Vardon and Ted Ray in the 18-hole play-off for the championship. Now, making use of his Lincoln-Ford dealership in California, he saw to it that the visitors were well equipped. When they left California, they had to turn the car in; then, under their own steam, they bought themselves a Chevrolet for 'five ninety-five', which served its essential purpose, despite various altercations with the highway police, until the tour was over.

For Jacobs, the three months' visit provided several memorable highlights. In the Crosby at Cypress, there was the chance to play with Gardner Dickinson, Ben Hogan's one-time assistant and protégé, who was later to be a US Ryder Cup team member, and with whom he was later still to be associated on the panel of US *Golf Magazine*.

According to Jacobs, 'Gardner dressed like Hogan and imitated him, and for 14 holes in that tournament he played superbly. But he couldn't hole anything. Near the end of the round and close to exasperation, he missed another short putt. After tapping it in, he picked the ball out of the cup and crashed it down again at the hole.

"Introduce yourself," he muttered.'

It was at Palm Springs* in the Thunderbird Classic (later the Bob Hope Classic) that things 'came good'. Apart from Jacobs's satisfactory, top-ten finish in the tournament itself, his team was second in the pro-am, played in conjunction with the first two rounds of the main event.

'Each professional had three amateur partners and there was a big selling sweep before it. There were twenty-four teams and the amateurs bought their tickets in the auction. The pool, I remember very well, produced a total of $137,000, a great deal of money in the mid-fifties. My amateur partners had bought our team, which scored 58 and 56 net to finish second. They gave me $1000 from their winnings. This, together with the $400 I won for my seventh or eighth place in the tournament, helped to swell our kitty and keep us going. We hadn't won a bean up till then and were beginning to think we should have to come home.'

$1400, against the $2000 for the tournament winner, was a sizable boost for the Dunlop-sponsored British contingent's cash flow. But beyond the monetary gain, there was another bonus from the Palm Springs event: it was played at the Thunderbird Golf and Country Club, which, fortunately, was to be the venue for the Ryder Cup match that year. Byron Nelson, the Fort Worth marvel, whom Ed Lowery had helped to set up at the start of his career, was present as an invited celebrity. He was then forty-three and his health had forced him to retire from competitive golf with his honours thick upon him. His eleven consecutive tour wins between March and August 1945, when set in the frame alongside his US Open, Masters and PGA Championship victories, still make an astonishing record. Jacobs was lucky to strike up a friendship with Nelson at that time:

'John Pritchett and I played with Byron for three days in a row, a wonderful opportunity for each of us. He hit the ball absolutely dead straight for the whole of those days. He had a personal golf swing – very straight up and down. It would normally have been too steep, but he sank right into the ball, his head dropped well down in the hitting area and his knees went all soft, so that he almost scraped the turf through the ball, keeping it very wide and close to the ground.'

Twelve years later, in 1967, Jacobs and Nelson were together again

*There were two courses at Palm Springs in 1955, Thunderbird and Tamarisk. Ellsworth Vines, fine tennis player and good golfer, was the golf pro at Tamarisk. Jacobs reminded him that, as a boy, he had seen him at Lindrick pre-war, when he and Donald Budge, US and Wimbledon Champion, came into the shop.

at Hoylake, the scene of that year's British Open. Each had a television commitment. Never one to miss a chance to probe a great golfing mind, Jacobs played the diagnostician's card:

'I told Byron I had read his book and judged from it that he must have been, in his early days, a flat swinger. Nelson at once took up the running. "Yes," he said, "that was so." He won tournaments with a rounded, flat swing. But he would win one week and miss the cut out the next. He knew he could and ought to play much better.

'He then told me that he decided to take six months off – six months away from tournaments altogether, quite a decision – and remodel everything. He remodelled his swing totally. "After that," Byron remarked, "I knew that I would never play badly again." What a wonderful thing to be able to say.

'If now I was asked, after all these years, who was the best hitter I ever saw, I would have to say Byron Nelson.'

Donald Steel, the golf-course architect and journalist, whose well-informed writing in the *Sunday Telegraph* and *Country Life* commands a strong following, has a knack of picking out a signal feature in a golfer which others may well have missed.

As a member of Ted Dexter's Cambridge golf team which invited Jacobs to spend a week with it at Rye in the winter of 1957–58,* he recalls the experience:

'We used to spend fascinating evenings in the pub at Rye just listening to John talking about golf and golfers. Naturally, he helped us on the course and on the practice ground with our games, but what struck me as the most beneficial aspect of having him as a coach was the chance to hear him talk – not so much about the technical side of the game but about how to play a match, how to get it round – and to listen to his stories of his Ryder Cup conquest in 1955 and of the Middlecoffs, the Sneads, the Nelsons and the Hogans and what made them great . . .'

Jacobs registers what he sees and files it away in his mind. Talk to him about a player, a style, a fashion, or discuss with him a developing

*Jacobs was invited to give a hand with Oxford as well as Cambridge at Burnham, in Somerset, the following year. In the university match at Lytham St Annes in 1960, both teams again asked him to be present, but Lytham refused permission for him to attend . . . A curious contribution to the cause of university, and amateur, golf, particularly for such a distinguished and respected club. Apparently the committee thought he would be trespassing on their own professional's domain.

trend in the game, and there will be a new reflection, a fresh slant on what may well be an old theme. His mind cuts through the game like a laser.

What had he discovered, then, from his first US visit about the Americans' long-established attitude to playing golf?

'One thing I learned competing alongside them during that tour was the way they forgot about a bad shot. If they hit a poor one, they just seemed to go straight on with playing the next one. I always felt so embarrassed if I hit a really bad stroke. But they weren't in the least inhibited by what had happened.'

It was this ability, as much as any other, which gave Walter Hagen the first of his four British victories at the Open Championship at Sandwich in 1922 and, with it, a cheque for £75 which he at once endorsed and handed over to 'Skip' Daniels, his caddie.

There never was a player better able than Hagen to put the hard knocks behind him. Maybe someone had reminded him of the famous lines

> To mourn a mischief that is past and gone
> Is the next way to draw new mischief on.

The 1955 US tour, and notably his experience at Thunderbird, was to pave the way for Jacobs's inclusion in the Ryder Cup team that year. His place in the side, and especially his maximum points in the contest, contributed significantly to his colleagues' choice of him, a quarter of a century later, as captain of the first combined British and European team.

Two years earlier Jacobs had been close to a place in Henry Cotton's team for the match at Wentworth. After reaching the semi-final of the *News of the World* match-play championship only a short while before, he had been added to the sixteen who were to play trials in advance of the team's selection.

Cotton's plan was to send the trialists out in fours on the West course at Wentworth with everyone putting a pound into the kitty. The low medallist in each of the four rounds, which were played over two days a fortnight before the match itself, would scoop the pool.

Jacobs, then twenty-eight, was placed in a key game on the first day – he, Peter Alliss, twenty-two, and Bernard Hunt, twenty-three, going out with the captain in the morning. His 68 in the first round and 69 in the afternoon were good enough to collect the pool, £16, each time.

For a while he thought he might be picked, but in the event others were preferred: 'Obviously, I was disappointed not to be in the side after winning two of the four medal rounds – disappointed, but not more than that. I wasn't sure then that I was quite good enough for a place as there were some very fine players in the team.'

There was a lighter side to the team's selection which probably contains a moral for all selectors.

The sixteen trialists were staying at the Dormy House, at Sunningdale, two or three miles down the road from Wentworth. They sat down to dinner each evening at small separate tables; Alliss, Hunt and Jacobs managed to sit together. They were thus able to compare notes at the end of each day and check what individual selectors had, quite wrongly, been telling them about their chances of being picked. Jacobs recalls what they found out: 'Each one of the three of us had been assured by each selector individually that he had nothing to worry about and that he could count on a place in the side!'

It was hardly a responsible way of picking a professional team to represent Great Britain against the United States. It led in the end – and Jacobs was one of the prime movers in getting the system changed – to the 1955 team being taken from the first seven in the averages, with three more being chosen by the executive committee. With his own seventh place in the order, Jacobs was thus automatically selected.

Jacobs believed that the US team at Wentworth in 1953 was probably about the strongest the Americans had ever sent to Britain. More venerable judges might contend that the 1937 side, with Nelson and Snead included for the first time, was its equal. The 1953 team, however, undoubtedly possessed one overriding advantage.

It was then roundly twenty years since the United States Golf Association had introduced the 1.68 inch diameter ball into general use in America, so a generation of US golfers had grown up never having known the smaller, 1.62 inch ball. The resulting US advantage was obvious from a comparison of the two teams' actions at Wentworth just as it had been four years earlier in the Walker Cup match between the two countries at Winged Foot, New York.

From his own observations, Jacobs had already formed positive views about the merits of the big ball and its effect upon the US players' striking: 'Their swings were altogether firmer and more solid as a result of the prolonged use of the 1.68 inch ball. They were firmer at, and right through, the ball. They swung their arms better and there was less independent hand and wrist action – less flicking.'

A dozen years were to elapse before the British PGA made the use of the 1.68 inch ball obligatory in its tournaments. It was more than twenty before the Royal and Ancient Golf Club took the plunge and made the larger ball compulsory in the Open Championship of 1974.

Ben Hogan's Open at Carnoustie in 1953 had a special interest for Jacobs. After driving Peter Alliss up to Scotland in his spacious Lincoln Ford, which he had brought back from Egypt the previous year, Jacobs arrived at the clubhouse to find he had been allotted a locker next door to Hogan's. The superman from Fort Worth, Texas, had become a powerful world character, whom the sports writers of the day were apt to call 'the Hawk':

'I was nervous about opening up a conversation, but Ben was always courteous and pleasant, saying good morning and passing a thoughtful word before changing and going out to practise or play.

'Naturally, I dashed out to watch him at the first opportunity. I had read his book, *Power Golf*,* written just after the war. This had shown him to have a very strong left-hand grip, and the first thing one noticed was the change which had come about. Here he was now with a very weak, one-knuckle grip with his left hand, fanning it open going back and getting his left wrist underneath the shaft at the top to give him a marvellously open position. From there, he could let fly and hit it as hard as he liked without fear of hooking the ball.'**

Hogan's four rounds at Carnoustie – 73, 71, 70 and 68=282 – played before a surging Scottish throng, over a big and searchingly difficult course, bore testimony to the worth of the change he had made. He won immaculately by four shots from his compatriot, Frank Stranahan, Dai Rees of Britain, Peter Thomson of Australia (then only twenty-four, he won the first of his five Opens the following year at Birkdale) and Antonio Cerda of the Argentine. This victory, when matched with his other two wins that season in the US Masters at Augusta and the US Open at Oakmont – three majors in almost as many months – set the seal on his supremacy.

*Nicholas Kaye, London, 1949.
**Byron Nelson confirmed to Jacobs when the two were together at Hoylake in 1967 that Hogan, his Texan contemporary, had started his professional career with a strong left-hand grip. 'I said to Byron that I felt Hogan had wanted to weaken his left hand for years. It had taken his dreadful car accident to give him time to master it. I remember adding that I bet Hogan had said to himself when in hospital, "If I can recover and play again, I'm never going to use a strong grip again." Byron confirmed that Hogan had practised with a weak grip for at least two years before he actually adopted it, but when he got out on the course he changed back.'

But there was more to those sterling rounds than that. This man, who, only four years before, had been crippled in a dreadful highway collision, and whose legs thereafter would be critically affected, had been close to the limit of human endurance.

Two years later, when Jacobs had made the 1955 British Ryder Cup team at Palm Springs, he witnessed a bizarre little incident involving Hogan. The tourists had stopped off at Tulsa, Oklahoma, to take part, with a team of ten specially chosen Americans, in a charity event for the Cancer Research organization. Jacobs was fortunate in the draw:

'We played at Southern Hills and all one day I was in the match directly in front of Hogan. It was a treat to turn round and watch his seconds dropping time after time around the pin.*

'There was one longish hole on the back 9 where the second shot had to be laid up short of a hazard; this left a short pitch to the pin. The next tee was quite close to the green. I had hit my drive and was walking off the tee just as Hogan was playing his 9-iron or wedge to the flag. He had about sixty or seventy yards to go. He hit the ball clean off the socket – right off the pipe of his pitching club. It flew sharply right and, as a matter of fact, very nearly hit me as I walked forward. I thought to myself at the time: I bet there aren't many who have seen Hogan hit a full-blooded shank.'

Jacobs's performance at the Thunderbird in the subsequent match against the US was a personal triumph, although Britain was heavily defeated by 8 points to 4. He was wholly or in part (with Johnny Fallon, his foursomes partner) responsible for 50 per cent of the team's points and the only man in the side to record a 100 per cent result in the series. A couple of Jacobs's experiences from the two days' play are worth recounting.

It was a natural for Dai Rees, the British captain, to pair the two Yorkshiremen, Jacobs and Fallon, together in the foursomes. They were old friends and knew each other's game from tee to cup. Their victory over Jerry Barber and Chick Harbert on the thirty sixth green with two rounds of 70, against a tight par of 71, was the visitors' only point on the first day. It was not easily gained.

Britain were one up going to the final hole – a par 4 of over 450 yards as it was set up for the match. Both pairs were through the green with their seconds. Jacobs was away, confronted with a testing little

*A US sports writer described the process with a colourful metaphor: 'like a machine stamping out bottle caps'.

pitch up a steep bank and then down to the pin, with the green sloping away:

'It was an uptight moment. I remember having visions of Peter Alliss's pitch to the thirty-sixth green at Wentworth in his match against Jim Turnesa two years before. Then, suddenly, a thought came to me (it's strange how these things do when you're under pressure). If this was the tenth hole at Sandy Lodge in a weekend game, and I was way down below the raised, plateau green, I would simply take a sand iron and flip it over the top. I actually pitched it well to within seven or eight feet of the flag.

'The US ball caught the top of the bank and rolled all the way back, whereupon blow me if Jerry Barber didn't chip it in for a 4. But Johnny, bless him, knocked a brave putt into the back of the hole for a half in 4 and the match. The result made such a difference to my attitude to the singles the next day.'

Jacobs's game with Cary Middlecoff was a hard-fought, truly professional affair:

'We both hit the ball very well and putted extraordinarily well.' Dormy 2 up standing on the thirty-fifth tee, with two par 4s for a 65, the British player reckoned he had just about got the match won. Both were on the penultimate green in 2. With Jacobs lying dead for his par, Middlecoff shaped up to his eight-yarder. 'I was quite certain he would hole it, and he did.'

One up with one to go, Jacobs's second to the final green was a solid long iron to the back of the putting surface. With the pin on the left-hand front of the green, there was still plenty of work to do:

'I hit a good putt from a difficult position, with the ball pulling up some six feet short – shorter than I had expected when I hit it. With Cary's ball now stone dead for his par, I suppose everyone round that green thought I would miss mine and the match would be halved.

'When I looked the putt over, I had no doubt at all that I would hole it; I was quite certain that it would go in. (How does one know sometimes, even under extreme pressure, that a putt is certain to drop and that others will miss?) Anyway, I knew that one was going straight in, and it did . . .

'I suppose that, at that moment, Middlecoff was just about the best in-form player in the United States. He was at the peak of his playing career. I just stood there all day and admired him as a golfer. I feel pretty sure that if we had been playing on a bigger golf course I wouldn't have seen the way he went.'

True or false, Jacobs's 134 strokes for the 36 holes, under the whip, suggested that by then he was more than a match for the great occasion.

At the end of the tour, a stop in Washington on the way home enabled Jacobs to indulge his lifelong penchant for seeing historic places and, when there was a chance, listening to successful men.

'I was able to see President Eisenhower's famous Oval Office in the White House. Unfortunately, the President wasn't there as he was recovering from one of his heart attacks. But I did notice that, as a golfer, he had had constructed a very nice-looking putting green right outside his office window.'

Once they were on board ship, and homeward bound, Lord Brabazon,* then the president of the British PGA and a wartime member of Churchill's coalition cabinet, invited Rees and Jacobs – the captain and the most successful team member – to dine at his table. There were only the three of them. A man of rare talent and diverse interests, 'Brab', as everyone knew him, was in the first three of Britain's 'after-dinner' speakers. His wit and originality had appealed greatly to his American hosts at the various functions the team had attended. Jacobs comments:

'Lord Brabazon had been absolutely superb. He seemed to make a mark effortlessly with his speaking and with his presence, giving a lead whenever it was needed. He brought so much authority to an occasion. For me, he was a Churchillian figure, and to be able to listen to him at dinner that evening, talking about his experiences and the great figures and events of his life, was something that I shall never forget.'

In fact, Brab had singled out Jacobs from among his playing contemporaries as the one whose intellectual qualities, background and acumen were the most likely to serve the PGA when it was looking for a leader from the tournament side of the organization. It was a prescient judgement, and Brab's opinion of him was to prove useful to Jacobs in the future:

'When a few of us were pressing for a better representation for the tournament side on the club-dominated executive committee, his

*Lord Brabazon of Tara, 1st Baron of Sandwich, who later became captain of the Royal and Ancient, had a house at Sandwich Bay in the inter-war years. He was a golfing enthusiast. Friends staying with him in the early days found themselves having to play three rounds in a day – at Deal, St George's and Prince's. When Prince's, where Gene Sarazen won his Open in 1932 with a total of 283, was commandeered by the military in World War II, an ignorant commanding officer allowed the putting greens (among the finest and truest in all the world) to be used as targets for mortar fire. Someone told Brab. 'My God,' he exclaimed in disgust, 'it's like throwing darts at a Rembrandt.'

lordship asked me several times to go along and see him privately in his office in Berkeley Square. He wanted to hear at first hand what those for whom I could speak felt. I admired the way he picked up the things that mattered and discarded the rest. I felt sure he was on our side and in sympathy with what we were trying to do. It was a privilege for me to be able to talk in confidence with him like that.'

1955 left another interesting legacy. The Open that year was played at St Andrews. Jacobs was about to tee off with his Ryder Cup partner, Johnny Fallon, for a practice round when a young South African approached them. Courteously, he introduced himself as Gary Player. He was nineteen and had been a professional for two years. He had neither a starting time nor a partner. 'Would you two gentlemen allow me to join you?' he inquired.

It was Jacobs's first meeting with the wiry, whipcord-tight, pocket figure whose competitiveness and plain guts would, before long, take him to the summit of the game:

'It was Mr Jacobs this and Mr Fallon that, and there were the endless questions. Gary asked us about everything – our thoughts on the game, our swings, his swing, the course, how each hole should be played, the clubs we used. But it was plain from just that one practice round that here was a young man who was going places. You could see he was dedicated to the game and everything about it. He was out to learn every scrap he could.

'Although he had that rather peculiar, very flat, rounded swing, it was repetitive. He hooked everything, but he hooked it well – that was the point. The ball always came down soft.'

That round marked the beginning of a long friendship. Player occasionally used to stay with relatives of his countryman Trevor Wilkes at Pinner, in Middlesex, only a few miles from Sandy Lodge. 'When there wasn't a tournament on, Gary would come over to the club and hit balls for hours on the practice ground,' remembers Jacobs. 'In his first season or two in Britain, he would often ride with me in my car to the tournaments. He lived every moment of every day for his golf.'

John Jacobs's decision to quit the all-embracing life of a club pro-fessional in the early 1960s was taken rationally and deliberately. He concluded, with his wife, for whose down-to-earth, innate Yorkshire nous he has always carried so high a regard, that his career up to this point had run its course.

The breadwinner had gone as far as he felt he was likely to go as a tournament player. He was widely experienced at home and abroad. He had done well, on occasions very well, to make his mark and establish a platform for whatever might lie ahead. But he hadn't made it to the top. Nor, as he approached forty, did he think the picture would alter: 'I had realized by then that I could teach the game better than I could play it. I had total confidence in myself as a teacher. I never had quite the same feeling as a player.'

Those who directed the affairs of Sandy Lodge during the Jacobs years felt that between them and their professional there had existed a special relationship. It was essentially an adult understanding, founded on genuine respect. One who saw it all at first hand was my own elder brother, Ian Lucas, who was then secretary of the club. As a director and shareholder of the company, and one of the club's longest-serving members, he held office for some twenty years, half of which covered Jacobs's time. The association between them was friendly, fruitful and devoid of conflict. It was also straightforward. (Jacobs is allergic to devious back-stage dealing – as others elsewhere have discovered to their cost.) Lucas's background helped. Brought up at Sandwich in an 'establishment' atmosphere, he had absorbed the game in boyhood and understood its traditions. An accomplished journalist, he had spent a quarter of a century in Fleet Street, starting as a junior reporter on Northcliffe's *Daily Mail* before moving on to Reuters, for whom in the 1920s and 1930s he covered the royal tours to distant lands. As the accredited correspondent on those journeys, he had won the trust and confidence of those members of the royal family whose activities he reported. Later, he took his place on the London editorial staff of the worldwide agency.

With a reporter's eye for the meat of a story, he could identify the distinguishing features of the Jacobs reign:

'The point about John was that he got involved with the club. Apart from all the playing and the teaching, that was where he really scored at Sandy Lodge. He had a pride in the club and the members knew it. They felt he was playing in the team, not watching it. He had a good commercial brain and ran his shop like a business. He delegated responsibility to his assistants, whom he picked well and carefully. They were invariably well-trained, disciplined young men with good manners. In this he set the example and they followed it naturally. When he was away – and he was away a lot when the tournaments were on – things ran on normally. The two assistants knew what was expected of them and, between them, they provided the service. I do not recall a complaint because of a lack of cover or service during John's absence. He had laid down a standard and it was followed.

'He was, of course, lucky after a while to get his mother to come down from Lindrick to join him and take over the running of the shop. People would go in and buy equipment from her when they hadn't intended to. She was an exceptional saleswoman and we were all very fond of her, just as we were of Rita, his wife, who was a member of the club and a real asset to him.

'John was tough about money. He had his price and stuck to it. He kept looking for ways of increasing revenue and making suggestions to the club for doing so. He would put up an idea to me and I'd say that I would take it to the committee. He might not always agree with the decision, but he would accept it when once he knew it had been properly represented and considered. He was firm, very firm, in his convictions but he was prepared to see the other side's point of view.

'I am not aware that John and I ever had a difference in the time we worked together which we weren't able quickly to resolve. When he left the club in 1963, he kindly gave me a copy of the book which he and John Stobbs had then just published.* He wrote a short inscription in it which I have always valued: "In sincere gratitude for ten years of complete harmony."

'It was, indeed, a harmonious period because each of us dealt directly and openly with the other. John is a direct and open person and we got on, I believe, because we treated one another in just that way. If there hadn't been that kind of understanding between him, the committee and myself, then, I suspect, things could have been much more difficult. As it was, John and Rita and his mother – Mummy J – were all friends of the members and that was the basis on which it all evolved.'

As John Jacobs played out his innings for the club, another overseas visit came his way, which was to have important consequences.

Air Marshal Asghar Khan, commander-in-chief of the Pakistan air force and, at the time, also president of Pakistan International Airlines, was something of a golfing nut. He took lessons with Jacobs at Sandy Lodge whenever he came to London on business. Encouraged by his own experience, the air marshal ('a corker of a man, he was still flying aeroplanes, quite late on, at mach 2') decided that his air force

---

* *Golf*, Stanley Paul, London, 1963.

should be given the chance to learn to play golf. The Sandy Lodge professional and ex-Royal Air Force aircrew graduate was tailormade for the job.

In no time, Jacobs was flown out to the stunningly beautiful north-west frontier of Pakistan. There, in Peshawar, close to the Khyber Pass and the rugged Afghan border country, the air force was given the rudiments of the game. The air marshal was aware of the pro's predilection for country pursuits: 'I taught golf four or five days a week and then the C.-in-C. and I would fly off up-country in his helicopter to fish water that others had never fished before. The beauty of it all was startling.'

On a different occasion, just before he returned home, the thoroughgoing countryman was able to indulge another love – a day's partridge shooting:

'It was a very fine shoot, just north of Karachi. There were plenty of birds and at the end of it the air marshal asked me if I would like to take a dozen brace with me back to England. Of course, I said that I would, but that I doubted whether customs at Heathrow would allow me to take such a consignment into the country. He claimed that they would, and at once all manner of papers were prepared to facilitate the entry. The birds were then put in the ice box on the flight to London.'

As he had expected, when Jacobs declared the package at Heathrow, the customs officer refused entry. 'You can't bring those birds into the country,' he said decisively.

'I'm not sure that you're right,' retorted Jacobs, sticking in his toes. He then produced the impressive documentation which had been prepared in Pakistan. The customs officer bore it off. Half an hour later he returned. 'It's in order for you to bring in the birds,' he said, deadpan.

A year or so later, the air marshal had another package of birds flown in to Heathrow for Jacobs. It was backed by the relevant papers. Customs called him at his home. There was a package of two dozen partridges, addressed to him, which had just arrived from Pakistan: 'We've had to destroy the birds as they cannot be brought into the country.' 'You're wrong to do that,' countered Jacobs, and told the officer to whom he was speaking the previous story. He asked to be called back. The officer did indeed telephone to admit the mistake. 'But by then,' says the frustrated recipient, 'it was too late.'

After the success of the first visit, Asghar Khan asked Jacobs to return to Peshawar a second time. The C.-in-C. had, by now, become number two in the government and in charge of tourism; so, in addition to the teaching, he wanted five new courses designed and constructed. The demand for more and better facilities made manifest the increasing popularity of the game. This had been fuelled by the presence on the north-west frontier of Royal Air Force officers who were still there helping with the changeover following the partition with India. The liaison between them and their opposite numbers in the Pakistan air force was close and profitable.

Jacobs was well acquainted with the terrain from his first visit; with this local knowledge and the large-scale ordnance surveys which were available, he was able to put down on the maps the outline of the course designs that were needed. Once on the site, he had no difficulty in adjusting individual holes to suit the ground's contours and the architect's receptive eye.

In later years, course and golf-centre design has become an appealing feature of Jacobs's work both at home and overseas. He likes setting examination papers to which all classes of player will respond.

The relative exclusiveness of the game in Pakistan was shown by a revealing incident which occurred towards the end of Jacobs's second stay. He had already redesigned the front 9 holes of one of the Peshawar courses on his previous visit. Now he had returned to complete the second half. To help get the feel of it, he was playing the holes with the C.-in-C. and two other air force officers.

Jacobs and his party were about to play their tee shots to the 180-yard eleventh hole. Before the gaze of five or six hundred uninitiated spectators, an Englishman, playing with the local professional, shouted across that his pro had just holed the sixteenth in one. Before hitting his tee shot to the eleventh, Jacobs called back: 'If you watch carefully you will see how it's done.' The 3-iron went straight into the hole! 'The amusing thing was that most of the spectators who saw the shot, not being golfers, thought that it was intended!'

That same evening, Jacobs was flown by helicopter to Lahore to dine with Ayub Khan, Pakistan's president. It made a good story over dinner. The president, himself a keen golfer, was well aware that 3-irons cannot be made like that to order.

Holes in one have an attraction for Jacobs. Maybe it is because his own 'aces' have occurred in unusual circumstances. There are two more to set beside the strange affair in Peshawar.

Soon after the Ryder Cup team returned from Palm Springs, Frank Pennink, a highly competent British amateur before the war and, after it, a distinguished golf-course architect, rang up Jacobs at Sandy Lodge. Pennink was then writing a weekly golf column for the *Sunday*

Express and hit on the idea of playing a round with each member of the team, picking out the particular club with which the player was identified. He asked Jacobs what he might do with him which was different from the rest:

'I didn't hesitate. There was a very strong wind blowing that day so I said to Frank, "Why don't you feature long-iron play in the wind?"'

The two got round to the fifteenth, a good one-shotter straight into the eye of the wind. 'Here's one to test us today,' commented Jacobs as he prepared to drive a 2-iron at the green, low under the wind. Drilled navel-high, straight at the stick, the ball pitched once just short of the flag and rolled slowly into the cup.

But, of all his strange 'aces', perhaps the most bizarre occurred at the short seventeenth on the New course at Sunningdale. It was midwinter and Jacobs was playing with the local assistant against the two Hunt brothers, Bernard and Geoffrey. The golf, as he remembers it, was exceptionally good:

'There were birdies galore. Pars were of little use. 3s and 2s were the order. My partner and I were beaten 3 and 2 on the sixteenth green.

'I had originally talked Bernard into playing for a fiver, so I said to him on the seventeenth tee, "Come on, £10 or nothing on the bye."'

Hunt accepted the challenge with just a hint of misgiving. 'All right, Jacobs,' he countered, 'but with a nose and a name like yours, you'll probably get a one.'

A few moments later, they were picking Jacobs's 6-iron out of the cup.

4
Crossing the Rubicon

EXECUTIVE DECISIONS

John Jacobs was thirty-nine when he made the break from Sandy Lodge and, with it, the life of a club professional, to set out along the rough road of business. The severance came, not with misgivings because it had been thought through and pondered carefully, but with a real recognition of what was being left behind. There were the enormous experience he had gained and the friendships which none could take away. And there was the nostalgia, for Jacobs sets lasting store by his personal relationships and working associations. He does not turn his back unthinkingly on the past. For him – and, indeed, for his wife – the Sandy Lodge years had been special.

The invitation to join Athlon Sports Ltd, a company with interests in leisure, arose through a turn of fortune. The Jacobses had recently acquired a new neighbour at Sandy Lodge. Leslie Dobson, a businessman, was friendly with one of the directors of Athlon Sports. He knew that Jacobs was now casting about for a new job. He therefore mentioned to his contact that, as the Athlon campany was apparently bent on exploiting the commercial potential of golf, the organization might do a lot worse than approach his neighbour.

Without delay, Algernon Llewellyn, Athlon's managing director, contacted Jacobs. He explained the company's belief that, with the expansion of the game on the back of television, the widening use of the motor car and increased leisure hours and spending, it was time to enter the golfing market. The appeal would be primarily to golf's new clientele as well as to its established followers, for whose needs existing facilities were already inadequate. The parent company would form a subsidiary, Athlon Golf Ltd, specifically to pursue this aim. Llewellyn and his colleagues hoped that Jacobs would agree to join the board of the operating subsidiary, become its golf executive (that was to be his title) and bring his specialist knowledge and teaching ability to bear in overseeing and promoting the new operations. Covered, floodlit driving ranges, which had already made a mark in Japan and America, would be the first priority.

As frequently happens with new ventures, initial progress fell far short of hopes. Suitable sites were difficult to acquire on reasonable terms; and when they were available, problems with planning consents abounded. Delays followed.* With little income accruing from the company's other sources, dangerous inroads were being made into the original £120,000 or so of capital funding.

Eventually, Jacobs and his colleagues found an answer to their difficulties by using racecourses as sites. They embarked on developments in the centre of Leopardstown, near Dublin, and at Sandown Park, near Esher in Surrey. These were followed by another operation on the periphery of Gosforth Park racecourse, near Newcastle upon Tyne, while a smaller going concern was acquired at Norbreck, near Blackpool, and expanded.

However, before Athlon had begun to find its feet and move forward, a succession of traumas had to be overcome. It took John Jacobs less than three months from his arrival on the board of Athlon Golf to realize that, confronted with numerous difficulties, the company was getting nowhere and that his talents were being totally wasted. Beyond this, it was apparent that between his approach to the company's problems and the managing director's there was a widening abyss. To Algie Llewellyn's portfolio in the parent company had been added the managing directorship of Athlon Golf. As the two executives of the operating subsidiary, Jacobs and Llewellyn were incompatible. The temperaments and workstyles were a long par-5 apart.

Llewellyn, a man of outward charm and a facile tongue, did not possess the hard cutting edge and practical vision which Jacobs thought to be essential in the senior management of such a venture.

The golf executive therefore took two steps which required some courage. First, he told the managing director that he wished to have an early opportunity of putting his views to the parent board, which was composed of a number of substantial independent people well versed

*During the hiatus, Jacobs and the company made six fifteen-minute instructional films, at a cost of £30,000, for showing in golf clubs and, later, at Athlon's centres. They were the forerunner of an outstandingly successful series made for Yorkshire Television.

in the wiles of company life. He was dissatisfied with the course of events and the lack of positive direction. He wished to be able to state his case to his senior colleagues and outline the action he believed to be required. He would support his submission with a previously circulated paper so that none could be in any doubt about his opinions. Unless there was a swift executive response, he would be picking up his cards.

He further proposed that, until there were golf operations for him to supervise – and, therefore, places where he could teach those who were daily seeking his advice – he should take a cut in salary and be allowed the time to enter those PGA tournaments which would suit his, and the company's, schedule.

At the meeting Jacobs went straight to his case and was listened to attentively and, he felt, with respect. He sensed that there was much sympathy with his point of view. The upshot was that he was at once asked to join the parent board and given the additional powers which would go with the directorship. Further, his request to take a salary cut in exchange for time to play in selected tournaments was also granted.*

Much more remained to be done, however, to get the company off the ground. Harold Wilson's first Labour Government had recently been elected and the City of London was gripped in the vice of a credit squeeze which thwarted whatever chance Athlon might have had of raising the fresh capital which was now patently needed. The board, right up against the collar, turned to GRA Property Trust, the entertainment, sports promotion and property group, its principal shareholder. GRA, seeing a commercial future in golf for the masses, and knowing the attraction of Jacobs's name, had taken a substantial stake in Athlon.

For GRA's board, the options were starkly plain: do nothing and say goodbye to the investment or acquire the company, provide the cash and management to realize Athlon's initial programme and create the first comprehensive golf centres in the UK. The board of the publicly-quoted company, familiar with risks and encouraged by John Sutton, its aggressively-capable managing director, elected to take the

---

*His competitive excursions during this time produced, in the circumstances, some surprisingly good scores. Notable among his performances was his finish in the Braemar, seven-club tournament at Turnberry in 1964, a bold first putt to tie on the seventy-second green hitting the hole to leave Lionel Platts the outright winner. For Jacobs it was 'hugely enjoyable being able to play a tournament with seven clubs'.

second course. Llewellyn resigned as Athlon's managing director and was replaced by W.B. Shepherd, GRA's finance director. A Scots accountant, Bill Shepherd had originally been recruited from the leisure and property group's City accountants, Peat Marwick. Jacobs, a shareholder in both companies, was given a new five-year contract with latitude to expand his own interests. He was made responsible for completing as quickly as possible the centres at Leopardstown, Sandown and Gosforth Park, each of which would carry his name.

A fourth major centre, to be developed at Delapre Park, Northampton, for the forward-looking local borough council, came under his purview. Opened in the second half of the seventies, this successful product of public and private enterprise had been managed since the start by John Corby, who worked with Jacobs throughout the Athlon years, taking charge, first, of the Leopardstown centre and then Sandown Park. To his eye for good customer relations, Corby added a teaching ability which has won him a strong following.

As the work progressed and the new centres were opened, two things became clear. First, there could be little commercial future in driving ranges alone. An acceptable return on the investment would only be obtained if the open-to-all, pay-to-play centres became truly comprehensive enterprises. Experience quickly showed that the centres required not only a floodlit, covered, multi-bay range, but also short (par-3) and conventional-length, nine or eighteen-hole courses, backed by supporting amenities – attractive equipment-merchandizing and club hire, and limited catering and entertainment facilities; this, with Jacobs-trained teaching staff always available, was the necessary formula. Driven hard, with good management and imaginative promotion, such a centre could soon become viable.

Second, it was obvious within a year that Jacobs and the managing director were at cross purposes. Shepherd, although able with figures, possessed neither the resilience nor the man-management skills needed to handle an executive of Jacobs's personality and adamant views. Shepherd thought that to assert his authority he must adopt an unyielding stance against a strong opinionated colleague. This only exacerbated an unhappy relationship.

As chairman of Athlon, I could see that there was one suitable place for Jacobs: in the managing director's hot seat, carrying responsibility directly to the chair, and through it, to the group's executive board for the discharge of the subsidiary's business. Jacobs was much more at home as a number one. That was his natural slot. He wasn't an accommodating or compliant number two.

With the expiry of his second five-year contract late in 1976, Jacobs decided not to renew his association with the group, but rather to set up his own company, John Jacobs Golf Consultants Ltd, geared to offer the same services and expertise as Athlon had provided during his time. Shortly after its formation, he invited me to take the chair, thus continuing a personal and working relationship which had proved effective and satisfying for both of us. Also from GRA and Athlon came John Corby, by then an experienced executive in this specialized field.

The principle of the comprehensive golf centre which Jacobs and Athlon had pioneered was probably ten years ahead of its time and not at first widely understood or accepted. Nearly a quarter of a century after its inception, with its use greatly expanded, it offers incontrovertibly the best vehicle for carrying pay-to-play, open-to-all golf to the community, from the beginner (and his family) to the proficient player. In its well-sited, properly designed and managed form, it surpasses, in terms of potential viability, any comparable golfing facility. Unless there is a real-estate content, no other type of public golf provision possesses the same opportunity for obtaining such a comparable and attractive financial return.

The GRA and Athlon experience had an important effect upon Jacobs's performance and future. It gave him the administrative ability and the confidence to meet the British tournament players' plea in 1971 to set up and run, on their behalf, an autonomous tour division of the Professional Golfers' Association. He was the original architect of what has now become the immensely successful PGA European Tour.

In the four or five formative years Jacobs spent as director-general of the division, the competitive scene was transformed from a relatively narrow, UK centred operation into a broadly-conceived, European command. Having encouraged the televising of the golf tour, he sold it to sponsoring companies as a new and telling way of advertising their name and their products. He dealt directly with group chairmen, managing directors and group promotions managers and not, initially, with their staff. He persuaded them that a common market was opening in golf and that, via television, they could reach a captive audience of several millions for a fraction of their advertising and promotional budgets.

It wasn't all a freeway. In time, the opposition to change within the old-established trade union became intense and sometimes acrimonious. It was to bring much personal animosity down on Jacobs's head.

Jacobs began his television broadcasting work during his time with Athlon, initially with the BBC and then with ITV. In 1964 he was at Porthcawl, in Wales, to look after the British team in the ladies' Curtis Cup match against the United States. The BBC asked him whether, when once the contest was under way, he would do a commentary for them. Without pausing for thought he said yes. The arrangements, by comparison with the present, were primitive, as Jacobs recalls:

'I was asked to report to the television people half and hour before the broadcast. I was completely on my own and was sent up a very tall ladder to a station at the top. There, I just had a television set to look at and a chair. It was bright sunlight and, being exposed to the brightness of the sky, it was very difficult to see the picture. A little boy kept running up and down the ladder with information about the state of the matches. I remember being told to say welcome to the viewers from racing at Wincanton.'

'I would hear a voice in my ear saying "And now we will go to the third green where such-and-such is happening." Then, just as I was about to say something about the players on the third, a voice would cut in: "Sorry, we've lost the camera on the third, you'll just have to go on talking." With all the experience I have had since, this kind of thing can be looked at differently. But as an introduction to broadcasting, it was quite the worst nightmare one could imagine. Still, the programme went out live for two hours, and that was that.'

The next assignment came at the Walker Cup match against the US at Sandwich. It was 1967 and Joe Carr, the Irishman, was captain of the home team. Henry Longhurst and Bill Cox (W.J. Cox, the Ryder Cup international, then the club professional at Fulwell) were the BBC's two accredited commentators. Jacobs was invited to provide 'the expert opinion'. Later that summer, with Cox and Longhurst unavailable, Jacobs took on the coverage of the Daks tournament with David Coleman at Wentworth.

There followed a strange affair at Hoylake, the venue of the 1967 Open Championship – Roberto de Vicenzo's year. This was Jacobs's first experience of working with Longhurst in a straightforward commentating role.

For its coverage, the BBC had stationed Bill Cox and the American, Mark McCormack, at the back of the fifteenth green, while Longhurst and Jacobs shared the pitch behind the eighteenth. But 'share' is hardly the word:

'Whenever coverage was switched from the fifteenth to the eighteenth, Henry at once took over and never left the microphone. I was not allowed to say a word. Eventually, Alan Mouncer, a thoroughly able golf director, came through on the earphones: "Is John Jacobs in the box behind the eighteenth green?" I pressed the key and said, "Yes, but he can't get in a word."

'I then heard Alan instruct Bill Cox on the fifteenth to say, as they switched over, "Come in John Jacobs on the eighteenth." But it made no difference. Henry just picked it up and went on talking away. In the first two-hour broadcast I did from that championship, I never had the chance to say a word.'

On the face of it, Longhurst's attitude was uncharacteristic. But it should be remembered that golf on television was then in its infancy. The technique and coverage which are a commonplace today were light years away. The response of non-golfers to the corporation's broadcasting of golf, with its limited audience measurement, was critical. Anyone who sat on BBC's general advisory council in those days, and heard the criticisms, will remember that it was a long way from becoming established. It required some stout support from the back benches in that curiously assorted body to keep the ball in play.

The coverage and, to a lesser extent, the commentators were still very much on trial. Longhurst, who was later to provide a consistently brilliant spoken portrayal of the spectacle on the small screen, had not yet cut out for himself a place in sports broadcasting history. He knew that Jacobs was also, at that time, being offered a contract by the BBC and that he himself was the only other BBC golf commentator who had one. It is possible that he wanted to lose no opportunity of sewing up his own position beyond doubt. What is interesting is that he could ever have thought that, with all his skills, wit and humour, it was necessary to 'prove' his prowess.

In the event, those who were directing the programme made it clear to him that the pitch at the back of the eighteenth was to be a shared arrangement between him and Jacobs, and that he wasn't to hog it. The difference was soon settled as his colleague well recalls:

'Henry apologized to me and was very nice about it. It was quite absurd that he should ever have thought that I might be usurping his position. It was out of the question. Anyway, once it was sorted out, we got on fine and, from my point of view, he was a joy to work with.'

Towards the end of that year, after the season was over, Bryan Cowgill, who was then responsible for, among other things, the coverage of outside events for the BBC and who subsequently became managing director of Thames Television, asked Jacobs to lunch. He had with him Alan Mouncer, the corporation's golf director, and Slim Wilkinson, the producer. The purpose was to discuss terms for a contract. Understanding was reached and the details were to be embodied in a formal agreement. 'Then,' says Jacobs, 'nothing happened. Several weeks passed and no agreement arrived.'

Jimmy Hill, himself a golfer, had then recently gone to London Weekend Television. He knew Jacobs, understood his appeal in golf and had heard his commentaries for the BBC. He asked him directly, 'Have you got a contract with the BBC?'

Jacobs explained the position. The two discussed the services which LWT would want and the terms which would be offered. 'I'll have a contract sent round by hand to your office this afternoon,' said Hill – which he did.

That afternoon, Jacobs telephoned Cowgill from his office at GRA's White City Stadium, next door to the BBC television centre at Shepherds Bush. He put the cards down on the table, face up. 'We agreed terms some weeks ago which were to be embodied in a contract, but I've never been sent a contract. Now I've got a contract from LWT lying on my desk.'

Within an hour or two, the corporation's agreement had been delivered to the White City by hand.

There was much in LWT's proposals which was attractive. Apart from the coverage of golf, there would be an opportunity to make a series of instructional programmes for the network, first in black and white, then in colour. This weighed heavily on Jacobs's mind. Making instructional films was right down his fairway. But up till then, the BBC had made all the running with the coverage of golf; the commercial network had had little or no experience of it. From various points of view, however, not least from the standpoint of the PGA, Jacobs could see merit in encouraging a competing interest in golf on television. On balance, therefore, he decided to treat with LWT.

Although Cowgill conceded that the corporation had never sent Jacobs a contract, they had, he claimed, reached verbal agreement on terms and other details. It was wrong now to be dealing with the 'other side'. Athlon's managing director was equally tough. What Cowgill had said was perfectly true, but an agreement wasn't secured until documents had been signed and exchanged. There was no formal contract.

Cowgill was incensed; a chasm opened up between the two. Hill, on the other hand, reckoned he had scored a bullseye. Was Jacobs right to have dealt with the commercial company and turned his back on the BBC?

Looking back over twenty years, the wisdom of his action is at least debatable. Certainly, the exposure Jacobs received from the three immensely successful, thirteen-part instructional series he made for Yorkshire Television took his teaching to a far larger audience than would otherwise have been the case. The BBC had had no plans for a similar production. And, as Colin Snape later confirmed, the association's competitive position was transformed by the existence of a second interest with which to do business: 'Before, BBC was apt to pat the PGA's head and say: "There, there," whenever a proposal was put to it, "we'll see if we can do anything to help." It was a patronizing attitude. When John came along and was able to offer the Ryder Cup to ITV as well as BBC, it was a different ball-game altogether.'

That said, ITV's coverage of golf in the earlier years was much inferior to BBC's. Apart from the technical considerations, there was one very good trade union reason for the discrepancy. For Jacobs, it could hardly have been more frustrating:

'The union insisted that when a professional tournament was being covered in one area of the country, the director of the programme and the cameramen would have to be supplied from within that region. As the tournaments were moved about the country, it meant that the director and the cameramen were constantly being changed. It prejudiced the coverage because no one team was being built up with the necessary expertise.

'It wasn't until we came to an understanding whereby Yorkshire Television provided the director and the camera crew for golf coverage for the whole network that things really improved. In my time as director-general of the tournament division of the PGA I was therefore able to insist that, under the terms of the agreement, ITV's cover of the Ryder Cup would be handled by the team which knew all about presenting golf as a television spectacle. It made a great difference.'

Nevertheless, despite all these arrangements and the improvements which were made in the commercial network's coverage of golf, Jacobs's decision to throw in his lot with ITV was probably misguided. The BBC's extended and greatly improved coverage of the Open Championship each year, the hours which it devotes to professional tournaments and other events, uninterrupted by commercials, and the magnitude of the corporation's golfing operations, have outstripped the efforts of the independent network. And when ITV dropped its regular coverage of tournaments and restricted its golfing programmes to prestige events in the United States, there seemed little doubt that the wrong horse had been backed. But it hadn't seemed that way at the time.

Television commentators attract their share of praise and criticism. The ability to embellish and decorate with originality the spectacle which is being broadcast is given to few, and Jacobs is not among them. This is strange, considering his undeniable aptitude for talking colourfully about the game and vividly describing a player's action. His strength as a television commentator lies in his capacity for analysis, dissection, diagnosis. His reading of a man's mind, the picking out of strokes which turn events, and the noticing of apparently nondescript things in a round, set his personal comments apart.

This is his métier – not the descriptions of the high drama which usually surrounds the closing holes of a hard-fought tournament. The voice ('like a fall of Yorkshire soot' as some wag once had it) tends not to lend itself to that style of comment. And yet, the surprising thing is that Jacobs has seldom been used in the manner best suited to his analytical skills. Renton Laidlaw, golf correspondent of the *London Standard*, and broadcaster, probably saw this more acutely than others when the two worked together for ITV. Laidlaw, with a journalist's eye for an opening, set up the opportunities which the diagnostician's mind could exploit. It was, of course, this special flair which Cowgill saw in Jacobs when he was trying to pull off the BBC deal.

Although the two differed widely in temperament and personality, a combination of Longhurst's commentating, with all its originality and colour, and Jacobs's faculty for instant diagnosis and assessment, together with his thoughts on the game, would have been difficult to beat. But it was not to be.

The subsequent pairing of Peter Alliss with Longhurst, however, was a master stroke of television casting. The two had much in common – not least humour – and worked comfortably together. Beyond that, it gave Alliss a marvellous opportunity. He had the intellect and the sensitivity to absorb much of Longhurst's style and merge it with his own. As Jacobs says, 'The truth is that, nowadays, a blend of Peter with Bruce Critchley, Clive Clark and Tony Jacklin gives the BBC a balanced commentary team which anyone anywhere would be hard put to match.'

RIVER, COVERT AND CONTROVERSY

John and Rita Jacobs had, by the early 1960s, begun to hanker after a family home in the country. Their childhood in the Yorkshire countryside had left its traces. It had been out of the question for a busy club professional to live far from the shop. But now that Jacobs's work style had changed, and he was no longer tied to one place, he felt that chance had come to realize a mutual desire.

He and Rita had enjoyed such short holidays as they had been able to take with Joanna and Jonathan in Hampshire's New Forest, with all the opportunities which were offered for country pursuits. They therefore resolved that, when they sold 7 Sandy Lodge Lane, they would move to the Lyndhurst area of Hampshire. When the Old Vicarage at Emery Down came on the market, they had no difficulty in deciding that it was the house for them.

For a few years, both before and after their move, Jacobs kept a small flat as a *pied à terre* in Melcombe Street, close to Baker Street, in the NW1 district of London. From here he daily conducted his quickly expanding business affairs. In time, as he became more and more his own master, involved with his own private companies, he found he could give up living and working in London during the week, a practice which he much disliked. He therefore transferred his office to Lyndhurst as soon as he could and made his country home his working base.

With Heathrow little more than an hour's drive up the motorway from Emery Down, he was still well placed for the increasing flights he was obliged to take abroad and within the UK. Whatever inconvenience he suffered by giving up his London pitch was more than compensated for by the gain in personal and family happiness.

Boyhood at Lindrick, and the long summer days spent on neighbouring Deepcar Farm or at Welbeck, had left him with a lasting love of animals. Ever since their Yorkshire days, he and his wife have kept a varying assortment of dogs and cats, ponies, budgerigars and the rest. They have always been a part of the household. There isn't a member of Sandy Lodge during Jacobs's time with the club who does not remember the professional's Irish setter, Skittles, ranging widely round the course or sitting beside his master on the practice ground, viewing the comings and goings of the pupils through lugubrious and disdainful eyes.

If Jacobs isn't working – and his leisure time is still inordinately short – he is happiest out of doors with rod or gun and with a working dog at his side. He often stays with Angus Nudds, gamekeeper on Sir Peter Crossman's 3000-acre Tetworth Hall estate, near Gamlingay, a dozen miles or so west of Cambridge. Nudds recently wrote a book entitled *The Woods Belong to Me** which exposed, in engagingly perceptive and unadorned English, a man's affair with the countryside. Only someone who had had the country bred into him, and was at peace with it, could have written such a work. For Jacobs, the visits to Angus Nudds and his wife, Audrey, are firm forward entries in his diary: 'The hours I have spent with Angus, at varying seasons of the year, just walking round Sir Peter's estate, are treasured times. Sometimes I have been with him in the late spring and early summer, after getting back from a hard spell of work in America, when he is tending his hen pheasants, breeding and rearing the young birds from eggs. But usually it's August and September, when we fish together, that I can spend most time with him. Then, I'm as keen as he is to know how the pheasants have done and whether there will be any partridges this year.

'It's wonderful just to be able to walk about the estate with someone as knowledgeable as that, who can tell you everything and who seems to notice any little change from normal – a piece of bark that's missing from an old tree here, a new working in a hedgerow there; Angus will tell you at once what bird or animal has been there and whether it will be back again . . . A man of the countryside, it's a delight to be with him.'

There are times when the keeper at Tetworth can invite his friends for a 'cocks only' day with the pheasants later on in the season. An old cock bird, driven high over the guns, and coming fast on the turn down a brisk December or January wind, will test the very best. There is an entry in Nudds's game book of January 1967 which captures the spirit of such a day:

> It was the first time that John Jacobs had shot at Tetworth and he turned up with a brand new Spanish-made gun** which he hadn't fired before. The first drive of the day was what we call our high drive. As I started the beaters, an old cock bird that knew the drill got up, stood on its tail to gain height, then headed over the guns in the bottom of the valley, making for Weaveley Wood. As he

*The Blandford Press, Poole, Dorset, 1985.
**Nudds's original comment on seeing his guest's purchase of a Spanish, rather than a British-made gun was characteristically colourful.

crossed over the guns at a tremendous height, a solitary shot rang out and the bird crumpled in the air and fell stone dead. It was a real gallery shot.

I called to my flank beater on the right: 'Whoever shot that bird, it was out of range?'

'It's that pal of yours, John Jacobs,' came the reply.

I remember saying that I didn't believe it, or words to that effect; but when we finished the drive I found it was true. What a way to start the day on a strange estate!

It was Nudds, too, who introduced Jacobs to Danny Northrop and his wife, Ruth, and to their home, Church Farm at Barrington, in Cambridgeshire, a dozen or so miles east of Tetworth. It wasn't long before he was invited to become a member of the shoot there, fitting in easily with Northrop and his farming friends. For a decade and more, the days at the farm have been ringed in the calendar: 'I have been very much the golfing interloper, but they have been hugely enjoyable times and I have always been made to feel so welcome.'

P.G. Wodehouse once claimed that 'golf, like measles, should be caught young.' So, too, for that matter, should shooting. Jacobs's boyhood days at Lindrick, walking with cousin Jack, the dogs and his precious .410 over the common and surrounding farmland, have left their mark. For one who gets relatively little practice, he shoots, as Nudds has it, 'naturally and with a good style. When John is shooting well, he kills his birds cleanly.' But Nudds sees more in it than that:

'I have noticed, whenever I see him following his own profession – taking a clinic or teaching an individual pupil – that he is very much the man in charge; always courteous and helpful, but still firm. Yet, when it comes to someone else's profession, he is not too proud to take advice from a fellow pro.'

The move from Hertfordshire to Hampshire in the early seventies gave Jacobs ready access to his first love (apart from golf): fishing. On the River Test, close to his home, there is perhaps the finest trout fishing in the world. Mention the Test to a keen fisherman anywhere, even in the United States, and it will stir him in the same way as talk of St Andrews will at once arouse the interest of his golfing counterpart. The proximity of such a river means much to Jacobs:

'It's a blessing to feel there is a stretch of water only ten or fifteen minutes away. To be able to slip away at mayfly time for an hour or two's fishing after a day's work in the office is a wonderful relaxation –

like going out for nine holes in the sunshine after tea.'

Fortuitously, Jacobs's golfing expertise has brought him into contact with some of the best fishermen in the land. His first meeting with the late, illustrious Richard Walker was as fruitful as it was unexpected:

'I was teaching golf one evening at Sandown towards the end of the 1960s, and I noticed a man sitting at the back of the covered bay, watching me. He sat there throughout the session from six until ten o'clock. His face seemed familiar. At the end of it, he introduced himself as Dick Walker. "What!" I said. "Not the *fishing* Dick Walker? If it is, I've got all your books." "Yes," he said, "that's me."'

Walker was himself setting up a course for fly-fishers – for those who were themselves teaching the art of fly-casting. He had heard all about Jacobs's prowess as a golfing instructor and he had taken the trouble to go down to Sandown Park and study the maestro's technique.

'Dick Walker invited me to join a course on trout fishing at Grafham, one of the big reservoirs south-west of Huntingdon. He was endeavouring to get the art of fly-casting well taught. I joined the course and enjoyed it immensely. At the end of it, Dick asked me to write a report for him on how I though the instruction had gone.

'I recall very well saying in my account that there was one instructor on the course who was specially helpful to me in casting a fly *because he hadn't told me too much*. He made his explanation absolutely clear and then would give me *a couple of positive things to do* as opposed to half a dozen, which would have confused me.

'That, after all, is the secret of teaching golf. When you're trying to get pupils to hit it, they can really only think of about a couple of things; more than that, and they will become confused. That's why, after the diagnosis and the explanation, the correction must be short and simple – and correct the first time.'

There was a similarity in temperament between fishing instructor and golfing teacher. Like Jacobs, Richard Walker had a strong character and firm and decisive views on his own pastime. His disciple is unequivocal in apportioning credit: 'Dick brought so much of his own expertise into the art of fishing and many of us who learned from him will always be in his debt.'

After the meeting with Richard Walker, there was an introduction to the Hardy family, makers of the best-known fishing tackle in the world. The company, Hardy Brothers of Alnwick, in Northumberland, winners of the Queen's Award for Export, had written to

Athlon's managing director in the late 1960s to say that they had made up a set of golf clubs with fibreglass shafts similar to the material they were using in their rods. They wanted to know whether he would try the shafts and give them an opinion.

Jacobs's reaction was favourable, but the leading players did not want to use the new clubs, and this was bound to colour the ordinary golfers' attitude. Jacobs warned the company of this problem in his report. He also added that, as a keen fisherman, he was not himself prejudiced against fibreglass because he was well aware of its properties from using Hardy's rods. This brought an early response from James Hardy.

'The next thing that happened was that Jim Hardy took up golf and used to come to Athlon's centre at Gosforth Park for lessons when I was there', says Jacobs. 'Jim gave me, in return, tuition in fly-casting . . .'

There was a fortunate rub-off from the Hardy connection. When Hardy's were taken over by Harris and Sheldon, a manufacturing conglomerate based in the Midlands, the group chairman and chief executive of the predator, James Miller, soon took the chair of the renowned fishing-tackle producer.

Through James Hardy, Jacobs got to know Miller, 'another mad keen fisherman'. Then began a rewarding relationship of the sort that has become a feature of Jacobs's golfing career. Every autumn, for years now, he has had three salmon days on the Tweed with Miller; and then, late in the following spring and early summer, when the mayfly is out, the chairman of Harris and Sheldon visits the Jacobs's in Hampshire for a return encounter on the Test.

Fishermen, like golfers, are drawn to old haunts.

Jacobs's fishing associations mean much to him. In addition to those with Richard Walker, in his lifetime, James Hardy and James Miller, he has others with men whose names are respected throughout the fishing world. 'It is a joy to fish with the best and I know how lucky I have been to have done so.'

He rattles off the names rather as he would select at random the stand-outs among his contemporaries in the golfing scene, adding a comment here and there when a special quality occurs to him.

'Pat Russell and Brian Clarke, surely two of the best dry-fly fishermen in the country . . . Barry Welham . . . Alex Behrandt, who started still-water trout fishing. After being a German prisoner of war in Britain, he married and settled here; an extraordinary person, now in his seventies, he gives seminars every autumn; he runs a fine business and gives great pleasure to people . . . Then there's Kenneth Keynes on the Avon – a marvellous river, it has got everything from the biggest coarse fish to a wonderful run of spring salmon and, later in the year, sea trout. What fun I have had on it with Ken Keynes . . . He knows it backwards. If you're ever in doubt, he'll tell you what bait or fly and where to fish it . . . A tremendous help, these guys. Like having a good caddie.'

Away from his leisure hours, there was one executive decision of some significance which the managing director of Athlon took in the mid-1960s. At the height of the controversy which was then raging over the adoption or rejection by Britain and Europe of the 1.68-inch diameter, US-size golf ball, Jacobs backed his judgement and went nap on the bigger ball for the floodlit driving ranges at all the company's centres. As one centre after another became operational, the bulk order amounted, in time, to well over a quarter of a million range balls.

As mentioned in the previous chapter, it was Jacobs's long-held belief that the United States' world supremacy in golf at that time owed much to the use of the 1.68-inch ball throughout the North American continent. With few exceptions, the rest of the golfing universe was then using the small 1.62-inch British bullet.

Jacobs had concluded early in the 1950s that the Americans' generally superior, and altogether firmer, striking was the product of their adoption of the large ball two decades before. He had repeated his opinion both in the press and in talks at golfing gatherings throughout the 1950s and into the 1960s. With Henry Cotton, Leonard Crawley, the British amateur and golf correspondent of the *Daily Telegraph* and *Field,* and a few other contemporaries in the United Kingdom, he never missed an opportunity of urging upon the authorities the adoption of the large version in the tournaments. He had summed up his arguments in his first book.* The words formed the basis of an article which was published in the magazine *Golfing* in 1959:

> I am convinced that it is high time we came into line with our American friends and conceded that theirs is the better-sized ball to play with . . . The real point is that if the large ball is not quite 'middled' it flies considerably less far than the small one from the same sort of stroke . . . This is a good thing. It may be the reason

Golf, Stanley Paul, London, 1963.

why the best American players use an action which keeps the club-blade squared for longer in the hitting area as opposed to the more common method in this country in which the wrist-flick and roll have been over-emphasized.

This type of 'blade square for longer through the ball' we call 'driving the ball' . . . I am absolutely certain . . . that to drive the ball is by far the sounder method . . . Generalizing then, *we* flick the ball: *they* drive the ball . . . To get results, the US large-size ball has to be driven; and, therefore, right from the start, it encourages a sounder method . . .

I very much believe the weekend golfer would eventually find it an easier ball to play with and one which would sooner or later automatically improve his game.

The great Samuel Jackson Snead once made a telling aside to Henry Cotton when he was playing at Wentworth. Snead was then well past his prime and the British bullet was still in use in the professional tournaments. 'You know, Henry,' he said, 'I like playing golf over here in my old age. I can miss this small ball of yours and still get away with it.'

For the tournament player, the large US ball required more exacting control; yet, for the average golfer, it had undoubted benefits – which was why the Americans had adopted it in the first place. Market research at Athlon's centres confirmed that the patrons preferred it.

Predictably, all through the controversy, the British manufacturers kept up a barrage of opposition to suggestions for a change. While they made the 1.62-inch bullet well, they were fully aware that the 1.68-inch ball made in small quantities in Britain fell far short of the first-class American product. It would be expensive and take a long time to close the gap.

In the end, spurred on by Cotton, Jacobs, Dai Rees, Tommy Horton and others in this country and, overseas, by the likes of Tommy Armour, the old Silver Fox, who had seen it all in the States, Palmer, Nicklaus and Player, the British PGA rejected the soft option and, in the mid-1960s, plumped irrevocably for the 1.68-inch ball in its tournaments.

As is explained below, for the first time, the whole hullabaloo need never have happened.

One evening in 1966, Roger Wethered and his wife were dining at my home in London. The arguments and counter-arguments about the ball were still at their height. The PGA had only then just taken its decision in favour of the 1.68-inch size and given the lead which others would later follow. With Cyril Tolley, Wethered had formed half of the pair in what, in the Golden Age of amateur golf after the First World War, had become known as the 'Tolley–Wethered era'. Historically, it matched the 'Jones era' in the United States. Roger could play golf; and behind a winning modesty, there lay a deep knowledge of the game. When he did talk about it seriously – which was seldom – it was generally always in private.

Wethered had tied with Jock Hutchinson for the 1921 Open Championship at St Andrews. He lost the 18-hole replay the next day – and, with it, a promised day's cricket in the south. He won the Amateur Championship at Deal two years later and stayed in Moore-Brabazon's (later Lord Brabazon) house at Sandwich Bay for it. The chambermaid called him with a pot of tea at 7.30 on the morning of the final, ensuring that the curtains in the bedroom were fully drawn back before she closed the door. An hour later, his host went up to find out why his eminent guest hadn't come down to breakfast. The tea beside the bed was untouched and cold. Wethered was still doggo.

After his victory, he was twice runner-up in the championship, the second time to R.T. Jones Jr at St Andrews in 1930, the Grand Slam year. In his prime Wethered was as good an iron player as there was in the game, amateur or professional. Had Jacobs been about in those days, he might well have fixed up Roger's somewhat wayward driving, and then he would have been well-nigh invincible, for he had a sensitive short game, a silken putting stroke and just the right, unflappable temperament for a champion.

The point is that Wethered knew about golf at first hand – an authoritative hand at that. He did not talk openly about the ball for he was not much enamoured of controversy, but he was an incorrigible protagonist of the larger version. He was well aware that I was active in its support.

As the diners left the table, he put a hand on my arm. 'If we could sit down for five mintues,' he said, 'I could tell you privately about the ball.' He then recounted his depressing story. A note which I made the next day and then locked away serves as an *aide memoire*.

Soon after the Second World War, Wethered had been made chairman of a small working party at St Andrews, set up, as he put it, 'to look at the question of the ball'. In particular, it was to examine the difficulty which arose from the United States using one size of ball and the United Kingdom, and its followers, another. The outcome of the study was still quite fresh in Wethered's mind.

'We did our work quickly. It was obvious that, if there was to be a change, then, in fairness to the manufacturers, notice should be given as soon as possible. Their factories were turning over from wartime to peacetime production and getting ready to meet the demand for golf balls, which were then in short supply.

'My group came up with one principal recommendation – that we should adopt the American specification for the ball which the US Golf Association had decided upon in the early 1930s, 1.68 inches in diameter and 1.62 ounces in weight. It wasn't difficult to get agreement and I'm quite sure we were right. I was convinced of it myself. It wasn't that we were blindly following the Americans; there were playing advantages with the 1.68-inch ball which were denied with the smaller one.'

It was now well into 1946:

'One day, Monty Pease [J.W. Beaumont Pease, an England and Oxford player, then Chairman of Lloyds Bank], who was the chairman of the general committee of the R & A, saw me in the City. [Wethered had stockbroking and finance interests in the City of London.] He explained that, as the Walker Cup match was being played at St Andrews the following spring and representatives of the USGA would be coming over for talks with the R & A, it would be courteous to them to defer a decision on the ball. It would be right to talk things over with them first. They wanted to carry the Americans with us, the aim of the two governing bodies always being to try to march in step.

'I said I thought this was quite wrong on timing. A different situation would arise by then with the manufacturers. They had to get on and meet the demand for balls, and once they were geared up to produce the small ball in large numbers, they would never want to change over to something else. It would cost them money. I said that if it was really felt necessary to consult the Americans then surely someone could go over there and talk to them. I was fairly sure the arguments about the larger ball weren't understood and its importance was mostly missed.

'In the end, I allowed Monty to talk me out of it. I should never have done so. Although I say it, I feel certain I would have got the backing to carry the thing had I dug in my heels. But I didn't want to go against the general committee and make difficulties. I am afraid, looking back, it was a terrible mistake. The opportunity had been lost. Now we've got all this row . . .'

It is easy to see now why Wethered was so certain that a fundamental misjudgement had been made. He knew that the use of the bigger ball promoted better, more solid striking and greater accuracy close to the green. By comparison with the advance of United States golf during the subsequent thirty years or so, the mistake put us at a disadvantage and retarded the first-class game in Britain and Europe for a generation. Beyond that, it compelled Jacobs and a few of his enlightened followers to mount and win a campaign in the 1960s which need never have been fought. But the effects of that victory were far reaching.

It is only in the last few years that the results of the adoption of the big ball in European golf have truly begun to work through. There has been an all-round improvement in the first-class game. A new gener-ation of players has grown up with the ball since childhood and thereby enjoyed an advantage which its predecessors never knew — and should never have been denied. Winston Churchill once described the Second World War as the 'unnecessary war'. Roger Wethered could well have said the same of the conflict which bedevilled the British game in the third quarter of the twentieth century.*

*It is worth noting that Raymond Floyd, 1986 US Open Champion, one of the world's greats and long conversant with British and European golf, was asked by *Sunday Express* correspondent Alan Tyne, in California in January 1987, why the gap between the United States and Britain and Europe had narrowed so perceptibly in recent years. He gave 'the introduction of the bigger, American ball' as his first reason. 'This,' he added, 'automatically made them better strikers once they got the hang of it.'

5
The Bowden Factor

ANGLO-AMERICAN ALLIANCE

Few successful men or women have got to the top without an ally. In golf, the last seventy years have been studded with notable alliances: Harlow and Hagen, Keeler and Jones, 'Toots' Cotton and her husband, Henry, von Nida and a youthful Peter Thomson, McCormack and Palmer, George Blumberg, the South African, and an emergent Player . . .

For John Jacobs the ally has been Ken Bowden, journalist, author, magazine editor and one-time service manager. It is debatable whether, without Bowden to open the transatlantic route, Jacobs would have got the chance to make his mark on the thinking and the teaching of the game in the United States. Certainly, it could not have happened in the way that it did without Bowden's intervention.

Ken Bowden was born in New York City of British parents on 11 July 1930. He thus became an American citizen under US law. This was a key to his acceptance, thirty-nine years later, of the editorial directorship of the US magazine *Golf Digest*, the game's largest-selling periodical. Without this qualification, his purpose might well have been thwarted. He had been brought up in the UK when his parents returned home. His education, training and working experience had all been gained in England; and permission for an Englishman – or any other foreign national, for that matter – to work permanently in the United States is not readily granted. American immigration authorities play the 'green card' close to their chests. Two advantages, however, stemmed from this English upbringing. First, he enjoyed, like Jacobs, the benefit of a British grammar school education – in his case at Dartford, in Kent, a privilege which, somewhat incongruously, he shares with Mick Jagger. There, he obtained a better basic education than he was likely to have received in America. Second, he was able to learn the arts and artifices of journalism in the best journalistic school in the world. Local newspaper reporting with the Bexley Heath *Observer*, sub-editing, a stint in Fleet Street with the old *News Chronicle*, and ten years with the Temple Press, contributing to and producing a succession of their technical journals, gave him the base – and the independence – to begin freelancing.

Beyond this, by the start of the 1960s, Bowden had become a golfing 'nut', and as consistent a hooker of the ball as could be found. He read everything he could lay his hands on about the game. Most of the instructional stuff he found was ill written and, if not unintelligible, then difficult to understand. To a magazine man's trained eye, the golfing periodicals of those times appeared, by comparison with their US counterparts, drab and unappealing. So when, in November 1961, Charles Brett offered Bowden the chance of becoming the founder-editor of *Golf World*, and one of its three principals (Ron Downs, formerly of the *People*, one of Fleet Street's large-circulation Sundays, was the other), he took it – and, with it, the risk. 'No room for another golfing mag,' the knockers claimed at the time.

The first issue of *Golf World*, backed by a strenuous promotional and marketing campaign, was published in March 1962. It sold more copies than any golf magazine had sold before in Britain. But, as Bowden recalls, there were no illusions about the achievement. 'It was as much a measure of the weakness of our then competitors as a testimonial to our editorial and publishing genius!'

In the golfing 'literature' he had read, Ken Bowden had spotted the instructional pieces which Jacobs had been writing for the monthly magazine *Golfing*, which John Stobbs was then editing: 'I noticed this material of John's for its logic, commitment and simplicity. I liked its directness. I could understand what he was saying. It caught my eye particularly because, apart from Bobby Jones's books, all instruction seemed to deal with the mechanics of the swing and positions, and what these were supposed to achieve. John, on the other hand, started from the other end. He stated what had to be achieved by the player and worked back from there.'

Bowden was determined to establish *Golf World* as a good instructional medium. 'I wanted to make it, if I could, the outstanding teaching magazine. I aimed to make that side of it different from the usual run, and easy to understand. I ran a lot of American copy because, frankly, I thought it was livelier, more positive and compelling. It was set out better and the illustrations were more appealing.

But, above all, I wanted to get John as a contributor.'

Jacobs is under the impression that his first meeting with the editor of *Golf World* took place over dinner in London with Charles Brett present. But this wasn't so. Bowden's account explains the mistake: 'I originally telephoned John at his home at Sandy Lodge and explained what I wanted. He was very sceptical. He was content to be writing for another magazine. He had just done his book with John Stobbs and he couldn't see why he should be changing horses. It was quite understandable, but I wasn't leaving it there. In the end we agreed to meet at Walton Heath, where he was shortly to be playing.'

The first meeting, from Bowden's standpoint, was neither easy nor encouraging: 'This was very much John in a hurry. He was still sceptical and fairly uninterested. And when John gets a fixation he's difficult to shift. He can be obstinate. I didn't feel I got very far. The meeting made little impact – that's why John has forgotten it.'

Bowden persisted and eventually got Jacobs's consent to set up the dinner party in London with Brett present. After a lot of subsequent exchanges, the former Ryder Cup player agreed to join the new paper and contribute to it.

Towards the end of 1966, nearly five years after he, Brett and Downs had set their hand to *Golf World*, Bowden received an unexpected request from John Jacobs. The shoe was now on the other foot. The Athlon company had been taken over by GRA and the parent was intent upon driving the golf-centre business forward. The Jacobs centre at Sandown Park had, after two years or so, been partially completed. But the management was unimaginative and the operation was still losing money. Jacobs, responsible to the Athlon board for the success or failure of the enterprise, saw that if the business was to be turned round and its potential realized the local management would have to be changed. He therefore asked the company's chairman whether he might approach Bowden about taking on the job of manager.

The *Golf World* editor and the Athlon executive had been working closely together on regular instructional articles for the paper. The magazine was now strongly established and advancing. Jacobs believed that Bowden, with his restless temperament, might well be receptive to a new challenge.

The Athlon board agreed to the proposition. Bowden accepted the offer and started work at Sandown, as the centre manager, on 1 October 1966. He was also to advise on the marketing of the rest of the company's golf-centre business in the UK and Ireland. His stint with the organization was brief but effective.

Bowden left Athlon no more than three years' later, in the autumn of 1969, to move to the United States with his wife, Jean, and take up the editorial directorship of *Golf Digest*. By that time, Sandown had been built into a profitable and successful business, earning a steadily improving return on capital. Jacobs, with his name and teaching genius, had attracted attention to the centre. The centre manager, with his direct-shot advertising through the local press and a variety of marketing ploys, had consolidated its image.

A frequent witness to the professor's teaching clinics at Sandown, Bowden had himself learned all about the 'geometry' of the ball-flight laws. He had come to understand thoroughly the Jacobs teaching doctrine and his thoughts on golf and its players. His own game had profited notably by the association. Because of the grounding, and his clean and expressive English prose style (with a splash or two of American idiom thrown in), he had developed the ability, in Jacobs's words, 'to put me down on paper better than I could do it myself'.

In May 1971, *Golf Digest's* new editor invited Jacobs to join him in the Bahamas. The magazine, putting Dick Aultman and Bob Toski in the driving seat, had just run the first of the golf schools which would become a feature of its external promotional work. Bowden was anxious that Jacobs and Toski should spend time together and strike up a working relationship. He also had another motive: 'I had a feeling by that time that all the material which John had produced for *Golf World* and other publications was, in its way, so fresh and original that it ought to be collected and put together in an authoritative and readable whole.'

The two spent days 'sprawled on a lovely Caribbean beach, working on the manuscript, putting the copy together and fashioning it into its proper sequence'. When it was finished they had to find an illustrator. Anthony Ravielli had produced brilliant drawings for Ben Hogan's book, *The Modern Fundamentals of Golf*. He was pre-eminent in this rarefied business: 'John and I both felt that he was so much the best at this sort of thing that we must get him if we could,' says Bowden. 'The problem was we couldn't really afford him.'

Jacobs and Bowden decided, however, that whatever the difficulties, they should at least let Ravielli see the manuscript and then have a talk. 'As things turned out,' says Bowden, 'Tony was so impressed with John when he met him that he seemed to warm to it. Eventually, we found a way of agreeing terms which were acceptable to him, and the work went ahead.'

Thus was *Practical Golf** born. With all its foreign-language translations, it has become, internationally, almost certainly the most successful instructional golf book ever written. Sixteen years after its initial publication date, pay cheques from the royalties continue to flow in.

REMEMBER JONES

Bowden gave Jacobs the opportunity to convince the *Golf Digest* teaching panel of the validity of his doctrine. But he could not insulate him against the opposition which his heretical British views initially aroused.

The panel consisted of Snead, Middlecoff, Runyon, Toski, Flick, Merrins and Wiren – as formidable and broadly based a sextet as could have been marshalled in the United States at the start of the 1970s. Having thrown Jacobs in at the deep end, Bowden was concerned not only that he should acquit himself well but also that he should ultimately get his concept accepted. After all, he had gone out on the line in the first place in inviting Jacobs over. Such apprehensions as Bowden may have harboured were, however, strongly counter-balanced by his conviction that his choice of British nominee for the panel was sound.

The details of that day-long opening session – the first , as things turned out, of a number of similar annual gatherings – are still fixed in Bowden's mind:

'John ran into a lot of opposition – not jealousy, the American mind is too open for that – because he was teaching a different concept. He was starting from the point where the ball reacts to the clubface, and how the flight of the ball tells you all you want to know about the swing path, the angle of attack and the set of the clubface.

'He eventually broke down the resistance because of his logic and his total commitment to his theme. He is a dogmatic man and they couldn't shift him. His simplicity of expression and his articulation meant that they had no doubt whatever about his meaning.

'*John turned the panel around to his way of thinking as soon as they realized that they could learn from him. They resisted him until, from*

*Stanley Paul, London, 1971. The New York publishers Atheneum republished the book in the US in 1983, eleven years after its original publication in America. This edition is now in its fifth impression with a sixth coming up.

the pure logic of his argument, they accepted that he was right. If you follow it through, he changed the thinking of the Golf Digest *panel and, thereby, he changed the mass of American thinking about the golf swing.*

'*It has all been forgotten now because the majority of teachers in the States today start from the point of impact – the point John was starting from when he first began to explain his theory at the beginning of the seventies.*' (Author's emphasis.)

Bowden puts this into historical perspective:

'What John was telling them in 1970 was really little different from what Bob Jones had been saying years before. It's all there in his books. If you read them you will see the extent of the common ground there is between the two men. Jones talked as freely as John does about the way the ball reacts to the clubface and the lessons to be learned from the flight of the ball.

'But then Nelson, Hogan, the cult of the square-to-square method and Nicklaus intervened to obscure the Jones concept. The Americans are a practical, mechanical, statistical society. In golf, they were thinking in terms of methods and set-piece positions. They had lost sight of the end-product. In a word, they had forgotten Jones. What John did was to remind them of that heritage. He took the stiltedness – the mechanicalness, if you like – out of their golf game.'

Brief extracts from Jones's *Golf Is My Game** make Bowden's point (and Jacobs' case) for him:

> I kept on hammering at that pesky ball until I found a way to make it behave . . . I watched other players . . . and when one of them made a shot I specially admired, I would . . . try to produce the same result. But I didn't observe how they took the club back or measure the 'body turn'. I watched that clubhead strike the ball and saw how the ball responded. Then I tried to make the ball do the same thing . . .
>
> Golf is played by striking the ball with the clubhead. The object of the player is not to swing the club in a specified manner, nor execute a series of complicated movements . . . nor look pretty . . . but primarily and essentially to strike the ball with the head of the club so that the ball will perform according to his wishes. No one can play golf until he knows the many ways in which a golf ball can be expected to respond when it is struck in different ways.

The words might have been lifted straight out of *Practical Golf*.

*Doubleday, New York, 1950.

There are other similarities in the two men's thinking about the game – concerning the set-up, for a start. Just as Peter Thomson, the Australian, had once gone out to Sandy Lodge simply to get Jacobs to check his position to the ball, so would Jones, now and then, invite Stewart Maiden to give him a considered view. Those who know of Jacobs's insistence on the importance of a player's set-up will find an echo in a small incident which Jones himself relates. Jones's long irons had been playing him foul. A few hooks would be followed by a blocked shot 'a mile to the right'. Stewart Maiden, emigrant from Carnoustie, was, fortuitously, close at hand. Jones sought his opinion. 'Hit a few,' he said. Jones complied. Maiden intervened. 'Wait,' he said, and tapped Jones's left arm two or three times just below the shoulder with the club he was holding. The player automatically moved back behind the ball. 'Move back,' said Maiden. Jones recalls, 'I moved back some more, then looked up. "Stewart," I said, "I'll knock this ball straight into that left-hand bunker." "Never mind," he said, "back some more." "What do I do now?" I asked. "Knock hell out of it," said Stewart. The ball almost landed in the hole. I hit another straight at the flag . . .'

The speed of Maiden's correction recalls Tony Jacklin's reflective verdict on using Jacobs as a mirror for his own action. 'I just wanted John for five minutes. I didn't want him for thirty. He saw it all with me so quickly . . . Attack on the ball, and what it was giving. Then alignment, set-up, shoulders, ball position . . . That, and tempo. It was all there in five minutes . . .'

In the end, it all comes back to what Michael Bonallack, with his acute golfing intellect and authority, has to say about the Jacobs teaching concept. He has the personal experience to go to the heart of it. 'John has almost taught the game backwards. Instead of starting with the address and the swing, he begins by seeing where the ball has gone. And when he has found out what the ball is doing and what is happening to the shots, then everything is worked backwards from there. He was the first person I came across who taught you to think about golf that way.'

The years that Ken Bowden edited *Golf Digest* were critical for Jacobs in establishing his US presence. By the time Bowden had decided to quit the magazine's editorial chair (he has remained to this day a contributing editor and closely linked with the journal) to freelance again and begin a long-term association with Jack Nicklaus, Jacobs's international reputation was secured. Consolidation would take time, but the process was hastened by Bowden whose conviction that an antidote must be found to the heinous square-to-square craze which was then sweeping the United States led him to match Jacobs with Dick Aultman and Jim Flick; he felt that, in this way at least, a balance could be struck.

Aultman, a graduate of Northwestern University, and co-author, with Flick, of the book *The Square-to-Square Golf Swing*, had already become one of America's leading sports writers, with a leaning towards golf. He had edited *Golf Digest* for a dozen or so years, when he first met Jacobs. A left-handed golfer, with a low handicap, his action soon came under Jacobs's scrutiny: 'Dick was an effective player, but a flat swinger and a short hitter. He rolled the face open in the backswing and then left it open coming through. He cut everything, but he cut it straight. He was a good chipper and putter, and he got results.'

It was quite a while before Aultman came to accept the force of Jacobs's arguments. A dedicated protagonist of the square-to-square theme, he wasn't prepared to be swayed easily. Bowden saw to it that the two shared a room at the 1970 Masters at Augusta. Jacobs remembers the days – and nights: 'Dick and I argued and argued during our time together. But we never fell out. That's one of the joys of talking with these guys in the States. It was the same with the *Golf Digest* teaching panel. One had to be very forceful, to battle really hard, to get one's thoughts across the table. But there were never any hard feelings – not like there were with all those arguments with the PGA's executive committee at home. The behaviour and manners of those guys were impressive.'

Aultman was to become a convert to Jacobs's ways and, later, a preacher of his gospel. He was with the British tutor at the first *Golf Digest* school Jacobs ran. It took place on 19–25 March 1972, at the Carefree Inn, at Desert Forest, Arizona. Endless similar enterprises were to follow under one banner or another – *Golf Digest*'s, *Golf Magazine*'s (temporarily) or Practical Golf Schools'.

Aultman's conversion was the result of first-hand experience: 'John watched me hit a few balls. "Dick," he said, "I'd like you to hit a shot for me when you actually aim to hit the turf with the clubhead an inch or two behind the ball." The instruction really startled me. I felt I must bury the clubhead in the turf behind the ball.

'Anyway, I did as John said and to my surprise I hit the ball as far as I ever remember hitting it – and maybe further. I had, of course, been one of those guys who had always swung the handle of the club too far ahead of the clubhead so that the face was always open to the flight-path. The thought of digging into the turf just behind the ball got me hitting it earlier and squaring the face up at impact. It made all the difference to my game.'

Dick Aultman eventually became Jacobs's number one teaching assistant for some five years, until the mentor left *Golf Digest* ostensibly to perform a similar function for its US rival, *Golf Magazine*. In that time, he had seen the British professional in varying situations. Aultman says:

'When we first started to talk about the square-to-square golf swing, John made it quite clear to me that he thought it was so much garbage and that the message would actually harm the golfing public. To be honest, I wasn't quite ready for such a candid opinion. It was frightening. But, as the years went by, I found his candour was his strong suit. That's all right if you're correct in what you're saying. In my experience, whether one liked it or not, John was almost invariably correct.'

Aultman makes another observation about the forthrightness of the Yorkshireman's character:

'John will tell you that he is always more patient working with pupils in the United States than he is with his students in England. Possibly it's true that he feels he has got to be on his best behaviour when he's over here. But that hasn't stopped him from being very firm with a student when he thinks it's necessary. I've seen a pupil do or say something which he just can't tolerate, and he hasn't hesitated to take the person aside (he would never do it in front of a class) and tell him, or her, that he or she is out of line.

'I remember seeing him teaching a student at one of our schools who was an inveterate slicer. John had done a yeoman's job with the guy. In a few moments, the slice had been eliminated and the student was actually hooking the ball. After a while, he turned to John, somewhat displeased: "I came here with a slice, now I'm hooking 'em."

'When the session was over, John took the pupil aside. "My dear sir," he said, "if you want to strike the ball better than we've got you hitting it now, you will either need a new body or a new teacher." Sometimes fellows needed that kind of treatment to improve.'

Aultman's comment upon the effect on his own teaching of working with Jacobs gives support to Micklem's contention that 'he taught the pros to teach'.

'If I've seen John teach one student, I must have seen him teach a thousand. What this has done for me is to make me feel, when I'm teaching, that I am John giving the lesson. I see him in my place, doing my job. How I diagnose, how I explain and how I provide the correction is modelled on how I visualize John would do it.'

Two other qualities of Jacobs particularly impress Aultman:

'I have been amazed sometimes at John Jacobs's stamina. A golf school, with maybe thirty students, lasting several days, is quite a test of endurance for the teaching staff, with the work starting early in the morning and running on till late at night with all the socializing. John is a hard-working teacher in daytime, yet he will still have the strength to play a full part in the evening's activities. His sense of fun and outgoing manner, and his ability to communicate, from the welcoming cocktail party at the start of a school until the final evening, are striking. He gets the students going and sets the tone; and there is always fun to be had with his very English language.

'There was a lady student, I remember, who came to us with a chronic slice. "Never mind," he said to her one evening, "have no worry about that slice of yours. I promise you that by the time you leave here you will have been turned into a consistent hooker."

'All the other students at the bar fell about laughing. In our phraseology, a "hooker" is a lady of the evening.'

Jacobs and Aultman combined to assemble, in book form, twenty-five lessons designed to diagnose, explain and correct the average golfer's shot problems. Jack Nicklaus wrote a foreword for the book and Anthony Ravielli provided the illustrations. Published in 1979, it was entitled *Golf Doctor* in the United Kingdom and *Quick Cures for Weekend Golfers* in the United States.* Successful though the book has been, Jacobs disliked the American title. He thought it conveyed an impression of 'quackery' which ran counter to his fundamentalist ideals.

Of one thing, however, he is convinced. To have two journalists of the professional and technical calibre of Aultman and Bowden to represent his views in their written form was a piece of special good fortune.

A somewhat bizarre incident occurred before Jacobs finally took his

*Stanley Paul, London, 1979; Simon and Schuster, New York, 1979.

leave of *Golf Digest*, and its golf schools, to move over to *Golf Magazine*. The *New York Times* had by then acquired *Golf Digest*, but William H. Davis, the periodical's founding father and prime architect, remained the editor-in-chief. It was Bill Davis who had encouraged Ken Bowden, at the end of the sixties, to quit Britain and pursue his work in the United States. With a handicap of six at the time, Davis was entitled to his own firm views on the golf swing. Someone suggested, however, that it would perhaps be appropriate if he let Jacobs have a look at him. The British professional was then engaged with a golf school at Innisbrook, near Tampa, on the west coast of Florida.* Aultman, Shelby Futch and Bert Buehler were teaching with him. Students at the school had been hitting balls all day. The ground in the hitting area was worn; there was little grass left.

Davis, with a 5-iron in his hand, took a few practice swings. According to Jacobs, 'It was a very solid, rounded swing . . . in-to-out . . . a bit flat . . . rather shallow.' Davis then started to look for a decent piece of turf.

'I promise you,' says Jacobs, 'people don't have to do any more than that to let me know exactly what to expect'. Having watched his practice swings and then seeing Bill Davis searching for a good lie, the picture was all there:

'"Bill," I asked, "how long have you hooked the ball?" There was a trace of indignation in the reply. "I don't hook the ball." "What," parried the teacher, "not at all?" "No," came the reply. "OK, then," said Jacobs, "just hit a few."'

Davis hit three strokes from carefully-picked lies. Jacobs comments: 'They were three very good shots. All were struck cleanly, from in-to-out. They started about twenty yards right and then hooked back to the target to finish roughly on it. But the balls had no back-spin. They would either have gone straight through a firm green or would have had to be pitched well short and allowed to run. The important thing, however, was that, although they had all finished on the target, each ball had moved fifteen to twenty yards, from right to left, in the air.'

The striker was well satisfied. 'There you are, John,' he said, 'you see, I don't hook the ball.'

The professional onlookers could hardly contain their mirth. But Davis wasn't having it. He wasn't trying to fool anyone. Those three balls had landed just where he wanted them. In his judgement, he hadn't hooked one.

*Mike Souchak's club: the former US Ryder Cup player is credited with having one of the best cellars in America.

Jacobs spoke: 'Bill, would you please just swing up to the top of the backswing and hold it there.'

Jacobs then stepped forward. The club was laying off to the left of the target, with the left wrist flat and straight: 'I just took hold of the shaft and pointed the club at the target – got the clubhead much more open and in the right direction. This would at once have the effect of narrowing the downswing, making the angle of attack steeper. "Let me get out of the way," I said, "and then you hit it from there."

'He swung the club down, took the ball first and then a divot – something that he hadn't done for years. The ball started straight on the target and stayed there all the way. He repeated it three times in a row.'

Usually, when a player is asked to do this – and it's an exercise which Jacobs often employs – the shot is mis-hit. It's not easy to hit a ball from a stopped position at the top: 'Normally, he will have to hit two or three shots before he gets the perfect one. But Bill Davis had hit three one hundred per cent shots straight off.

'"Well, there you are," I said, "that's all you need."'

But Davis had other ideas. 'Oh no,' he said, 'if I'm going to do that, I'll have to cup my left wrist at the top of the swing [get the left wrist under the shaft at the top of the backswing], and that's against the magazine's teaching policy. It's our belief that a straight left wrist at the top of the backswing is fundamental.'

Poor Mr Hogan and Mr Cotton, thought Jacobs, and left it there.

BEAR COVERING

Ken Bowden gave up the editorial directorship of *Golf Digest* in 1972, the year that he and John Jacobs published *Practical Golf*. He had already struck up a fruitful working relationship with Jack Nicklaus. The two had combined effectively to produce the 'Lesson Tee' series, which was then beginning to appear in the magazine. In contrast to Palmer and Player, Nicklaus had, two years before, left Mark McCormack's agency to set up his own business group, Golden Bear Inc., headed then by the American lawyer Putnam S. Pierman. 'Put' Pierman and Nicklaus were on the lookout for a part-time writer just as Bowden was himself making another start. His new freelancing activities, allied with the rapport which he had already established with the stable, made him a natural for the job.

Fifteen years have passed since the connection was formalized. The output of written work which Nicklaus and Bowden have produced in that time has been prodigious. Leaving film and television interests aside, but taking three paperback strips into account, nine books in all have been published, with Nicklaus's autobiography yet to come. Worldwide sales are well in excess of a million. So, when all the literary works with which Bowden has been involved, both with Nicklaus and with Jacobs, are placed together, the international golfing spread is probably without parallel. It would, of course, have been difficult for Bowden, from the standpoint of modern golfing literature, to have latched on to a more fertile pair than the duo from Lindrick, in Yorkshire, and Columbus, Ohio.

Bowden introduced Jacobs to Nicklaus at the end of the 1960s, when Nicklaus was going through a rough time. He hadn't won a major championship, either in the United States or in Britain, for almost two years. His good finishes (and, make no mistake, he had had them) had come more from his courage and superb course management – his ability to save a poor round before it became a disaster and protect a good one just when it looked like slipping away – than from his striking of a golf ball. He was, by his standards, which are inhumanly high, in a trough. The winner's spoils remained tantalizingly beyond his grasp.

The British Open that year was played at Lytham. Tony Jacklin was a thrilling winner with a 72-hole aggregate of 280 and a finishing round of 72, which Jacobs now describes as the 'most courageous round of golf I personally ever saw played'. Nicklaus was equal sixth, five shots behind.

Two or three days before the championship began, the American had been playing a practice round with his compatriot Gardner Dickinson, and Gary Player. Jacobs had gone out to walk a few holes with them. He had played with Dickinson in the Bing Crosby tournament at Cypress Point fourteen years before, while Player was an old friend. He had only quite recently come to know Nicklaus.

Nicklaus was palpably unhappy with his game, as Jacobs well recalls: 'On the second tee, Jack got his neck over the ball, rocked and blocked, and pushed it way out to the right. In fact, it cleared British Rail's line to Blackpool with some yards to spare. He put down another ball. Again, he rocked in the backswing, but then he turned from the top and knocked it yards left, right over the fifteenth green.'

He fared little better on the third tee, whereupon Player and Dickinson offered counsel. 'For goodness sake, Jack, you've got to turn more to get the club more on the inside. You must turn more in the backswing.'

Jacobs, standing behind on each tee, said nothing. But it crossed his mind that he had seen Nicklaus as a 'hugely promising' nineteen-year-old amateur, with a crew-cut, playing at Muirfield in 1959 in his first Walker Cup match against Britain: 'He had been swinging the club better at Muirfield than he was at Lytham.'

The threesome reached the tee on the long, par 5 sixth: 'Jack hit another huge push-fade, missing the fairway by seventy yards on the right.' He turned to Jacobs, watching silently from behind the tee. 'Come on,' he said, 'you're supposed to know something about it. What do you think?'

Jacobs had already made up his mind that, if asked, he would say exactly what he thought.

'Jack,' he said, going straight to the trouble spot, 'has anyone talked posture to you?' The sentence was interrupted in mid-stream: 'What d'yer mean, posture?'

Jacobs explained. 'The back of your neck is virtually parallel with the ground as you stand to the ball. Your head is so much *over* the ground that you can only rock and tilt your shoulders, which will take the club straight back and up. And it's no good these two gentlemen here [Player and Dickinson] telling you to get inside. You can't from that address position.'

He had touched a tender place. 'Dammit,' said Nicklaus, 'when I was growing up, Jack Grout* used to put his fist under my chin as I addressed the ball and tap it to make me get my head up and stand taller. He still does it sometimes when I see him . . .'

They stayed on Lytham's sixth tee, hitting balls, for all of fifteen minutes. 'If I were you,' said Jacobs at the end of it, 'I'd go and see Mr Grout when you get home.'

'When I get home? There's a championship on this week and I'd like to win it. What are you doing this evening?'

Jacobs could see a problem. 'Of course, I'll come and watch you hitting balls on the practice ground. But there'll be hundreds of people milling about and I really don't think it would do for me to be seen standing there with you. But I'll just stay in the crowd and watch you, and then we can talk about it afterwards.'

Nicklaus at once saw the point, and that's what the two did.

Two months later, the Ryder Cup match was played at Birkdale, to the south of Lytham, across the Ribble estuary. A couple of days

*Nicklaus's lifelong teacher.

before the match, Nicklaus spotted Jacobs standing beside the club-house as he got out of his car. 'Hey,' he said, 'I believe I've got it now. I think you'll approve. I'm going down to the practice ground now, come and see what you think.'

There were again crowds of people moving about. 'Jack,' said Jacobs quietly, 'there's nothing I'd sooner do than come and watch you. But this is the one moment when I just daren't be seen with you and your golf swing, two evenings before the Ryder Cup. They'd never leave it alone.'

Nicklaus made it easy. 'Sure,' he said, 'I understand.'

By 1979, ten years later, despite the intervening moments of triumph, Nicklaus's golf had become, for him, downright bad. He was then thirty-nine, with an unmatched and unmatchable record behind him. The faithful Grout had been on at him for some time about the need to make changes if his game was to be restored to its full effectiveness. In truth, he had reached the crossroads: one signpost pointed to 'change'; the other to 'quit'.

Five years earlier, in 1974, he and Bowden had produced their book *Golf My Way*,* in which Nicklaus had been curiously critical of Jacobs's theory. He had claimed, in so many words, that 'the distinguished British teaching professional', as he called him, had tried to get him to flatten his swing: 'John's point may be valid for some golfers, but I'm going to have to say that it isn't in my case . . . To me, the accuracy factor of the upright plane is too valuable to be easily discarded.'

This was, in fact, a misrepresentation, or perhaps a misinterpretation, of what had been said. Jacobs was adamant that at no time, when he saw Nicklaus at Lytham in 1969, had he advised him to flatten his swing. What he had said was that his posture, with his head over the ball and neck virtually parallel with the ground, made it inevitable that he would rock and block – with the right shoulder rising up in the backswing and the left lifting up as the club was swung down and through. It was preventing him from getting inside. His advice had been to raise his head at the address and so improve his posture. This, of itself, would help him to turn *the shoulders* flatter. He hadn't suggested that he should *swing* flatter.

Since the 1950s, Jacobs has been quite clear about it. There are two

*Simon and Schuster, New York, 1974.

distinct planes in the golf swing. 'The shoulders go back and the arms go up' has been his consistent cry. As a corollary, he has long stressed the point that the shoulders and arms are *not* married together to move in one and the same plane. Indeed, it was one of the things which astonished him when he first began his discussions with the *Golf Digest* teaching panel that there was then no proper understanding in America of this principle: 'They hadn't seemed to realize that you couldn't possibly have the shoulders and the arms working in the same plane, whether that be too upright or too flat. There were drawbacks to both.' In the first four months of 1980, Nicklaus, just turned forty, spent much of his time with Jack Grout at Lost Tree Village and Frenchman's Creek, near his Florida home, engaged in what Bowden now calls 'his remake'. Nicklaus and Bowden tell the story in their book *The Full Swing** published two years later.

The introduction, 'An Easier Way to Swing', describes the case for change, and the adjustments which were required to achieve it. It reveals a man who, having dominated the game for a quarter of a century, was big enough to admit that there was still something to learn – or, more accurately, to relearn:

> . . . I accepted the need for certain changes that I hoped would reverse more than ten years of gradual deterioration in my full swing . . .
>
> The first and probably the most critical change I had to master was to stand taller to the ball at the address . . . maintain my height . . . throughout the swing. The more inclined the body at address, the more the shoulders and hips will tend to lift and head to dip during the backswing. The greater these tilts and dips, the harder it is to genuinely turn the upper body and arms away from the ball and behind yourself, and thus the more upright the swing plane will be.
>
> Even in the good old days I had to watch a tendency to get too inclined or 'over' the ball at address . . . Now, set up as tall as Grout wanted me, I felt at first like a soldier on parade – virtually standing to attention.

This, and much else in the book, sounded potently reminiscent of the Sermon on the Sixth Tee at Lytham ten years before.

Bowden, a witness to the Golden Bear's rehabilitation and a long-term confidant of Jacobs, put the point one day to Nicklaus, *en*

---

*Golf Digest/Tennis Inc., a *New York Times* company, 1982.

passant. 'Didn't John Jacobs tell you that all that time ago?' Nicklaus murmured assent, 'Uh huh, yes he did.'

PART TWO

NEW WORLD

6
Director-General

'... AND IN TODAY ALREADY WALKS TOMORROW'

The graph of a successful career charts many changes – the high points may come early, never to be repeated; they may come, more commonly, in the middle years, thereafter coasting undramatically along; only rarely will the pinnacle be reached in later life. That Jacobs now rests upon an international high is undeniable. Comfortably placed, but without, perhaps, having gained the ultimate riches which could have been his had he been ready for a McCormack to exploit his genius, he lives his own full life. Working hard and travelling widely, much is packed into a working year. But his leisure, such as it is, is still equally fully used. With son, Jonathan, married now to his wife, Sheila, making his successful way as a skilled musical engineer, absorbed with the production of electronic sounds which support the highly-publicised modern groups, and daughter Joanna, now engaged in the health farm business after a spell working with Practical Golf Schools in America, Rita and John Jacobs can enjoy the benefits which toil, reasonable luck and success have bestowed.

On 10th October 1971 John Jacobs became director-general of the PGA's Tournament Division, and over the five years from 1971 he masterminded and built up what has since come to be called the PGA European Tour.

The roots of his achievement were planted back in 1954, during a tournament at Harrogate. Jacobs, then twenty-nine, and carrying the banner of Sandy Lodge, was standing behind the eighteenth green waiting to collect the players' signatures as they finished their rounds. There was discontent at the way the tournaments were then being conducted. The players wanted change, yet the bulk of the twenty-

113

eight-strong PGA Excutive Committee, heavily loaded with the 'old guard' of club professionals, blocked the way.

Twenty-nine tournament players signed a requisition which was heard at the PGA's convention in London on 25 November 1954. Jacobs and his fellow-signatories, 'speaking for all the younger guys' wanted to know:

1. What the executive committee of the PGA was doing about the 'continued loss of major tournaments'.
2. What action was being taken to encourage new sponsors and new tournaments.
3. Whether the PGA would go to existing promoters and tell them that it would be 'to the advantage of promoters, the PGA and golf generally if prize lists only included the first thirty players, along with more encouraging prizes for young assistants.'

The PGA bulletin of February 1955 credited Jacobs with saying that manufacturers 'would only promote tournaments if there was something in it for themselves in the way of publicity'. He had added that 'the present liaison with the press was very poor . . . and an improvement in publicity might well improve the chances of new tournaments.'

Some vigorous discussion was eventually closed with the undertaking that the executive committee would give the matter 'favourable consideration'.

Jacobs was on his feet again at the association's 1960 annual general meeting, held at the Royal Automobile Club in Pall Mall on 23 November. He spoke in support of a letter which, the bulletin of February 1961 reported, he had written to the secretary 'on behalf of Messrs. P. Alliss, B. J. Hunt, H. Weetman and himself'.

The letter had complained about an ineffective resolution which had earlier been passed by the executive committee about the promotion and control of tournaments. This, the critics observed, 'in no way changes the situation about which we have been complaining'. A kick and a threat were contained in the tail. After noting that the all-powerful executive had apparently no intention of delegating suitable authority to sub-committees (in this case the tournament sub-committee), Jacobs and his mates reached for the driver and teed it up:

> If this is so, we wish the executive committee to understand that we shall do all in our power to change the . . . rules . . . so that the . . . committee . . . shall in future comprise . . . a fairer and more balanced representation of the different categories of our

A company day at Woburn, on the Duke of Bedford's estate: John Jacobs with Severiano Ballesteros, twice Open Champion, twice US Master Golfer

The practice ground at Birkdale on the evening before the final round of the 1971 Open. Tony Jacklin, the 1969 champion, had asked Jacobs 'to have a look at him'. A brave 71 the next day left Jacklin third on 280, two strokes behind Lee Trevino, the winner

'Jacobs is happiest when he is out of doors, with rod or gun. From the Test to the Tweed, from Ireland to Pakistan's north-west frontier, he has, literally, cast his net wide . . .'

'Scoring' on the Tweed with Gareth Edwards (right), Welsh rugby's immortal

A day on the famous Lough Sheelin, Southern Ireland

Angus Nudds (below), Sir Peter Crossman's 'keeper' at Tetworth, and Danny Northrop (left) at Church Farm, Cambridgeshire, two of John Jacobs' close friends

Bottom: Man at peace . . . On the north-west frontier of Pakistan

Right: 'Come on,' said Nicklaus to Jacobs on the sixth tee at Lytham, 'you're supposed to know something about it, what do you think?'

Below: Jacobs will take his Practical Golf Schools to Golf del Sur, the new 27 holes golf, leisure and real estate complex at San Miguel on the island of Tenerife. The Dutch developer is Robert C Schumann, on the right

It was Emma de Garcia-Ogara (second from left), non-playing captain of the 1986 winning Spanish women's World Cup team in Venezuela, who persuaded the Spanish golf federation in 1969 to appoint Jacobs as coach to the country's national teams. The 1986 players were (left to right): Maria Orueta, Macarena Canpomanes and Mari-Carmen Navarro. Michael Bonallack, secretary of the R & A (background right) applauds their victory

Craig Bunker (left) with Practical Golf Schools' original teaching quartet, South Carolina, 1980: second left to right: Jim Hardy, John Jacobs, Shelby Futch (now president) and Bert Buehler

USA today: Some of Jacobs' 32-strong teaching staff of Practical Golf Schools in the US. Left to right (if you can discern them):
Back row: Joe Eldridge, Matt Zeman, Tim Smith, Randy Burkhardt, Shelby Futch, Bert Buehler, John Joseph, Marc Boggia
Front row: Donald Crawley, Teresa Weinshilboum, Mike Lafond, Bob Augustine, Todd Howard

'"Say," he said with a twinkle, "what was that you were good enough not to tell me [about my game] that evening at Walton Heath . . .?"' Tom Watson, five times British and once US Open Champion, and twice US Master Golfer

'. . . Jacobs' brief was to tell *Golf Magazine's* readers what three of the world's greats were currently working on. Greg Norman was one he checked with. The Australian didn't hesitate. "It's to do with what you told me when you saw me originally . . ."'

Golf course architect: Jacobs planning the new South Course at Wentworth with Bernard Gallacher (first left), Gary Player (second left) and David Pottage (right), managing director of John Jacobs Golf Associates, October 1986

association.

Our view is [that] the executive should consist of the following:

4 club professionals
4 tournament professionals
1 senior professional
1 assistant professional

This committee to be freely elected by postal votes by all the categories concerned.

(They had in mind a committee of ten, properly representative of all the factions, in place of the cumbersome, unwieldy body of twenty-eight whose survival rested upon the largely sympathetic proxy votes of the club professional in the association's eight sections.) Ernest Bradbeer, a much respected member of a fine, West Country golfing family, who, like Henry Cotton, was always sympathetic to the pleas of the younger tournament players, moved that 'Messrs P. Alliss, B. J. Hunt, J. R. M. Jacobs and H. Weetman, now serving on the tournament committee, be elected to the executive committee.'

The proposal was agreed, but such was the continuing imbalance of the controlling executive that the quartet found it could, effectively, get nowhere. Bradbeer had done his best, but it could only be a palliative. The elections did no more than treat the symptoms of the disease; the root cause of it was left untouched.

More than fifteen years would pass before a PGA management committee structured very much on the lines of the proposal outlined in Jacobs's original letter, was formed. It embraced three club professionals on the one side and three tournament players on the other, with an independent amateur in the chair.

In golf, as in other sports, the trick is to keep ahead of the game. Once a ruling entity allows itself to be overtaken by events, the initiative is lost and, with it, authority. Trouble usually follows. In 1960, Jacobs, Alliss, Hunt and Weetman, and those who were playing to their tune, were ahead of the game; the executive were half a dozen holes behind. It would be some 14 years before the players were able to extract the full price from their initiative. But by then it was too late to prevent a split. The PGA, founded in 1901, was being ripped down the middle, with the 'establishment' and the club professionals on one side grinding up against the tournament players on the other. It was a time of emotion and bitterness. Nothing quite like it had occurred in the organization before.

Such was the scenario with which Jacobs, supported 100 per cent by the tour, but vehemently opposed by a strong majority of the remaining members, was confronted. How it all happened, and how it was ultimately resolved, makes a compelling chapter in trade union history. Those who are conversant with the corporate side of business life, with contested take-over bids and the deviousness which surrounds them, with charge and counter-charge, rumour, allegation and innuendo – and just plain dirty tricks – will find much in the saga which is familiar. Indeed, to the initiated, it may all seem to have been fair game. In the staid citadel of the PGA, however, earth tremors tested the foundations at their base.

Jacobs had entered the fray, when it came, with several advantages which were unknown to, or at least underestimated by, his opponents. The rough experience he had gained as Athlon's managing director, working within an aggressive public company group, had taught him all he needed to know about in-fighting. The value of the well-drafted memorandum or minute to substantiate a verbal understanding wasn't lost on him. His paperwork through all the turmoil bore the Athlon and GRA stamp. Allied to this, he was, by now, quite used to the ways of the 'establishment'. He was acquainted with its bark, and not in the least intimidated by its bite.

The start of Jacobs's tenure as director-general of the tour was propitious. It certainly gave no hint of what was to fellow. He had been reluctant to accept the director-generalship of the tour but, egged on by the players who were desperate for improvements, and encouraged by John Bywaters, the association's secretary, he undertook the task as a duty to his colleagues. One thing was plain. At a salary of £5000 per annum, it wasn't the money that attracted him. He was contracted to give 50 per cent of his time to the work, but he knew very well that, initially, it would demand more than that. His backers wanted him to do the job full-time. This was unacceptable because he was also contracted to Athlon for some 50 per cent of his output. Such was his loyalty to the company, and his interest in the golf-centre business, which was now gathering pace, that he had no intention of seeking a release. His board colleagues, recognizing his worth and the company's financial limitations, were happy for him to spread his wings.

Jacobs made one overriding proviso in accepting the director-generalship. He insisted on being given a completely free hand to drive the work through. He knew he couldn't succeed on any other basis. Having served for a spell on the executive committee, he was well aware of the likelihood of interference from that quarter. This had to be avoided. Bywaters gave him the verbal undertaking he sought, confident that he could obtain the necessary consent.

The director-general-elect was in Portugal on a brief holiday with his family when Bywaters's cable arrived. 'All confirmed,' it read. 'Start 1 October 1971, as proposed.'

The first three months in the job were 'hugely successful'. By mid-December, with the help of George Simms's public relations organization, who gave him throughout stalwart support, he was able to tell the press of the Christmas present he was offering the tour. Michael McDonnell, the *Daily Mail*'s golf correspondent, gave the news in the first two paragraphs of his story. Under the headline, '£443,000 bonanza for British golf', he reported:

> John Jacobs, the man with the job of raising more cash for British professional golf, delivered the goods yesterday and promised a £443,450 bonanza next season. This is almost double the £266,215 that British tournament pros earned last season.

However, even allowing for 20 per cent inflation rate in the mid-seventies the advance was itself later dwarfed by the total which accrued at the end of Jacobs's five-year run at the head of the tournament players' division. Mark McCormack, whose International Management Group handles many of the game's leading players, put the size of the increase in perspective. Writing of the British tour in his golf annual of 1973, *The World of Professional Golf*,* he gave his assessment:

> Whereas Jacobs had originally stated his belief that a sum of about £700,000 was as much as the market would bear in the foreseeable future, he quickly revised that estimate to a whopping million-and-a-half in five years' time

Protected from interference by John Bywaters, and with the forward path smoothed for him, the director-general had, by 1973, largely sold the tour to the chairmen and managing directors of sponsoring companies. He had offered a circuit resting not upon the narrow British base, but on one with wider horizons, embracing Europe and Scandinavia, where he had already had so much teaching experience with the professionals and the national teams. This, and the interest he had aroused in the television producers, meant that a much more

*Collins, London, 1973.

appealing package was on offer.

Jacobs was able to enter his negotiations with an extra ace in the pack. By then, Tony Jacklin had done something that no other home-based, British professional had accomplished since Ted Ray's victory in the US Open at Inverness, Toledo, Ohio, fifty years before: he had beaten the Americans in a major championship on their own soil. Jacklin had been slogging it out on the US tour in the latter part of the 1960s with a singleness and resolve which set him apart. Top-ten finishes in the most exacting competition of all, culminating in victory at Jacksonville, Florida, in 1968, had made him whipcord-hard and prepared him for his success in the British Open at Lytham in the following year. Less than twelve months later, he had added a second 'major' to his record with his exceptional triumph in the US Open at Hazeltine, by Chaska, in Minnesota. With these, and his other starred performances at home and abroad, Jacklin possessed a drawing power which was unrivalled on the British tour.

But Jacklin was managed by Mark McCormack, as tough and as astute a lawyer as can be found in the agency business. This led to a number of hard but realistic negotiations for Jacobs: 'I had some terrific battles with Mark. But I actually enjoyed them and the challenge which they offered, because I found in our dealings that he was both fair and absolutely straight. Over the use I wanted to make of both Tony Jacklin and the other leading players he had on his books, he offered real help. He understood exactly what I was trying to do with the British and European circuit to mould it into a single, large entity. Easy to say that he helped me because by helping me he was also aiding his own clients. Whatever the reason, Mark McCormack was a big factor in enabling me to get our show so strongly and quickly on the road.'

Jacklin himself was in no doubt of his worth to Jacobs at this formative time:

> '... *I was blind to my natural instinct to slow down ... but I stayed on the lucrative treadmill, encouraged ... by John Jacobs and the PGA European Tour officials who knew I was a major drawing power in the early days of the circuit ... I never doubted I should help ... I wanted to ...
>
> Some of the younger players forget that the European Tour was not always the way it is today. It would never have developed as it

*Tony Jacklin with Renton Laidlaw, *Tony Jacklin. The First Forty Years.* Queen Anne Press, London, 1985.

did but for the vision of John Jacobs who saw the potential of the untapped marked on the Continent and had the foresight . . . to forecast and cash in, to all our benefits, on the growth potential . . .'

The director-general, and the association, were dealt an unexpected blow in the spring of 1973 just as the season was about to move into top gear. John Bywaters, who had served the PGA as its secretary for eight years, died suddenly in his headquarters office at London's Kennington Oval. Bywaters was known to have been unwell, but the surprise of his death shook his colleagues and none more so than Jacobs, for the two men had become close friends. Under the secretary's benevolent eye, 'everything had, up till then, gone swimmingly' for the director-general.

The executive committee, acting with commendable speed, soon appointed a successor. Colin Snape, a comparatively recent recruit for one of the two administrators' posts in Jacobs's tournament division, had already made his mark. An outward calm hid a tidy, well-trained and ambitious mind. This was supported by a *curriculum vitae* which suggested that, with his accountancy background, he could be just the man to take hold of a sprawling, old-fashioned and top-heavy organization and modernize it. By the time Snape got the job, he had already formed his own pungent views on the restructuring which was required. In a phrase, the place needed turning upside down. Given the chance, he felt he could do it.

As a first measure, the executive committee invited the new secretary to commit his thoughts to paper. This he did with breathtaking directness and dogmatism, basing his proposals upon his own highly critical assessment of the association's administrative machine.

The director-general was not consulted during the preparation of the memorandum. This was clearly a mistake. As the head of an increasingly successful and well-publicized division of the association, Jacobs felt that there should have been an opportunity at least for an exchange of views. The secretary, on the other hand, had been given his remit. As far as he knew, it was his views on the reorganization, and no one else's, that the executive committee wanted to see.

Snape's paper was considered on 9 August 1973 by the advisory council of the PGA at Calcot Golf Club, near Reading, where a tournament was then beginning. The council, as its name suggests, was an advisory body on which sat three senior professionals — Geoffrey Cotton, Bernard Hunt and Dai Rees — plus Three Wise

Businessmen who had been brought in from commerce and industry to offer advice. The president of the association, Lord Derby, presided at the meeting, which was attended by the chairman of the executive committee, Douglas Smith, a long-serving club professional, a native of Stafford Castle in Staffordshire, where his father had been the professional. Jacobs, on holiday at the time with his family in the New Forest, drove up from Hampshire, expecting to contribute to a useful and constructive meeting.

The paper was circulated only a few minutes before the meeting. It made an instant impact upon the director-general: 'It gave me the shock of my life.' Not only did it appear to him to cut clean across some of the provisions of his formal agreement with the PGA; it also seemed to fly straight in the face of the 'completely free hand' on which his acceptance of the tour directorship had depended. He doubted whether the new secretary had read his contract before committing his views to paper.

The effect of the memorandum's proposals, if implemented, would have been to remove Jacobs's authority over the tour and concentrate strength at the centre, which, in practice, would have meant the secretary's office. Little of importance would have fallen outside this orbit. Players of the calibre and status of Jacklin and Oosterhuis (they were actually cited in the paper) – and their agents or managers – were to be brought to heel. They would be obliged to take the party whip – and the chief whip would crack it.

The paper was a transparently obvious attempt to weaken the director-general's hold over the tour and transfer power to a caucus at the heart of the association. As such, it was the antithesis of what the tournament players wanted and, therefore, a blueprint for strife. It looked at the time to be an ill-conceived and unwise document. Fourteen years later, there appear to be no grounds to alter the judgement.

The consequence was an unhappy meeting which acted like vinegar on personal relationships. It was the start of a two-year fight which would polarize the two sides of the association and throw the opposing camps into open and frequently acrimonious conflict.

At the first opportunity after the Calcot meeting, Jacobs consulted his solicitors, Herbert Smith. Armed with their advice,* he followed

---

*Originally, Jacobs was advised by H. W. (David) Higginson, a Cambridge golf blue in his day, and one of the best corporate lawyers in the City of London. After Higginson became senior partner of the firm, the work was dealt with by another partner, David Bolton.

his usual custom by representing his views in writing to members of the advisory council, the chairman of the executive committee and the secretary. Enclosing selected items from this correspondence, he wrote, on 15 August 1973, to the PGA president, Lord Derby. He made two comments which he regarded as crucial:

> '... The reason my own contract with the PGA gives me such tremendous authority over the whole tournament scene is because, like yourself, I have never had any confidence in the PGA management structure. I felt ... I could only be of use to the PGA as long as I was given a free hand. I knew it would be quite impossible if I were to become bogged down in either committees or [with] personalities.'

Referring specifically to the outcome of the Calcot meeting, he added:

> '... You can understand my consternation when it seemed to be accepted by all present that the new secretary should advise not only on Europe but over the whole field of rules as they appertain to the tournament players, the duties of the tournament committee, press and public relations, future tournament staff, etc, etc.'

Twenty-four months would elapse before the two sides came together, in the somewhat incongruous precincts of York University, for the inevitable showdown. Meanwhile, the PGA continued to do the splits across an ever-widening abyss.

MEN IN THE MIDDLE

It was clear that the old order of the PGA had run its course; it had lasted too long already. The pity was that the upheaval, when it came, had to develop in the way that it did. With greater prescience, and a readiness to accommodate the thrust of younger minds, it could well have been averted. The entrenched reactionary, however, is always hard to shift. The tournament committee's young progressives of the 1950s – the 'Messrs P. Alliss, B. J. Hunt, J. R. M. Jacobs and H. Weetman' – had learned that frustrating lesson.

The PGA president, Lord Derby, had been in office for nine years when the fracas began. He had succeeded to the presidency in 1964 with the demise of the widely experienced and worldly Lord Brabazon.

Distinguished son of a distinguished father, a decorated wartime Grenadier Guards officer, and already following his family's tradition of public service, Lord Derby had his own distinctive thoughts about the organization's need for change. When the split appeared and looked like developing into a chasm, his prime aim was to hold the two sides together. But things had, by then, moved too far. The tournament players – a new breed of professionals whose gaze, under their director-general, was now fastened not upon an insular national tour, but on European horizons, were resolved not to be fettered. They would brook no interference. They wanted their own autonomous division. The tide of opinion was running too strongly to be stemmed.

The chairman of the association throughout the conflict, from 1973 to 1975, was Douglas Smith. He had served Worsley, one of Manchester's old-established clubs, as its professional for eighteen years before moving on to Dunham Forest. Later, he was to turn south, to Harpenden, a stone's throw from the cathedral city of St Albans in Hertfordshire. A paragon of the club side of the profession, Doug Smith carried a heavier load through these troubles than any of his illustrious predecessors had previously been asked to bear.

Geoffrey Cotton, a former chairman (1968–69) and captain (1969) of the association, was another who, in these unpredictable days, was playing a significant, if less conventional, role. Articulate, and able to think well on his feet, Cotton's interventions in some of the decisive meetings were nicely timed for effect. Speaking more often than not from the cross-benches, he took a progressively independent line in the exchanges, thereby exasperating club colleagues while at the same time bringing succour and hope to the tour. Cotton was a controversial and key participant in the ultimate stages of the struggle.

Ranged with the 'establishment' and offering it guidance on tactics, was the association's increasingly active secretary.

Snape had established in his own mind that, come what might, the strength and control of the organization must be retained at the centre. He had seen at first hand, in the short time he had spent as a tournament administrator, what would happen if a brake was not quickly and effectively applied on the tour and, more importantly, upon its director-general. He saw that, if power continued to slip away from headquarters, impotence would follow.

Here let it be said that with the remit he had been given, and the circumstances with which he was faced, Snape would argue that he was wholly justified, as secretary, in pursuing his selected course. That was the way the chairman, and an overwhelming majority of the club professionals on the executive committee, saw it and, indeed, wanted it.

By comparison with the depth of golfing experience and authority possessed by the tournament side and its director-general, Snape's own background was relatively thin. Few knew, however, that, for nine years before joining the PGA's tournament staff, he had acted as honorary secretary of his local golf club, Walmersley, in Lancashire. He did the work in the evenings, after long days in the office, and at the weekends. When he volunteered to take on the job, the club, with fewer than two hundred members, was effectively broke. When he left it, nearly a decade later, the membership was nudging four hundred and the operation was financially strong. It was a record which the selectors had taken into account in appointing him to one of the two tournament administrators' posts. Even so, none could deny that when he was lined up alongside Jacobs, his golfing credentials appeared weak.

To mitigate this deficiency, Snape had to go out of his way to build up his own following within the association. His administrative talents were unmistakable, but to strengthen his own position he required the clout which a good, solid phalanx of club professionals would bring. It wasn't difficult to muster such a band. The exceptional success which Jacobs had had, by now, both as the tournament director-general and in his own commercial right, had aroused jealously and animosity, which would mount sharply as the conflict developed. While the players were behind Jacobs to a man, opposition to him, and even enmity, were rife in the other camp. Easy to see, therefore, from where support could be rallied behind the executive and to the secretary's side.

Some questioned Colin Snape's purpose at this time, likening it to that of the blindly ambitious man who was determined at all costs to build an empire and defend it. Others were not enamoured of his methods. But with the hand he had been given, and with the state of the game as he found it, his posture was understandable. Nevertheless his tactics put him on a collision course, wittingly or otherwise, with the tournament director-general.

Given the policy which the association's leadership was now following, and recognizing the incompatible temperaments of the two men, there was plainly no way that Jacobs and Snape would be expected to work together in harmony. And when to John Jacobs's dogmatic and resolute ways was allied the determination of the two successive chairmen of the tournament committee, Bernard Hunt and Neil Coles

– and the disarming efficiency of Ken Schofield as tournament secretary – there could never be any question of the tour representatives compromising, still less of giving in.

The fact remains: Snape's Calcot paper had effectively pulled the rug from under Jacobs's feet. Surprisingly, it was backed by some at the summit who, frankly, might have been expected to challenge its wisdom. More charitable perhaps now to say that the penny didn't drop until it was manifestly too late.

... AND, NOW AND THEN, IN THE ROUGH

The grumble of thunder moved steadily nearer after Calcot. Then the first darts of lightning flashed down on the Hill Barn Club, at Worthing, on 10 May 1974. It was the time of the Penfold tournament, which Tommy Horton was to win. The competitors, at loggerheads now with the executive committee, asked to speak with the tournament director-general. With all the sponsorships he had brought to the tournaments, Jacobs was, in the eyes of the contestants, riding the crest. But they sensed blocking tactics, and wanted to be rid of them. Aggressive and go ahead, they were well aware of what had happened recently to the restructured United States PGA Tour and were resolved to follow suit.

There was only one difference between John Jacobs and many of the leading players: they wanted 'out' and he didn't. They dreamed of being shot of the rest of the association, which they saw as a bureaucratic, all powerful octopus, manoeuvring to retain an empire. The ideal for which they hankered was a completely autonomous tour, self-financing, self-administering and walking its own selected path.

The director-general went 85 per cent of the way with them. He, too, felt that the right solution was the establishment of a separate tournament players' division. But he stopped short of a complete break from the parent association. He wanted a new body to remain under its aegis. He had, after all, owed his allegiance to the association all his working life. Despite its imperfections, it still commanded his respect. He reminded the players that, when their days on the tour were over, many of them would become club professionals.

His advice, then, was along these lines: form your own division, yes; retain absolute control over its administration and its finances; elect your own executive committee, appoint your own staff and keep all disciplinary procedures in your own hands. Drive the division ahead in the direction you want it to follow without interference from anyone. But do it under the umbrella of the PGA; avoid making a finite break.

Jacobs's view coincided with that of Bernard Hunt. The players were sceptical, but they accepted the advice because they respected it. It was a dialogue which would be repeated several times at subsequent meetings between Jacobs and the players; when their patience with the 'establishment' wore thin, it needed all his power of persuasion to hold the line – but hold it he did.

The strange fact is that Lord Derby thought at the time, and indeed has persisted in thinking, that the director-general's desire was to see the players break clean away. Yet this was not Jacobs's intention. It was this belief – more, perhaps, than any simple incompatibility of temperament – that lay at the root of the tension which, in those days, undeniably existed between the two men. It was a most unfortunate misunderstanding and it called into question the quality of the advice which the president was then receiving.

The Worthing meeting with the players was followed by another, a week later, on 16 May, during the Sumrie tournament at Bournemouth. So important were the conclusions reached at these two discussions that the tournament committee felt it essential to record them in a letter, which was sent on 17 May by its chairman, Bernard Hunt, to Douglas Smith, the chairman of the executive committee. It was copied to the president and to the secretary. Nothing was left to doubt.

While reiterating the players' wish to see an autonomous tournament division established, Hunt stressed that this was 'in no way to be viewed as a breakaway from the PGA'. He expressed 'the tournament committee's hope that the formation of the new division could be completed *with the minimum of upheaval and in the best possible atmosphere.*'

The executive committee met on 11 June, with Geoffrey Cotton, deputizing for Douglas Smith, in the chair. The players' proposal to establish their own autonomous division was considered and unanimously approved, with Bernard Hunt representing the tournament committee's concern that the new entity should be brought into being before the end of that year's playing season.

In the event, *eleven months* elapsed before representatives of the two sides met – at Finham Park, Coventry, on 6 May 1975 – to discuss how the new division could be set up. The delay was fatal. It undermined what little trust the tournament committee still had in the executive's resolve to see the business through. John Jacobs, like those whose interests he represented, was by then disillusioned and exasperated.

Meanwhile, Lord Derby proposed a formula designed to hold the two sides of the association together. At the 1974 Open Championship at Lytham, he unveiled a well-intentioned plan to relieve the impasse. First, he persuaded the widely regarded American Joe Dey (pronounced 'die'), who was then at the end of his stint of running the reformed US professional tour, to come over and talk to the British players about the lessons to be learned from the US experience. Dey, a selfless, God-fearing man of special charm and presence, who was succeeded by Deane Beman as tour commissioner, had earlier served the United States Golf Association as secretary. Everyone trusted and liked him.

Derby then suggested his compromise. He proposed the formation of a top management committee, effectively a coalition, composed of three senior club professionals and three more from the tour. In the chair to keep the peace, and blow the whistle, would be a respected amateur golfer of impartial mind. He would be able to stand back from all the internecine strife and take 'the broad view'.

It was an admirable initiative. But it had one flaw. The president suggested that the committee's first chairman should be Gerald Micklem.

Micklem's credentials were impeccable. Former British Walker Cup international and captain, one-time captain of the Royal and Ancient, and holder of a host of the game's high offices, he looked to be just the man. But the tournament side knew that Gerald Micklem could be prickly. Temperamentally, he was well known to be terse and fairly sharp, particularly if the ball wasn't running for him. Clear-minded and an able organizer, his precision was often interpreted as abruptness. To some, he could be intimidating, yet, in truth, he possessed a kind and caring heart. It didn't take a genius to see why, apart from his track record, Derby wanted Micklem. He was a tough cookie and would make a good match for Jacobs.

It was widely thought that Jacobs alone scuppered Derby's selection and, thereby, the plan. There is little doubt that that is what the president – and Micklem – were led to believe. The truth was otherwise. An influential group of senior tournament players thought that the scheme wouldn't work with Micklem in the chair. They had already seen what had happened with Snape and Jacobs in opposing corners. Put Micklem in the same ring with Jacobs, *in the circumstances which each would then be dealing with*, and a gaping breach would widen further. They felt that in the present highly-charged circumstances a different personality was required as chairman. Jacobs shared this view.

After more to-ing and fro-ing, much of it peevish, the association's annual general meeting, held in London on 28 November 1974, formally endorsed the proposal which the executive committee, under Geoffrey Cotton's chairmanship, had approved for the formation of an autonomous tournament players' division. An executive meeting, held immediately after the AGM, agreed, as a matter of urgency, to consider the steps to be taken to implement the decision.

Before the AGM had taken place, the director-general had wisely written to Douglas Smith on 8 October clarifying 'our points of agreement' and 'the areas still left to be decided'. He summarized, in ten points, the way in which he and his colleagues saw a new division being structured. The fifth item on the list had a special significance. It confirmed the tournament committee's conviction that the tour's *administrative* offices should be based in, or close to, London. This would give the tour its best opportunity of successful development, particularly in respect of future liaison/negotiations with those involved in professional golf on the Continent.

Under the PGA's reorganization plan, a move of the association's headquarters from London to the Belfry, a smart hotel and leisure complex embracing two golf courses then being developed near Sutton Coldfield, in the West Midlands, was being mooted. Greenall Whitley, the brewery group, who would become the PGA's landlords at the Belfry, were encouraging the move, offering the association a rent-free lease of 99 years. Apart from the establishment costs and day-to-day outgoings, the terms looked remarkable favourable.* But the brewers were said to be insisting that any move would be contingent upon the whole organization – including the tournament side – being transferred to the West Midlands complex. This condition was spelled out in a letter from Chairman Smith to Jacobs dated 17 October 1974, which made it clear that the executive committee would expect the tournament players' division to move with the rest of the headquarters staff. The correspondence touched off another irksome round of strife.

*The British firm Accles and Pollock put up £100,000 – £50,000 to finance the move, and a further £50,000, spread over ten years, to sponsor the PGA training school at Lilleshall. The only proviso was that the PGA's national headquarters should be called Apollo House.

The tournament committee were convinced it was a try-on by the 'establishment' to cut the new division down to size and keep it on a tighter rein under head-office control. A subsequent meeting with the brewers did indeed clarify beyond all doubt that the company would certainly not insist on the tournament players' division moving to the Belfry from its London base notwithstanding the impression which had been given.

Thereafter, the PGA chairman and the secretary met the principals acting for the Belfry on 21 February 1975, to tidy up the heads of agreement covering the association's move. The document was then sent to Jacobs, in its final form, to sign on behalf of the tournament players. An old fox at this kind of thing, the director-general went through the contract word by word. To his astonishment and anger, he found that it specifically provided for office space to be made available for the whole of the tournament players' division at the Belfry, while no clause had been inserted to cover the basing of the division in, or near, London. After all the brouhaha he could hardly believe it. It was impossible not to read all kinds of dark motives into the insertion and the omission.

Jacobs insisted on various amendments being made to the Belfry agreement. One concerned the provision which, had it not been altered, would have resulted in an embarrassing obligation for the PGA to hold the 1981 Ryder Cup match at the Belfry. The tournament director-general and his colleagues had no doubt that the newly-constructed course could not by then be in a fit condition to host the event.

When Derby saw the changes which Jacobs had made to the contract, he wrote anxiously to the association's secretary. His letter, dated 28 February, the day he was required to sign the agreement, laid it on the line. 'I must confess,' he wrote, 'I am not at all happy about the amendments in paragraph 4 of the Belfry company document. It seems to me that the suggested amendments . . . give a complete let-out to any Ryder Cup or tournament ever being held at the Belfry . . . I feel you should show this to a lawyer as soon as possible.'

An engaging twist was contained in the final paragraph: 'I have a nasty feeling that this is John Jacobs up to his usual tricks.'

Tricks or not, the director-general got the president off what would otherwise have been a most uncomfortable hook when it came to the 1981 match. He would have been in one hell of a fix with Lord Aldington, chairman of Sun Alliance, the sponsors, had the game been required, by contract, to be played at the Belfry (where the association had moved in April 1977) instead of at the attractive Walton Heath, the sponsor's choice.

There was another significant consequence of Jacobs's resistance to a West Midlands move for the tournament players' division. It paved the way for the subsequent establishment of the tour's headquarters at Wentworth, hard by London, Heathrow, and the Continent – in every way an ideal location.

Events were now moving to a climax. It was the delay in getting any action which was annoying the players. Accordingly, the tournament committee, having discussed the implications with care, wrote on 21 March 1975 to the PGA chairman. Referring to the committee's 'expressed concern and dissatisfaction' at its meeting on the previous day, 'that the decisions taken at the annual general meeting on 28 November 1974 [four months earlier] haven't so far been acted upon', it was 'shocked to learn' that it was now proposed that 'the club side and the tournament side hold meetings independently', the results of which would be put 'to a special meeting of members as per Colin Snape's memorandum of 6 March, written on your behalf . . .'

After listing the points of contention, the committee slipped in a paragraph which would have far-reaching consequences:

> The tournament director-general, on a request from yourself prior to the last annual general meeting, has not communicated with the press since that time on PGA business. However, he and the committee now feel at liberty to represent their views, along with those of the tournament players' section, if and when required.

Douglas Smith did not acknowledge the letter. Six weeks later, however, on 6 May, Smith, together with the PGA captain, Harry Riseborough – who was soon to die prematurely in office – and the chairman of the trades committee, Jack Hargreaves, met three of the signatories of the letter – Coles, Peter Butler and Jacobs – at Finham Park, Coventry. It was the two sides' first discussion of the arrangements for accommodating an autonomous tournament players' division within a reorganized association.

Jacobs and the tournament secretary, Ken Schofield, burning the early morning oil, and aided, as ever, by Marina Bray, the tour's private secretary, had drafted a six-page paper for the meeting, covering all the principal points for discussion. When the time came, they seemed to make headway. Jacobs felt the meeting was amicable and constructive. Apart from minor matters, there appeared to be general agreement.

It was a false dawn. Six weeks later, on 20 June, Douglas Smith handed Butler, Coles and Jacobs a one-page document headed 'Summary of Executive Committee's Proposals on Draft of Tournament Players' Suggestions for New Constitution'. The paper's eleven points appeared to Jacobs and his colleagues to be dictatorially worded and to depart significantly from the earlier agreement that the setting up of an autonomous tournament players' division was desirable. The three felt instinctively that this was another deliberate manoeuvre to postpone the implementation of decisions taken in general meeting.

Jacobs and the tournament committee, of which Neil Coles had become chairman, were now determined to bring the dispute out into the open and force the executive to sit down with them and thrash out a constitution. There was unanimous agreement that a players' meeting should be called at Carnoustie on 8 July 1975, before the Open championship, to decide, by consensus, the route to follow. Subject to the outcome, the director-general was instructed by the committee and its chairman to meet the press and disclose findings and intentions. By its letter of 21 March to the association's chairman, the tournament committee had already reserved the right, if felt necessary, to speak openly to the press.

There was an overwhelming endorsement by the players of the committee's stance. Jacobs, acting on instructions from the committee, then met the press on 11 July. Keith Mackenzie, secretary of the Royal and Ancient Golf Club, the governing body under whose auspices the event was being run, had raised no objection to the conference, provided the news was embargoed until the following Tuesday. He didn't want a row during the championship.

The Carnoustie caper had precisely the effect which the tournament committee wanted. As a result of the subsequent publicity, the executive committee was pressured into agreeing to a meeting with the tournament side. This was scheduled to take place on 12 August at York University, next door to Fulford, where the Benson and Hedges tournament was being played. The executive committee, in agreeing to the meeting, insisted that all the tournament players should be invited to attend. Astonishingly, some of the more gullible members of the executive committee had actually been duped into believing that the players were at odds with the director-general. The requirement, therefore, suited the tournament committee perfectly.

Meanwhile, the executive met in London on 28 July. Douglas Smith was in the chair, twenty-two members were present, and two representatives of Clifford Turner, the association's newly appointed City solicitors, attended to offer advice. Hackles were up. After his Carnoustie performance, Jacobs was the target. The executive's main purpose was to satisfy itself, on advice, that by going to the press and making some pretty defiant statements, the director-general had breached his contract.

On the evidence which the solicitors had before them, the advice was that there had, indeed, been a breach. Accordingly, if the executive wanted to, it could terminate Jacobs's contract.

A prolonged and fairly acerbic discussion followed. The director-general clearly had few friends in the room – Dai Rees, Geoffrey Cotton and maybe one or two others – but certainly no more than a handful. Other 'friends' had turned harshly against him. The majority mood of the meeting could be described in a sentence: 'Get Jacobs – but watch it!'

The executive stopped short of firing him there and then. It would have been criticized sharply had it done so without giving him a hearing. Instead, a decision was deferred until a full meeting of the executive committee was held at York on 12 August, immediately after the discussion with the players.

The Fulford meeting was the showdown, the culmination of two years of conflict, doubt, suspicion and a fair measure of subterfuge. But, then again, it was the beginning of a new order which would take the Professional Golfers' Association into another world.

There was a good turnout. The executive committee was there in strength, supported by a sprinkling of club professionals. The tournament committee, looking steady on parade, was pleased to see a hundred or so tour players gathered in the theatre of the university. Clifford Turner were in attendance to offer counsel. It had the feel of an historic occasion. No minutes were taken, but the director-general had prepared full speaking notes. A dozen or so years later, they make a revealing record.

Jacobs knew he was performing under threat of dismissal, for it was his action at Carnoustie which had done much to provoke this meeting. He had briefed himself fully. Frequently, through the past weeks and months of turmoil, he had not hesitated to pick up the telephone and speak with the faithful David Bolton at Herbert Smith to clear up some point of law. He had seen to it, with Ken Schofield and Marina Gray, that a very full summary, covering all the constitutional points which would arise, had been circulated to the players. They, too, were ready.

When Jacobs got up to speak, he was confident he held an ace in his hand. Having opened disarmingly by saying that he was at some disadvantage in having to make his remarks under threat of dismissal, he then covered the necessary ground. '... I would hope, therefore, gentlemen,' he urged, 'that the proposals for a new PGA constitution can be agreed in principle today.'

He came to his personal situation. 'The minutes of your 28 July executive committee meeting,' he said, 'state clearly that, after this meeting today, the executive will then decide my future with the PGA and that the position of Ken Schofield, the tournament secretary, will also be reviewed ... May I ask you, Mr Chairman, whether it is still the intention to fire me without giving me even an opportunity to address the full executive?'

He left it as a rhetorical question. He then singled out the association's solicitor. Referring to the unanswered letter of 21 March 1975, which the tournament committee chairman had written to the PGA chairman, reserving the right to go to the press if necessary, he played his trump card. 'When you offered the advice that, by my conduct at Carnoustie, I had breached my contract and, therefore, had left myself open to dismissal, had you previously satisfied yourself that the tournament committee's letter had no bearing at all on that advice?'

It was a beautifully faded 4-wood to the stick. Whoever had briefed Clifford Turner had omitted, for reason or reasons unknown, to give them a sight of the unanswered correspondence.

After that, the meeting, which had generated emotion and anger, proved to be something of a walkover for the Jacobs side. Dai Rees had warned the executive on 28 July that notwithstanding what the executive's 'advice' might have been, the players at Fulford would be 100 per cent behind the director-general. He was right. Armed with Jacobs's and Schofield's comprehensive paper, they presented a united front.

Eventually, the constitutional points were hammered out and agreed. What the tournament players wanted, and what they had come to the meeting determined to get, was granted them. The mild communiqué issued to the press afterwards gave no hint of dissension. In jargon befitting a spokesman for the Foreign Office, it had been a 'constructive meeting'; there was a 'useful exchange of views' and 'general accord' had been reached 'on all matters of common concern'. What the press weren't told was that effectively it was game, set and match to the tour.

After a tactful pause, Clifford Turner resigned as the PGA's solicitors.

The outcome of it all was clear cut. The principal decision was that a management committee would be formed to span the abyss. It would be composed of three club professionals on one side and three from the tour on the other. A respected amateur golfer would preside to see fair play and maintain the balance. It was a play-back of Lord Derby's proposal made at Lytham sixteens months earlier – with one variation. Michael Bonallack would become the first occupant of the hot seat. None envied him the task. Leonard Crawley, when he was golf correspondent of the *Daily Telegraph*, was apt to refer to Bonallack, in his playing days, as 'the Duke'. The job that he did for the PGA over the next five years was a ducal performance. It is at least arguable whether anyone else could have done it so well.

On reflection, the question may well be asked: How was John Jacobs able to contain his workload through these protracted upheavals? Not only was his plate apparently full as he wrestled with the director-general's responsibilities, he was also discharging his duties as managing director of an expanding Athlon company and at the same time teaching golf on an increasing scale both in Europe and the United States.

The answer is twofold. First, he had, by now, become adept at the process of delegation. Second, he had an asset without which he certainly could not have coped. He had acquired an unusually able secretary who could also administer. To Marina Bray fell the task not only of looking after the normal secretarial chores but also of maintaining for him an ordered programme. From this she artfully removed those things which, she sensed, he should not be bothered with . . .

And what of the fruits of all this effort?

From the base which John Jacobs created, the PGA European Tour has developed today into a highly successful, £7 million-plus enterprise, with its headquarters housed comfortably beside Wentworth's well-manicured fairways. With Neil Coles in the chair, and administered with unobtrusive efficiency by Jacobs's protégé and nominee, Ken Schofield, the tour walks tall in world golf.

Colin Snape has moved on to other fields after fourteen years as the executive head of the PGA. In his time he refashioned the association from a modest, early twentieth-century entity into a vehicle which now matches the advance of the modern game. He also gave the women's PGA tour a future at a time when it might only have had a past.

For Jacobs there was an unexpected reward. To his 'huge delight' he was made the first honorary life member of the European Tour 'for services as tournament director'. He was later joined by Dai Rees, Bernard Hunt and Peter Butler 'for services to the committee', by five Open Champions, Cotton, Daly, Faulkner, Ballesteros and Lyle, and by the 1985 US master golfer Bernhard Langer – all of whom were chosen 'for playing ability'.

How will history measure Jacobs's contribution to the establishment of the tour which at times brought him and his wife, who fought his corner with him, so much personal hurt and yet, in retrospect, such pride? Mark McCormack, who saw the director-general's work close to in that first extraordinary year in office, may already have got somewhere near the truth.

> '. . . You have to admit that the Jacobs plan worked . . . Almost immediately the mood of golf changed . . . He laid down minima for . . . prize funds. If a sponsor wanted to play his tournament in peak season, he had to pay for the privilege . . . The Continentals were coaxed into line . . . Golf had begun to believe in itself again . . .
>
> 'I, for one, do not doubt that [1972] was a year of high significance. It might be no more than a slight exaggeration to say that these twelve months saw British golf progress by a quarter of a century. And that is quite a trick.'*

*The World of Professional Golf, Mark McCormack's Golf Annual 1973, Collins, London, 1973.

7
Iberian Sunshine

'HE TAUGHT THE PROS TO TEACH'

Gerald Micklem has been one of golf's great activists since his undergraduate days at Oxford in the early 1930s. None has been involved with the game in so many different roles, at so high a level and for so long as he. A private benefactor, whose acts of generosity are cloaked in secrecy, his contribution has spanned half a century and more of the game's history.

At Moor Park in July 1985, during a spectating visit to the Carris Trophy, a 72-hole tournament in which many of the best of Britain's young golfing stock annually take part, I put a question to Micklem: 'You have seen as much golf as anyone during John Jacobs's career. How would you assess the mark he has made upon the game?'

The reply, delivered with a characteristic economy of words, touched the nerve-centre of the matter: 'John taught the pros to teach.'

The point is amply demonstrated by Jacobs's Spanish experience.

In 1969, at the behest of the governing body, Real Federación Española de Golf, Jacobs started his bi-annual teaching visits to Spain: ten days at Puerta de Hierro, in Madrid, followed each time by another ten at El Prat, in Barcelona. The federation's aim at the outset was to find an instructor who would help on three counts: with the country's national amateur teams, ladies and men's, and with the most promising juniors; with the assistant professionals and those in the caddie ranks who would soon join them; and with the established professionals whose teaching methods in those early days were, to put no finer point on it, 'individual'.

There were successful Spanish players – Ramón Sota, Severiano

Ballesteros's uncle; the two brothers, Angel and Sebastián Miguel; and others – but the standard of teaching was poor. There was no uniformity of approach. The Spaniards have a phrase for it: *cada maestrillo con su librillo* – every teacher by his book.

J. M. S. de Vicuña, a top executive of the Coca Cola company in Madrid, and the holder of a succession of offices in the federation, including that of president for seven years, has his own incisive views on the British instructor's influence on the Spanish game. As the president-elect of the European Golf Association and a vice-president of the PGA European Tour, de Vicuña can judge the contribution in its European, as well as its national, context.

It is no coincidence, as de Vicuña recognizes, that, during the eighteen years of Jacobs's uninterrupted association with Spanish golf, the country has climbed steadily to the summit. What factor led to his original appointment?

The Spanish authorities were not unaware of the results which Jacobs had been obtaining in Italy. There, for eleven years, from 1958 to 1969, he had provided promising young Italians, and the national teams with precisely the service which their counterparts in Spain now needed. His annual, month-long visit to Olgiata, in Rome, had brought recorded benefits and an awakening of Latin talent.

It was a package which, following some earlier sessions at Sandown Park, he was also to offer the Swedes over a four-year stretch from 1974 to 1978, at a critical period in the expansion of the game in their country. He taught, on his annual visits to Malmo and other Swedish centres, the ladies' and the men's national teams, and the juniors. Just as he was doing in Spain, he gave many of the country's professionals who attended his classes in successive years an extensive insight into the advanced teaching art. Jacobs's achievement is now finding its expression in the flow of well-taught Swedish players presently making their marks upon the British and European scene.

But the work which Jacobs was doing elsewhere in Europe wasn't the only pointer the Spaniards had picked up. As de Vicuña comments: 'The real driving force behind John's choice, and the person who helped to convince us in the federation of the contribution he could make to Spanish golf, was Emma de Garcia-Ogara. She later helped to organize and co-ordinate John's visits year after year, even acting, from time to time, as interpreter.'

Emma de Garcia-Ogara, herself a championship and tournament winner, had already experienced Jacobs's teaching. Her position in the Spanish establishment was not dissimilar to that of Lally de Saint

136

Sauveur (formerly Lally Vagliano, then Vicomtesse de Saint Sauveur and now Mme Patrick Segard) in the French hierarchy. Each knew the game and the form with Jacobs; and each employed that knowledge for the betterment of their respective national and European interests.

In the end, it was the brand image of the British product which ensured his selection. 'We picked John,' says de Vicuña, 'because of his known reputation as the pros' pro. But there were other attributes which worked for him – his warm character and sense of humour, his feel for the best way of dealing with people. He seems to understand the ego of golfers . . . how to tell a proud player that his method needs correction without wounding his vanity – a tricky business. In a game which is surrounded with mystique and confusion, John has such a straightforward approach.'

Jacobs scored, in this situation, with his memory for people and pupils. Seeing new faces – and swings – all the time could have led to a 'blanket' attitude. The point struck de Vicuña:

'We were amazed how he could remember individual actions and traits in a person's swing from one year to the next. If the player couldn't recall precisely what he had been told a year before, John would remind him and the reason for it. His photographic memory impressed our people greatly. It gave his teaching a personal touch.

'But I have always thought that one of John's strongest virtues as a teacher is his patience. He never seems to grow impatient with a pupil. He makes him or her feel comfortable and at ease. On the other hand, the moment he senses that someone doesn't want to listen or isn't receptive to his thoughts, diagnosis and advice, he makes it absolutely clear that he isn't prepared to waste his time. He is very direct.'

The former federation president tells a story about the American Fred Corcoran, a predecessor of Deane Beman as the director – commissioner is the preferred word – of the US tour, and the one-time manager of Sam Snead, Cary Middlecoff, Tony Lema and other immortals. Concoran had an appointment to see his friend Emma de Garcia-Ogara in Madrid on his way to visit Neuva Andalucia, in Marbella, to decide whether it would make a suitable venue for the World (then the Canada) Cup:

'When Corcoran found that Emma couldn't see him till 2.30 in the afternoon, as she was acting as interpreter for John Jacobs at one of his sessions at Puerta de Hierro, he asked if he might go along and sit in on the clinic. He spent the morning watching and listening to Jacobs, absorbed in it all. After it, he made a comment. "You know," he said, "there are only two people I like to watch teaching golf – John Jacobs and Sam Snead.''*

De Vicuña identifies another of Jacobs's characteristics: 'I am struck by the personal interest John takes in his pupils, running on from year to year. I know he had been very much impressed with the fifteen-year-old Mari-Carmen Navarro,** believing her to have a perfect golf swing and an exceptionally mature approach for one so young.'

When Jacobs began teaching in Spain eighteen years ago, his doctrine was not, at first, accepted without question. His subsequent experience in the United States, as we shall see, was much the same. As one of the chief protagonists of his selection, di Vicuña remembers the original reaction:

'John's influence, teaching methods and philosophy (he encourages people to *think* their way round a golf course; he calls their brain their "fifth wood") have now become deeply ingrained in Spanish golf. They are widely accepted by amateurs and professionals. The continuity with our players over so long a period, and his success with them, has obviously helped bring this about. But, to be very frank, his ideas were looked upon with a great deal of scepticism to begin with. He had to face quite a challenge from the professionals. It was a negative attitude, but it was there and there was no doubt about it; it naturally rubbed off on the amateurs.'

By his own admission, Jacobs was undeniably fortunate in having three of four highly regarded Spanish professionals who believed utterly in him and accepted his dictum once it had been explained.

Ramón Sota, the aforementioned uncle of Severiano Ballesteros,'† Manuel Piñero, José-Maria Cañizares and others among the playing alumni were always ready, at one time or another to be 'taught' in front of a class of aspiring assistants and young caddies, watched by a number of Spain's recognized professionals. Jesús Arruti, mentor of José-Maria Olazábal, another of the country's arresting prospects – of whom Jacobs said when he saw him as a teenage amateur at his sessions: 'There's a winner for you. That boy will win' – is another

*The thinking of the two on the fundamentals of the swing is substantially similar.

**The daughter of Juan Navarro, the professional at El Saler, in Valencia, himself an able teacher and regular attender of Jacobs's sessions at Puerta de Hierro, where he was once the assistant, Mari-Carmen Navarro is one of Europe's best hopes. At thirteen, she was a scratch player. When Jacobs first saw her at twelve, he was surprised: 'Her action was a model. There was nothing to tell her except to go on with what she was doing.'

†Ballesteros was twelve years old when Jacobs first began teaching in Spain and Uncle Ramón was a proven international player.

who was prepared to give a similar lead.

De Vicuña picks out Ramón Sota for special mention. Although he was then nearing the end of a distinguished playing career, he was still the country's number one player, and admired for it; de Vicuña comments:

'It surprised some of the younger professionals that someone of the calibre of achievement of Ramón should be seeking John's advice. Fancy, they thought, a man of his skill being ready to contemplate changes at such a late stage.

'Seve's uncle responded to this attitude by saying that he could only feel sorry for a professional who, never having achieved much on the circuit, was too proud to listen to Jacobs and take his advice. There's no doubt that Sota's example at that time did much to break the ice. He set a positive precedent for the other players to follow.'

Among Spain's ablest teachers Jesús Arruti was the one who was ready to accept the Jacobs doctrine when he had heard it explained, and had had the chance to think about it. According to de Vicuña:

'After Arruti had been won over, he was heard to admit with a chuckle: "Now I'll have to go back to San Sebastian and try to brainwash my pupils. Somehow I'll have to get them to forget the things I have always told them."

'The conversion certainly paid off for him, for he has gathered at his club an outstanding group of promising young players, among them José-Maria Olazábal, now a rising professional, but, in his amateur days, the winner of the British Boys' Championship, the British Youths and the British Amateur before finishing leading amateur in the 1985 Open at Sandwich.'

In speaking about his Spanish connection, Jacobs will never depart from his long-held practice of refusing to claim credit for this or that pupil's or player's rise to fame and fortune. It is convenient, therefore, to have a well-informed third party such as Johnny de Vicuña to fill in the Iberian background.

The British instructor won't thank him for it, but de Vicuña paints an interesting picture of the first time Jacobs saw Severiano Ballesteros as a teenager: 'He recognized at once the outstanding possibilities of this exceptional player . . . He saw he had all the potential to become a world champion . . . He commented upon Seve's quite upright swing and said at the time that this could, sooner or later, lead him into back trouble. This it eventually did and now Seve turns rather flatter than was his earlier custom.'

In the spring of 1979, the year of his Open win at Lytham,

Ballesteros was at Wentworth for an early-season tournament. He saw Jacobs there. 'Please,' he said, 'would you have a look at me? I slice everything.' 'My word,' replied that year's Ryder Cup captain, 'what an honour. Yes, of course, I will,' and the two set off to find a quiet spot. Jacobs remembers what he saw: 'Seve had the clubface ever so strong at the address. He was closing it going back – curling it under – and then opening it through the ball, which was producing the slice. He was rocking rather than turning and that, incidentally, wasn't doing his back any good.'

Shades of the 1976 Open at Birkdale – when, as a wonderfully compelling nineteen-year-old, Ballesteros finished second (tied with Nicklaus) to Miller with a brand of golf which had the Lancastrian masses chasing about the sandhills – still lingered . . . Somewhat wayward hitting, astonishing recoveries, sensitive pitching and a God-given putting touch.

At Birkdale, his swing had been in Jacobs's words, 'underneath, leaving the clubface open coming into the ball and then snapping it shut at impact . . . That's all right if the timing is right but, if it's not, the ball can go either way – sliced to the right if the face is left open, or hooked to the left if it is shut too quickly.'

Three years later, at Wentworth, the correction was as simple as the diagnosis: 'All Seve needed to do was to weaken the clubface a little at the address,* clear the right side to let his arms swing a little more inside and up in the backswing, and then let it go from there, turning through the ball in the downswing – clearing through the ball – to bring the clubface square at impact. In other words, he needed to make his action less *underneath* and his swing less of a *straight line*. Because we stand to the side of the ball and not over the top of it, the swing has to be from *inside-to-straight-through-to-inside again*. We can't swing successfully up and down a straight line.'

For two or three years afterwards, whenever he had to wait on a tee, Ballesteros would often be seen to be swinging the club back and forth at hip level – like a baseball striker on the plate: 'This was to get his back turning as opposed to rocking or tilting . . . A really super player, Seve has lifted British and European golf up by the boot-straps to altogether new levels . . . He has set new targets for our guys to shoot

---

*i.e., 'laid off' slightly as opposed to 'hooded'. Jacobs stresses the difference in angle between the top and bottom of the blade of an iron club. Follow the 'laid off' top line of the club and it encourages a marginally inside takeaway. 'Hood it' and it has the reverse effect.

at, lifted their sights and given them a belief in themselves, and the confidence to win. That's the measure of Seve's contribution to our game.'

Severiano Ballesteros is not alone in his family in his relentless search for excellence. Two of his brothers, Baldomero and Vicente ('like Seve, very strong characters – they wouldn't accept anything I said unless they saw it proved'), were frequent observers at Jacobs's earlier Spanish sessions: 'Also searching for knowledge, they came to listen, watch and make their own assessments.'

Micklem is entitled to his nod . . .

STARRED FIRSTS

The management at John Jacobs's Practical Golf Schools in the United States (see Chapter 10) calls them, somewhat perfunctorily, 'returnees'. These are the customers who, having tasted the treatment at a school one year, come back again for more the next. And the next. Great store is laid by them, for they are the people who spread the word. In this business, nothing promotes fresh custom more certainly than the verbal endorsement of the satisfied client.

Jacobs's Spanish classes have also brought their share of 'returnees' – Marta Figueras-Dotti, for example. She upset the form book – and a few of the paid sisterhood – by winning the 1982 Ladies' British Open Championship at Birkdale, as an amateur. Thereafter, having turned professional, she quickly cut out a niche for herself as a regular competitor on the demanding US women's PGA tour.

For Marta Dotti, daughter of the current president of the Spanish Golf Federation, the climb began in Madrid in the mid-1970s, when, as a young teenager, she first attended the professor's bi-annual classes at Puerta de Hierro. A decade or so later, in the autumn of 1985, she called in for a freshener when Jacobs was in Barcelona, teaching at El Prat. A few minutes was all she could be spared. Another six months on, when Jacobs was presiding at a Practical Golf School clinic at the Mountain Shadows Resort in Scottsdale, Arizona, she telephoned to say she would like to stop off on her way through to the next tournament in Palm Springs. 'Just a quick look' was all that she was after.

Jacobs looks back on Marta Dotti's advance:

'When I first saw Marta as a young girl, she left, to be honest, no special picture in my mind simply because she had been so well taught.* Her action was sound and solid. As with Mari-Carmen Navarro afterwards, there was really little to say except to go on with what was already there.

'I do remember her father asking me whether I thought it would help her to go to an American university. I said yes, it must do. Playing college golf, as they do there, seven days a week and competing every weekend could only do her game good, with such a fine method. She benefited from her time in the States and, when she turned professional, after Birkdale, she was not only a superbly orthodox player but also very experienced.

'When next I saw Marta in Barcelona in the autumn of 1985, she had had two or three years on the US circuit. Playing week after week, grinding it out under those pressures, she had developed much more of a straight-line swing than she had had before. Some "rock and block" had crept into her body action. This was in contrast with her earlier, flatter shoulder turn, her beautiful arm action which got the club *up* so well, laying it on the target at the top, and her inside-to-straight-through-to-inside swing line.

'All she needed was a bit of help in getting back to her old planes again. Hitting balls off a slope, practising with the ball above the level of her feet – such a good exercise for this kind of problem – assisted her. It got her back to a better plane again.'

In March 1986, six months and a number of US tournaments later, the professor found a not unexpected development:

'Marta had certainly got her shoulders turning on a much better plane, but now her arms and shoulders were locked together on the same plane. People often think (and sometimes even the good players fall into the trap) the shoulders and the arms should be married together in the same plane in the backswing. But this isn't so. If the arms are to position the club correctly at the top of the backswing, and then move freely in the through-swing, they must swing *up* as the body turns around.

'In no time, she was back again to her customary two-plane action, with the arms going up in the backswing and the right shoulder turning out of the way. She quickly began to play well again and score well. Her experience – the experience of a fine, orthodox player – has been repeated so often on the tour. Competing constantly under pressure can affect the swing in different ways.'

*Marta Figueras-Dotti had been taught by José Gallardo at Puerta de Hierro. Gallardo had earlier 'worked with' Jacobs both in England in the late 1960s and then afterwards in Spain.

Among Jacobs's male 'returnees' was Manuel Piñero. Twice a member of his country's four victorious World Cup teams* – once in 1976 with Severiano Ballesteros, and again in 1982 with José-Maria Canizares, when he was also the low, individual medalist – Piñero is a paragon of Spanish professional golf.

There are few in Spain these days prepared to back with their own cash the provision of public golfing facilities denied to those less fortunate than themselves. Piñero is among the few. He has said to the Spanish sports minister that, if the government or the local authority will provide the land, he will fund the rest – but to no avail. Now that the flow of boy caddies into the game is fast diminishing in Spain, due to the country's changing economic circumstances, he believes, with Severiano Ballesteros, that other playing opportunities must be made available for young enthusiasts who want to pursue the game but have nowhere to go.

Piñero uses the analogy of lawn tennis to make his point: 'The ball boys on the courts of Madrid and Barcelona in the 1950s became some of our fine players in the 1960s. It was their chance to advance and earn a good living. Now, the same type of boy from the poor family isn't there any more and what has this meant? We do not have the same high standard of tennis players. It is bad.'

The boy from Pueblo de la Calzada had himself just emerged from the caddie ranks to make the game his profession when, in 1969, he first stepped forward at one of John Jacobs's initial teach-ins in Madrid. He was seventeen, slight and spare of stature, but hard, acute and bright. The moment made a deep impression on him. Skilful with his feet, he had already been offered professional forms in the Spanish football league. With the glitter of Real Madrid in its great days, and the magic of Garrincha, di Stefano, Puskas and the rest still there, it was all a wise parent could do to stop his ambitious son from deserting fairway for stadium.

Born left-handed, Piñero's left was his strong hand. He wrote with it until, aged eight, he was made to change at school. Sometimes, even now, he follows nature's bent. His left eye is his master eye and he shoots driven partridges to a low handicap off his left shoulder. He plays tennis and throws a ball with his left. In his younger days, he could control a football with his right foot, but he took penalties and

*Spain's four wins in eight starts between 1976 and 1984 outstripped every other country during that period, including the USA. To these victories must be added Spain's triumph in the World Amateur Women's Team Championship in Venezuela in 1986.

free kicks with his left. When he put two hands on the grip of a golf club, his right went naturally into place below the left.

In all this, Piñero is the antithesis of Bob Charles, New Zealand winner of the British Open, who has played golf better left-handed than anyone else before or since. Charles is basically right-handed. His right hand, right foot and right eye are all dominant. At tennis, billiards, shooting, throwing and bowling a cricket ball and kicking a football, the right is always in play. But hand him a cricket bat or a golf club and the left hand will automatically stretch down below the right on the handle or grip. In truth, there has hardly ever been a really good left-handed golfer who hasn't been built that way. Mostly, they have been predominantly right-handed people.

So, when Piñero began hitting balls for Jacobs in front of forty or fifty of the country's professionals, who were there to learn from watching the Englishman teach, he had an unusual degree of ambidexterity. The memory of that first lesson is etched deep upon his mind:

> John stressed the importance of the position of the ball at the address and how this could affect the line of the swing. It is one of the fundamentals of his teaching. He said to me: 'You've got the ball too far forward and your shoulders are too open – too much across the line. This is affecting the line of your swing. You're coming inside and then over the top and hitting across the ball from the outside. That's giving you those sliced shots and loss of distance.'
>
> His correction was for me to bring the ball back, square the shoulders, turn in the backswing and swing the arms down on the inside. He told me this, and that I must watch my rhythm. When I started playing at eleven, I was not a strong boy. But I wanted to hit the ball as far as a strong boy so I tried to hit it hard and as fast. That gave me my quick swing.

There was a twinkle in those lively Spanish eyes: 'In fact, I tell you: sometimes I used to take a run at the ball to try to keep up with the strong boys . . . But I didn't tell John it was distance I wanted. He found it for me.'

Piñero practised throughout the rest of that first day: 'Maybe it was three hours, perhaps more. I could practise and practise, hitting balls all day long.'

He joined the class again the next day. He wasn't nervous any more about stepping out in front of his 'colleagues'. He felt, and knew, he was hitting the ball so much better – and longer: 'I've never forgotten what John said. He said, through the translator, because I couldn't understand English like I can now, "Tell this young man that, from now on for the rest of his career, I want ten per cent of everything he earns." It was wonderful for me. It's eighteen years since he said it. I've always remembered. It set me going.'

Jacobs gives his own view of that first session:

'I wouldn't say Manuel began with a lot of natural talent. He had a naturally good short game, yes, but in those early days he was the greatest in-and-over-the-top-200 yards-slicer you ever saw. With the ball miles too far forward and shoulders open, he took it back inside and then over the top to hit those short, powerless slices. He had a real figure-of-eight swing and was a terrible short slicer . . . But what a trier he was!

'All we had to do was to put him inside at the address . . . Ball further back, then turn him flat and get him to hit it early enough from the top – get him to swing it down early enough with his arms to hit it far enough. If he didn't hit it well enough, he wasn't going to be able to hit it far enough, that was the point. We had to get him to draw the ball to get the length he needed.'

That first contact in 1969 at Puerta de Hierro was the start of a long-term association, probably as beneficial for the one as it was for the other. Two episodes in their relationship are particularly illuminating.

Three or four years after that first encounter, Jacobs was at Wentworth doing the ITV commentary of a tournament which was to start the following day. As he walked down the steps of the commentary box at the back of the eighteenth green, Manuel Piñero was waiting for him at the bottom. 'Please,' he said, 'could you have a look at me on the practice ground?'

It was a repeat of the earlier session at Puerta: 'Manuel was moving the ball to the right, ill-spared length was being lost . . . He had become quite a short slicer again . . . We just had to put him inside . . . get him to turn rather flatter . . . and then to hit it early enough from the top to hit it far enough . . . As the flight of the ball improved and he hit it a better shape again, so his rhythm came back . . .'

In the autumn of 1984 Jacobs was back again teaching on his pitch in Madrid. Piñero was there: 'I wanted to see John; my golf was bad.' But, more than that, the Spaniard was anxious to give a lead to his professional compatriots:

'You don't have to be afraid, I told them, admitting you need help. Some people are – how do you say? – hesitant about being seen to be receiving instruction. They think some will say, "What, a top player taking a lesson, there must be something wrong." They feel it creates a stigma. I take quite the opposite view. These jealousies [he pronounced it, perhaps significantly, 'hellosies'] are stupid. I have no time for them.

'With John, most of that has been overcome, for he has had a great influence on Spanish teaching and now, in our national school, there are two excellent coaches, Carlos Celles, the president of our PGA, and Jesús Arruti, who believe in John's simple and natural understanding of the game and who have both worked with him. His message is being carried on . . .'

From Jacobs's standpoint, it was an exceptional advantage for the professionals attending the session to see a player of Piñero's record and status being prepared to stand out in front of the class and be 'taught':

'Manuel must have been out there for a good hour and a half while we worked together. The great thing was that the professionals could see why, after a long spell of very good golf, he had just gone through a disappointing time. It was so simple to show them what had happened in the face of all the pressures and why he was slicing the ball and losing length. It was equally easy, with a player like Manuel, to let them see the correction which was needed, and its effect . . . Ball and shoulder position to put him inside again . . . a rather flatter turn . . . and an early enough hit. The rhythm took care of itself.

'Manuel knew quite well the value of that "lesson" to the other professionals just as Ramón [Sota] did years before and, likewise, as José-Maria [Canizares] has also done. One's so fortunate having guys like that around. They're a joy to work with.'

It was also, no doubt, salutary that the professionals at that session should be able to follow Piñero's subsequent results: first or second in the next four tournaments he played in; seventh in the money list the following season, with £71,115 earned from twenty tournaments at an average of 70.93 strokes a round; and, perhaps best of all, four points out of a maximum five contributed to Europe's winning total in the Ryder Cup match against the United States at the Belfry.

It may just be apposite to recall in this context that, collectively, of Europe's fifteen points scored in the 1985 match, seven were down to Spain.

What are the views of the Spanish professionals whom Jacobs, over these past eighteen years, has taught to teach? Juan Mellado, one of their number, and now a highly successful teacher of the game, is well equipped to answer.

Mellado is the club professional at La Manga Club, a 1,100-acre leisure and real-estate development on the Costa Calida, in the southeast of Spain. Severiano Ballesteros represents it on the tour, while his brother Manuel fills the slot of golf director. The three of them make a formidable team.

With its two fine US-designed golf courses (and a third coming up), La Manga is the winter headquarters of the PGA European Tour. Set beside a wild and rugged stretch of Mediterranean coastline, where the winds shift about as unpredictably and as frequently as they do at St Andrews, it is an agreeable and testing place to play golf. As a resort development, it matches its counterparts in the United States.*

It could be argued that Juan Mellado would not have landed the La Manga job had he not graduated earlier with a 'starred first' from the Jacobs teaching academy. He was eighteen, and already a professional at El Candado, in Malaga, when, in 1972, he first took his place in one of Jacobs's sessions in Madrid. It was quite an introduction for a perceptive and impressionable young man:

'John was teaching Ramón Sota from the Pedreña club in Santander, in front of all the other pros. I've never forgotten it. I could see at once that here was someone who taught in a simple, uncomplicated and interesting way. He worked with a few fundamentals. He seemed so positive and confident in what he was saying. It was his authority which seemed to stand out.

'I noticed particularly that when Ramón Sota had finished and it was the turn of others, his approach to each person was different. There was nothing – how do you say it? – of the rubber stamp about his teaching. He told us he taught people, not a method. Much more interesting, he said, to teach people than a method. Specially with the senoritas . . .'

Juan Mellado broadened his golfing education by spending six months in Britain in 1976 and another six in California three years later. Nowadays, he possesses an encyclopedic memory for golfing detail. Ask him who won the US Open in '39, the British in '48 or the Spanish in '63, and he'll give you chapter, page and paragraph. He is the *Golfer's Handbook*, the *Guinness Book of Records* and *Mastermind* all rolled into one. As an attender for four years – 1972,

*One of Spains' latest American-style resort developments with which Jacobs has recently become associated is Golf del Sur at San Miguel de Abona in the south of the island of Tenerife, less than 200 miles from the north-west coast of Africa. Five-and-a-half hours' flying time from the US and four-and-a-half from the UK, it is tailor-made as a Practical Golf Schools location.

'73, '74 and '78 – at Jacobs's sessions at Puerto de Hierro, he can rattle off the names of all the Spanish professionals whom the mentor 'saw'; he also knows the names of those of their successful pupils to whom the message has been passed on.

For example: 'John saw Jesús Arruti first in 1969 and every year afterwards for so many years ... Carlos Celles, thirteen times a contestant in the British Open, was "seen" by John first in England and then for sixteen or seventeen years after in Spain ... The same with José Gallardo ... Salvador Balbuena, a beautiful player, he "saw" first in Madrid in 1969, when he changed his very strong, four-knuckle grip – Balbueno's death in Lyons on 9 May 1979, was a big loss for Spanish golf; José Rivero was "seen" first in . . .' The catalogue is endless, the impression left upon this receptive mind indelible.'

Mellado acknowledges his debt to Jacobs:

> I always knew and felt I could play golf well, but after taking part in John's sessions I just knew that teaching would always be – how do you say? – my strength. I just base my teaching on what I learned from him. Whenever he comes to La Manga – perhaps with the French, German or Walker Cup teams – I still go and watch him. He's so easy to follow, so positive . . . And look at the results.

With the aid of the Spanish Golf Federation, John Jacobs has turned his sessions in the Iberian sunshine into a form of workers' co-operative. All contribute to the end product. The young assistants and the caddie boys are taught in the morning, giving the professionals the chance to witness the teacher's art; both score.

In the afternoon, it is the turn of the amateurs in the ladies' and men's national teams – and the promising juniors – to be advised. The professionals stay on to watch. Many of them have pupils in this assembly of amateur talent. They thus witness, at first hand the professor's advice.

'The beauty of this,' says Jacobs, 'is that we are all working together to the same end. The professionals can see what I am saying to the amateurs for a couple of weeks in the year. They then carry on the work for the next fifty. This way, everyone benefits and there is continuity all the year round. Continuity is so important.'

The Spanish adventure has been particularly rewarding for Jacobs as he feels that he has now built up a special relationship with both the amateur and professional teams in Spain. When he goes there to teach he senses at once that he is working among friends. He identifies another particularly satisfying feature.

'The standard of instruction in Spain today is as high as it is anywhere, and probably higher. The game there is taught generally so well. If you take, say, one hundred Spanish professionals, thirty of them will teach it very well, another forty will teach it quite well and the other thirty won't do any harm. Percentage-wise, I doubt whether you could say that of any other country in the world.

'Compare it with America. Out of, perhaps, five thousand guys teaching the game there today, maybe one thousand will teach it well – the other four thousand not so well . . .'

8

Design For Pleasure

At the beginning of May 1985, John Jacobs was asked by the Royal and Ancient to address an international golf conference at St Andrews on the place of the golf centre in the modern game. The club had invited to this three-day convention representatives of all the principal golfing nations of the world. They came to the game's celebrated headquarters from Europe and Scandinavia, from the United States and Canada, from Argentina, the African continent, the Middle and Far East, from Australia and New Zealand and from the United Kingdom and Ireland. In golfing terms, rarely had there been assembled a broader international gathering.

Jacobs spoke for thirty minutes, setting his contribution in the context of the present-day game and its needs. He had worked for two days on his paper, writing the text out in longhand before having it typed – always his practice on such a 'set-piece' occasion. He stuck pretty closely to the script, varying it here and there to develop an argument or suit the mood. He had taken great trouble not only in deference to the assembly but also because he knew there would never be a more propitious moment to argue, with his own first-hand experience and authority, the case for a medium in which he utterly believes. Well though he knew his subject, it wasn't an easy ride. His problem was to speak with enthusiasm and conviction without, at the same time, giving the impresssion that he was plugging his own commerical interests. He was concerned to get the balance right.

His preamble struck an unexpected note. First, he referred to the game's young: '. . . I was fortunate, like many of you here today, in

150

being introduced to the game as a child, and although there have been changes for the better – and one applauds particularly the efforts of the Golf Foundation – it is true that the majority of young people everywhere still have little chance to play.'

He then took his distinguished audience along what, to some, may have seemed a reactionary path:

'I believe that golf, as we know it, does have its drawbacks: the cost to the individual, the amount of land it requires and the time it takes to play 18 holes – a far cry, indeed, from the two and a quarter hours I allowed for a round as a boy at Lindrick. I often played three rounds in a day. However, I only carried eight clubs in a light bag. How I wish eight clubs was the stipulated number today! Golf would, I am sure, be an even better game. Moreover, it would be less expensive, and, in terms of time, might once again be fitted into the normal pattern of breakfast, lunch and tea, with two rounds a day becoming much more usual.'

Jacobs then went to the kernel of his case. In a few characteristically short, direct and simple sentences he developed his golf-centre concept:

'It has arisen because of the need for low-cost golf for the masses, which cannot be supplied by the conventional golf course alone. Exactly as it sounds, [the centre] is a place where virtually all golfing needs can be catered for, from those of the novice right up to the international player's. It embraces everything, including a floodlit, covered driving range with as many as thirty-six separate bays, with outside playing positions; pitch-and-put and medium-length par 3 9- or 18-hole courses; and a conventional golf course, also of 9 or 18 holes.

'The variety of golf on offer, and the amenities which support it, are attractive to all types of player and, most important, they give the developer or operator a number of selling outlets and consequently a strong cashflow and the opportunity to meet financial targets . . .

'A golf centre can be tailored to suit individual circumstances. It can be adjusted to cater for local needs, available land and finance. A driving range and 9-hole par 3 . . . with functional, pavilion-type building, with bar and buffet, golf shop and changing facilities . . . can fit quite nicely into thirty acres and, according to its location and standard of mangement, be a viable proposition. On the other hand, a full-size, comprehensive centre can amount to anything from one hundred and forty acres upwards . . . Thus, not only can the centre offer flexibility for the golfer, it also provides it for the investor and

151

developer . . .'

After going through the detail of the design and build-up of a typical centre, Jacobs took as an example of a large-scale and successful enterprise the Hoebridge golf centre, near Woking, in Surrey, fifteen miles or so to the south-west of London airport. His company, John Jacobs Golf Consultants Ltd, had been responsible for the golf content of this 'latest development in the private sector'. Opened in 1982, it had, he said, been 'very extensively used' since the day operations began.

'The land . . . and capital was provided by Burhill Estates, backed by the Guinness Trust . . . I believe this centre to be, at this moment, the most comprehensive of its kind in Europe and probably the world. It has an 18-hole course measuring 6600 yards with a par of 72, an 18-hole par 3 course of some 3000 yards, extensive floodlit driving range, clubhouse and associated facilities, and was constructed for a figure in the region of £700,000 at 1980 values. Of that total, some £300,000 was attributable to the golfing amenities as opposed to the building and services.'

Stressing how the golf centre had been shown, in practice, to have a special application for the public sector and those local authorities which were concerned to offer, in the official jargon, 'suitable golfing provision for the community', Jacobs described his involvement with the local councils at Northampton and Stevenage in developing what subsequent results have confirmed to be eminently successful enterprises. He then listed, 'in order of priority', the benefits golf centres confer upon user and operator whether they be in the private or the public domain.

1. Properly sited, with capital costs kept to a minimum, and well managed, they are financially viable.
2. They [can] use a relatively small amount of land and can be designed to suit individual circumstances.
3. A much higher throughput of participants can be absorbed than [with] the conventional golf course.
4. Equipment can be hired and the customer only pays for the particular facility he or she uses. It is possible, therefore, to 'try out golf' before becoming committed to considerable expense.
5. The floodlit, covered driving range makes practice possible all the year round for players in all categories. The beginner does not suffer the awful embarrassment of standing on the first tee without any idea of what to do, while players of international standard can

work on their games ... when days are short and weather is inclement ... They are ideal places for giving and receiving instruction.

It is no coincidence that John Jacobs's rise as a world teacher has coincided, over the past quarter of a century, with the emergence of his golf-centre developments. Group and team instruction, clinics, golf schools and company days out are a natural corollary of these establishments. And no one has developed the art of group instruction to such a degree than the original architect of the golf-centre concept. He has turned his schools, clinics and company days into pure theatre spiced with humour and anecdotes.

Ted Ostermann, supporter of the Anglo-German cause, publisher in Hamburg of *Golf* magazine and a European golfing promoter, can speak at first-hand about the popularity of the British professor's instruction. In the five-year period up to 1985, Ostermann ran twenty-five golf schools with Jacobs, in Germany and in Spain. Every one of the thirty available places in each school was taken up by customers from Germany and other continental countries, Scandinavia, the UK and USA.

'I never had occasion with John to engage in international advertising compaigns to publicize these schools. After the first three, it was the word-of-mouth publicity which brought the custom. Frankly, the speed and spread of the personal recommendations made elaborate advertising unnecessary.

'This came about not only from the logic, simplicity and patience of this teaching but from his personality and his ability to handle customers and humour them. It was the attraction of his sense of humour and his ability to understand a pupil's mind – and *feel* it – which so much counted. We found that customers soon felt at ease with him and identified themselves with him. They felt he was working with them and not talking at them.

'We found, too, in these schools that his ability to handle people and communicate with them was more important to our customers than if he had been teaching some publicized system or method – which, of course, he doesn't do.'

Jacobs's group teaching has now become a well-rehearsed process. But that hasn't prevented him from preserving its freshness. The repartee, the asides and the noises off are too spontaneously original to give an impression of being contrived. It is all designed purposely to put people at their ease and have fun; in truth, he enjoys the fun himself:

'Now I don't want any of you to worry. When each one of you comes out in front here to hit your shots, we may well all have some fun together. But I promise you, you will never, never find me trying to put you down. I've missed them too often myself. So don't hold back . . .'

The banter bubbles on for a couple of hours:

'Now here's an American cocktail.' (Pause) 'A high ball.' Then it's a low one: 'This is what I personally practise a lot. I don't know about you, but whenever I play the wind always seems to be against.'

After some personal reminiscence, Jacobs looks quizzically at the group gathered around: 'Who's going to risk it now? I promise, it's quite harmless.'

Then levity is put aside. Plain-spoken, serious instruction ensues. A habitual over-swinger has produced a couple of weak, fairly ineffectual shots. There is no penetration. The diagnosis, explanation and correction follow: 'Now, sir, I want you to do me a short backswing, a tiny backswing, then turn through the ball. Exaggerate it. A short backswing and [the emphases is deliberate] turn through the-ball.'

Half a dozen shots are sufficient to instil fresh hope in the patient's mind. A chasing thought wraps it up: 'Work on that and, I promise you, you must improve your game. But remember this. For you, golf is the business of hitting the ball to the target, not hitting the clubhead to the ball. It's ball to target, not swing to ball . . . I'm sure you believe there's life after death . . .'

To the student who has difficulty in 'turning through the ball' or 'clearing the left side as you go through' Jacobs offers a useful *aide memoire*. 'Now, with this one, I want you to hit left – hit this ball left of the target – hit it at the left-hand side of the fairway – a Yorkshireman's left.' (Pause) 'I'll take the blame.'

As the pupil walks away from the practice tee, a supplementary thought follows him: 'You never want to play this game independently of the right side of the body. So just remember, to clear that left side, to turn through the ball, just think about hitting the ball left, hitting it left of the target.'

The instruction is repeated slowly for clarity. Maltby Grammar School, and the lessons which had to be explained by the teacher a second (or even a third) time, are vividly remembered. Not for Jacobs's pupils the need to come back after the class for another run-through.

A story about one of golf's greats is told to illustrate a point. The case of Hale Irwin, twice US Open champion, with an action to match, is cited to help a student who suffers from too much body action and too little use of hands and arms ... with all the resultant loss of accuracy and distance which it brings:

'In the golf swing, hands and arms are for clubhead speed, and clubhead speed means distance. Where we do our golf schools in America – in Phoenix, Arizona – my boys said to me when I got there a couple of years ago: "You've just missed Hale Irwin. He's been here for a week." "What a pity," I said, "he's such a nice guy."

'Then they told me that Hale had been there, hitting balls for six hours every day for a week, and they hadn't seen him hit one other than with his feet together – touching.

'So those of you who have a tendency to use too much body action just think of Hale Irwin and give yourselves a narrow base. Every time you go out and hit balls, practise hitting them with your feet together – right together.'

A little colour is thrown in for good measure: 'You'll all remember the late and much lamented Sir Douglas Bader. I recall Sir Douglas standing there at Sandown one day on his two artificial legs, hitting balls. He couldn't make much use of his legs, so we just had to get him to point the shaft of the club at the target at the top of his swing – lay the club on the target at the top. All he had to do from there was to give the ball an almighty clip with the clubhead ... Despite his tin legs, Sir Douglas played to a four handicap in his best years.'

Jacobs rounds off a demonstration by letting the group into 'one of my secrets'. The ruse can't fail to score. He had been helping an inveterate late hitter of the ball. The fellow left the clubhead so far behind in the hitting area that the clubface was always open. All he could do was to 'squirt' one ball after another to the right.

After getting him to hit early 'by using the clubhead to hit the bottom of the ball and even the turf an inch or so behind it – you won't hit the ground, but try to' – he lets drop the secret.

'It may interest you all to know that when I tell people at a clinic that I'm going to draw a ball (and I'd look a right Charlie if it didn't draw), I always *think behind the ball*. I concentrate behind the ball. After all, it doesn't matter if I overdraw it ... So, to hit early, *think behind the ball.*'

John Jacobs's comfortable ways with his pupils, allied with his teaching wisdom, has appealed to those golfing members of Europe's royal families who have sought his help. Like King Hassan of Morocco, they know they are assured of the professor's uninhibited, down-to-earth attention.

King Juan Carlos of Spain, in the days before General Franco's demise, appeared frequently at eight o'clock of a Madrid morning on the practice tee at Puerta de Hierro. There, he would get in his half-hour with the teacher before the sessions for the young Spanish assistants and the promising caddies, with the senior professionals looking on, began.

King Constantine of Greece was, likewise, a pupil at the centre at Sandown Park, ready to take his turn with the rest.

Prince Friso, son of Prince Claus of the Netherlands, another royal adherent, attends from time to time at Meon Valley, near Southampton.

The Belgian royal family play it differently. Their preference has been for Jacobs to stay with them for two or three weeks at their castle in the Ardennes or for a week or so at Laeken, in Brussels. That way they are assured of his undivided attention. For the late King Leopold, King Baudoin and Princess Liliane, Jacobs's visits have provided some diversion from the usual round.

An overnight stay in the 1960s with King Leopold at Le Zoute, some 60 miles north-west of Brussels, on the Belgian coast, a day's golf, an evening's discourse reinforced by shrimps and beer, 'was one of those times always to remember'. So, too was a drive together into the heart of Luxembourg for lunch at the castle, Colmar Berg, with the King's daughter, the Grand Duchess Josephine Charlotte, married to the Grand Duke Jean: 'Funny how these things stick in the mind – I shot a 66 that afternoon on the local course, not unlike an easier Sunningdale ... Whenever I teach visitors from Luxembourg at my schools in Spain, I am always reminded of that day.'

Rather more electrifying were the stays with the family in the Ardennes before the shooting season began in the autumn. The local golf course, six or seven miles away, was normally reached 'in an enormous shooting-brake along narrow, winding roads'. Once, however, the visitor was treated to a ride in the princess's 12-cylinder Ferrari. It was an interesting journey: 'Eighty and ninety miles an hour along those deserted, twisting lanes – I've never been so scared in all my life ...' A round of golf and six 3-putt greens later, a return lift was suggested. 'Only,' said the teacher, 'if I am allowed to drive ...'

Jacobs made it a feature of his larger golf-centre operations that there should always be available at each establishment good teaching assistants, trained by him, to help customers with their games. Personally taught to teach by him, those who made the grade, either in that or in a managerial capacity, had a special opportunity to absorb the teaching art. The competition to find a place in a John Jacobs golf centre was strong.

The examples of those who have gone on to establish themselves in their own right are many: Brian Plucknett, at Flackwell Heath, Buckinghamshire; Peter Ballingall, at Barnham Broom, near Norwich; Donald Crawley, late of Northampton and now with Jacobs's Practical Golf Schools in the United States; Sean Geddes at Worthing, Sussex; Robert Catley-Smith at Sandown; Alan Dobbins at Temple, near Maidenhead; and, rather specially, John Corby, the director of Delapre Park, Northampton, and the now widely experienced Vivien Saunders. A former Ladies' British Open winner, the first European to qualify for the US women's PGA tour, and currently in the top flight of instructors, female or male, Miss Saunders is presently teaching the English ladies' team and, at John Jacobs's suggestion, the Curtis Cup hopefuls.

Added to the list of successes are the three senior musketeers from Jacobs's Sandy Lodge years – Talbot, Fox and Patterson – and the teaching staffs at his schools in the United Kingdom, Europe and the United States.

Imitation in golf is important on two counts: for the young learning to play the game by watching the masters, and for the emergent instructors who are bent upon developing a teaching theme. Bernard Gallacher, who, from his teenage years, has been a witness to Jacobs's work in a variety of roles, and who possesses an acute golfing eye, is well placed to judge:

'The thing about John is his enthusiasm for the game – he really *likes* to play golf. And now that he is into his sixties, that is a great thing for him. It spills over into his teaching. Watch him when he is having a look at one of the tour players. John is working with him, carrying his load with him, understanding what's going on in his mind. You can feel his enthusiasm. It transmits itself to those whom he is helping. It's one of the reasons why he still has the motivation to go on travelling so much and working so hard.

'If John has a spare day in the winter, he'll ring up and come up here to Wentworth for a round. He's great to play with, because you feel he's enjoying what he's doing – and, what's more, he still likes to take the money. His appetite for the game is still as strong as ever.

'I know his teaching so well now that he has made it easy for me – and I don't doubt for a lot of others as well – to teach. In a word, I just teach what John teaches. It's as simple as that. It all starts from impact and what the ball is doing in relation to the clubface and the pupil's swing-path and angle of attack . . . what the two planes of the swing – the arms and the shoulders – are giving in terms of the flight of the ball . . . He has made it so logical and straightforward and uncomplicated that it's easy to follow – and to impart.'

It is Jacobs's enthusiasm for golf, and his transparent interest in seeing others obtain enjoyment from it – not least those whose upbringing was not as favoured as his – which has stimulated him in the creation of the golf-centre concept. For the golfing fraternity at large, he sees it as a design for pleasure. The satisfaction he has derived from watching these enterprises succeed, and seeing the principle accepted by the United Kingdom's Sports Council as a means of meeting the game's expanding needs, is the pay-off for the hard lessons which were learned in the embryo years.

The centre at Sandown Park, the first of its kind to be built in Britain, is particularly close to his heart. He spoke about it in his St Andrews address in May 1985. They were pioneering days, when budgets were tight and capital costs had to be pared right down:

'When the 9-hole, conventional-length course was constructed inside the racecourse (the driving range and the par-3 course had preceded it), we ploughed what was barley stubble in November and after a winter fallow the land was worked during the following spring. In August, I had two happy weeks riding on a bulldozer pushing the soil into position. A team of university students, on vacation, was hired with rakes, forks and other implements, to knock off the rough edges. The whole area was seeded in September of that year – 1968 – and was opened for play the following June.

'The total cost, at the prices of the late 1960s, was under £10,000. No one could have described it as a great golf course, but, at some 3000 yards, with a par of 34, it has given endless pleasure to many people. Those who began their golf on the range at Sandown and then moved on to the shorter par-3 course were eventually able to obtain, on the [conventional-length, 9-hole] course, an official handicap, which became their passport in the game.'

All that was some twenty years ago. Now the centre is controlled and managed by United Racecourses, owners of Sandown (and Epsom and Kempton Park), from whom the seventy acres of land had originally been leased. Peter Wynn, United Racecourses' commercial executive in the company's leisure development division, describes the current picture.

'We took over the centre in May 1984, and anticipate further capital investment to have reached £110,000 by 1987, concentrated mainly on the driving range, clubhouse and course machinery. This excludes a proposed £120,000 extension to incorporate a snooker club and a further £60,000 to £100,000 on extensive improvements to existing buildings, planned for late 1987–88. The return on the investment [pre-tax] is around thirty per cent.

'The number of golfers passing through the centre each year is in the order of 80,000. An estimated 50,000 balls are hit on a busy weekend day and some four million in a full year, a staggering total. Monthly takings from the golf shop vary [according to the season] from about £4000 to £11,000, with an average of around £7500. Competition is now very strong in this [merchandizing] area, and, related to capital tied up in stock, and administrative costs, this is not a great money earner for us.

'Lessons continue to be a crucial part of the business. This is largely attributable to John Jacobs's early work (ten years on, some people still refer to it as the John Jacobs golf centre) and to his "legacy", Robert Catley-Smith.* In 1986 Robert gave over 2500 lessons; 360 in one month alone.'

Market research recently undertaken by the company revealed some interesting facts for a centre of Sandown's medium size. The day and evening survey, taken between 8.00 am and 11.00 pm during the period 13–20 March 1986, showed that 79.1 per cent of users were male and 20.9 per cent female. Of the various age groups, 3.1 per cent were under eighteen, 36 per cent between eighteen and thirty-five, 42 per cent between thirty-five and fifty-five, while 17.8 per cent were over fifty-five, in a sample of 129 customers.

The social groups among the clientele were unexpectedly widely spread, as follows. 17%: A (higher managers and professionals); 10%: B (intermediate managers – bank managers and senior managers); 15.5%: C1 (supervisory positions, low-grade managers, foremen); 27.9%: C2 (skilled manual, plumbers, etc.); 3.8%: D (semi-skilled); 0.7%: E (unemployed); 24.8%: F (retired, housewives,

*Robert Catley-Smith joined the Sandown centre under Jacobs as an eighteen-year-old assistant in 1970 and learned to teach under the professor.

students). Such is the drawing – earning – power of a medium-size golf centre, built inside a racecourse.

Jacobs had learned in boyhood about land and soil. The hours passed on the course on Lindrick common, playing round and round and absorbing instinctively as he went the skills of the outdoor staff, taught him the rudiments of the greenkeeping art. Sometimes on a Saturday morning he would mow four greens by hand, treating each as if it was his own possession. Getting the lines of the cut dead straight was paramount; there must never be a visible deviation nor any sign of loose clippings left behind. Glancing back at the green as he left it, he felt a pride in the job he had done. It may not have been perfection, but that had certainly been his aim.

There is nothing which, in these later years, brings Jacobs greater pleasure than fashioning a new golf course, remaking an old hole to his taste, or putting together a golf centre on a piece of fertile land. The instinct was bred into him in the impressionable years. It follows that he sees the opportunity to design the new South course at Wentworth, in company with his old mate, Gary Player, and, indeed, the local district council's projected golf centre development at Wycombe, set high up in Buckinhamshire's Chiltern Hills, as attractive challenges.

Golf-course and golf-centre design work, which he and his associate, David Pottage, a civil engineer by training, do together, fits neatly into the pattern of Jacobs's busy round. The drill is always now the same. Jacobs, having seen the chosen land and committed its terrain and features to memory, puts his first layout down on plan. There will, perforce, be changes in detail, but that first impression will not easily be varied.

The thirty-nine-year-old Pottage, another direct Yorkshireman, with a fair share of practical, down-to-earth qualities, supplies the back-up – the technicalities, the admin and the executive needs. It suits Jacobs that this former local government officer has been prepared to found and fund his own company, John Jacobs Golf Associated Ltd,* and manage its affairs, thus leaving Jacobs free 'to paint on a broad canvas' untrammelled by detail and the time-eating chores of modern company life.

David Pottage in the United Kingdom, and Shelby Futch, the chief executive of the Practical Golf Schools in the United States, are

*Another interest must be declared. I am the non-executive chairman of David Pottage's recently-formed company.

nowadays the linchpins in Jacobs's business life. They shoulder much of the commercial load. Jacobs learned the process of delegation in the 1960s and early 1970s, in his time as Athlon's managing director. He saw what had to be done, picked the managers whom he thought could do it, told them what he expected and then gave them their head. It allowed him to carry out his duties as director-general of the PGA's tournament division and at the same time, 'earn a living outside'.

John Jacobs's statement at the Royal and Ancient's 1985 international conference at St Andrews was pitched, necessarily, in a serious key. It could not, properly, have been otherwise. But this is not his normal way. The talks and addresses he gives to his diverse audiences are usually in much lighter vein – and often laced with personal anecdotes told against himself.

He tells, for instance, of the visit he paid a year or two ago to a girls' school for the annual prize-giving. Having handed out most of the prizes, starting with the most junior forms and working up through the school, with a word of encouragement for each winner, he was beginning to run short of original thoughts.

Finally, up came the head girl, a good-looking and attractive seventeen-year-old, full of confidence and verve. She reached the platform to enthusiastic applause. 'And what,' Jacobs asked her, 'are you going to do when you leave school?'

'Well,' she replied after a pause, 'I had thought of going straight home.'

9
Ryder Cup Captain

1979: THE GREENBRIER, WHITE SULPHUR SPRINGS, WEST VIRGINIA

John Jacobs was fifty-four when, in 1979, he first captained Great
Britain and Europe in the Ryder Cup match against the United States.
The twenty-third contest in the series took place at the resplendent
Greenbrier, at White Sulphur Springs, nestling in the foothills of the
Allegheny mountains in West Virginia. Some held that he was on the
old side for the job, believing the forties, with the narrower age-gap
with the players, to be the optimum years for captaincy. But none
could deny that Jacobs was equipped and ready for the task.

1979 was the first year in which the Europeans were included in the
team alongside the representatives of Great Britain and Ireland. It had
been Jacobs who, immediately on taking office as tournament director-general of the PGA, had turned his eyes to Europe. He had known
that the narrow British circuit had to be broadened to embrace the
Continent and Scandinavia if British golf and the tour were to
advance.

Jacobs's teaching activities on the Continent, in Spain and in
virtually every western European and Scandinavian country, had
given him a special insight into contemporary Continental golf and the
potential of its performers. Just as his stewardship of the PGA tour in
the first half of the seventies had identified him closely with the home-
grown players (he had helped many of them, at some point, with their
games), so also had he come to know their counterparts in Europe, and
their golf. When, to this, was added his own 100 per cent record in the
1955 match, in America, the growing success of his schools in the USA
and his thoroughgoing knowledge of the transatlantic game, his
credentials could hardly be faulted.

Beyond this, he was a team man. The team games of cricket and football he had played in other days, in his native Yorkshire, and in the Royal Air Force, had left their mark and taught him something about team (and player) management. He needed that experience now. Professional golf, unlike the amateur game, offers few chances for teamwork.

Jacobs had another advantage at the time. With the television work he had been doing in the 1970s, both as a commentator and as a teacher with a long-running instructional series appearing weekly on the independent network, he had become a widely known and recognized figure. Indeed, such had been the growth of this side of his activities, with its accompanying effect upon the PGA's television policy, that it had brought him, the association itself, and its president, into controversy with Henry Longhurst. The dispute had a bearing on the Ryder Cup.

An outstandingly able commentator for the BBC, Longhurst was then at his peak. In his weekly golf column in the *Sunday Times*, which had, for years, commanded a diverse and devoted following, he had taken exception to the PGA's recently declared decision to switch channels to ITV for the television coverage of the 1973 match at Muirfield. 'Disquieting aspects,' he wrote darkly at the time, lay behind this intention.*

Declaring his own interest as one of the BBC's men on the box, Longhurst picked out two passages from the association's handout on the subject. The first was the statement that the PGA had selected ITV 'to establish a balance in the televising of major golfing events'.

'Why,' he observed, 'it should be any part of the professional players' trade union "to establish such a balance" is beyond me.'

He then challenged the association's insistence that the 'decision to employ ITV [to cover the match] was made in full committee and was neither made nor influenced by any single person'.

'Whoever could that be referring to?' he asked pointedly. 'Why, our old trusted and much respected friend John Jacobs, who took on the job – and how well he has done it – of rustling up sponsors for the waning British tournaments and especially of getting television coverage ... But Jacobs is also closely associated with commerical television ...'

Longhurst then concluded, 'If decisions are to be made by the PGA to "establish a balance" ... in televising major professional events,

---

Sunday Times, 3 December, 1972.

John Jacobs must surely resign forthwith from one camp or the other.'

This brought an instant rejoinder from the PGA president, Lord Derby. He put it straight to the *Sunday Times* the following week:* 'As chairman of the Ryder Cup Committee, I would like to assure you that we were unanimous in our decision and that we were in no way influenced by anyone. It is true that John Jacobs was at the meeting, but the case *for both sides* [author's emphasis] was presented by John Bywaters, the PGA secretary, and it was on that that we decided to opt for ITV.'

It was a tricky time. However, after one or two of his friends had reminded him that, as a former Tory MP, he should support free enterprise, competition and the working of market forces, Longhurst, having had his say, let the matter rest. The BBC's champion was never one for keeping alive differences. With his critical humour, he was a master debunker; but, having done the debunking, his agile mind was soon off in search of fresh game.

As it turned out, the introduction, at that particular moment, of a competing television interest, when before there had been a virtual monopoly, proved to be a most timely commercial break for the PGA and, for that matter, the Ryder Cup fund.

Selection of the Great Britain and Europe Ryder Cup team in Jacobs's time as captain rested on an apparently simple and straight-forward process. The first ten players in the order of merit were automatically selected. The last two members were chosen by a three-man selection committee made up of the chairman of the tournament players' division, Neil Coles, Severiano Ballesteros, the current leader of the order of merit in 1979 and the captain, John Jacobs.

Coles, a man with a comprehensive understanding of the game, extensive Ryder Cup experience (he played eight times against America) and still a class player, opened the 1979 proceedings. 'Come on, John', he said, 'you're the captain, you tell us who you want.'

Before Jacobs responded, he and Ballesteros inquired about the chairman's own position. Was he a candidate for the team? They both knew he was still worth a place. Coles was adamant. There could be no question of his being considered. He had a well-known aversion from flying; this, and the time factor involved in an Altantic sea crossing, to say nothing of the problem of internal transport within the United States, virtually ruled him out.

That settled, the captain, taking the chairman's lead, plumped for

Sunday Times, 10 December, 1972.

Peter Oosterhuis. Oosterhuis had a fine Ryder Cup record (he had never lost a single in the match) and was tournament-hard, competing week after week on the exacting US tour. For the last place, the twenty-six-year-old Irishman Des Smyth was preferred. He had just won the PGA match-play event and this in itself meant that he was close to being 'a must'.

These things are never easy, but the selection of the 1979 team, in contrast with the problems two years later, was generally trouble-free. The difficulties came during the match itself – principal among which was what Sherlock Holmes might have called the Strange Case of the Two Professionals.

In Mark James, then twenty-five, and Ken Brown, three years his junior, third and seventh respectively in the order of merit and, currently, two of Europe's leading players, Jacobs had a handful.

Bernard Darwin, years earlier and in a quite different context, was in the habit of asking, when an unfamiliar name came up for election to a rather special golfing society, 'Is he a tourable person?' The question sought to discover whether the candidate would make an agreeable playing and travelling companion on a golfing tour. In the case of Brown and James in those days (the situation is quite different today), the answer to Darwin would probably have been: 'No, but . . .', and then all their positive golfing qualities would, no doubt, have been trotted out.

The dress, manners and discipline of Brown and James fell below the required standard. This was accentuated by contrast with the model conduct of the two Spaniards, Ballesteros and Antonio Garrido, the first Continental Europeans to take part in the match. With all the subsequent achievements which stand to their credit, the memory of this period must make Brown and James recoil. Everyone makes mistakes, but only fools make them twice.

Thousands of words have been written about the affair and there is no point now in raking over the details. Suffice to say that, in Jacobs's judgement, it affected the team's results probably more than any, save the captain, could comprehend. Although the score-sheet read at the end of the three days: USA 16, GB and Europe 10, with two matches halved (Larry Nelson was the thorn in the European's side, taking a maximum 5 points, 4 of them against Ballesteros), the result was much closer than that. After two days of foursomes and fourballs, the match was finely poised, with the USA leading by 8 points to 7 with one game halved. There was still all to play for in the singles on the final day.

Jacobs had no doubt that, in the practice before the match, Brown and James, for all their strange behaviour, were playing as well as anyone in the team, and better than most. He saw the pair as one of his strongest suits. Then came the pulverizing reverse. In the foursomes match between Brown and James and Lee Trevino and Fuzzy Zoeller on the first morning, which the US pair won by 3 and 2, James pulled a muscle. In obvious pain, he could take no further part that day. After treatment, he tried hitting balls on the second morning, but he was obliged to tell the captain that there was no way he could continue in the series. Jacobs was compelled to pair Brown with another partner in the afternoon fourballs on the first day. He put him with Des Smyth, the PGA match-play champion. The consequences are writ in stone. Brown's behaviour towards his partner was, to say the least, uncivil. The two lost by 7 and 6 and the captain was obliged to offer apologies all round for the Englishman's conduct. It was a humiliating affair. No 'bloody-good talking-to' or other psychological approach was going to change a man in Brown's mood. He was unpartnerable; the captain couldn't risk him, after the performance with Smyth, with either the toughest, no-nonsense character in the team or with the most tactful and resilient. The fact that Ken Brown, pursuing his young, idiosyncratic way, was eventually one of only three British and European winners in the singles only compounded the wretchedness of the whole business.

There were those who said that Brown and James should have been sent packing on the first aircraft bound for London, and replacements obtained. Jacobs felt that, in the absence of military discipline, the idea was impracticable. His approach, to be fair the only rational one, was that the two players, nuisance that they were, would have to take their medicine later on. Which they did.

Nearly a decade on, the captain still thinks he acted correctly, although there were some among the press and the players who believed that, in the final reckoning, he should have been much harder on the pair. Jacobs takes a different view. 'It's all behind. Ken and Mark have married a couple of corking girls and now, according to their temperaments, they play it down the middle. Each has worked his passage since then and Mark is on the tournament committee and an influence for good on the tour.'

Some things in life have to be lumped, and this episode, for Jacobs, was one of them.

As things turned out, and leaving the pinpricks aside, the team played happily under Jacobs's captaincy. Moreover, the captain himself, and Rita, who had an easy way with the other wives and girlfriends, 'enjoyed it hugely'. At the end of it, Tony Jacklin, 'a superb team member', went with other of his mates to Lord Derby, chairman of the PGA's Ryder Cup committee to ask that the captain be reappointed for the match in two years' time. It was a generous accolade.

Two small, behind-the-scenes incidents added a piquant touch to the Greenbrier story.

On the second of the three practice days before the match, one or two of the British players, having seen the order of events in the programme, warned their captain that he was billed to play in a 'captains' exhibition' at 12.30 the next day, the eve of the match. The flag-raising ceremony would take place thereafter. No one had discussed this with Jacobs; there had been no message. It took him completely by surprise.

It was fifteen years and more since he had played tournament golf and, with all his teaching and other work, he was playing very little. He was, in any case, well past the age of consent. Billy Casper, the American captain, twice US Open champion and once a Masters' winner, had, on the other hand, been playing the tour regularly through the seventies.

'Billy,' Jacobs said to his opposite number, 'there's no way that you and I are going to play this exhibition.' He also let the press know his feelings. Instead, he suggested that the two captains should get their players to hit balls on the practice ground and they would talk about their respective teams. Casper agreed, but in a little while he was back. 'John,' he said, 'I'm sorry, but you and I are going to have to hit balls ourselves on the practice ground, as the exhibition has been advertised.'

There was little doubt that Casper and his confederates thought the Yorkshireman wouldn't want to do it and, if he had to, wouldn't do it well. In fact, this was just the thing that Jacobs was doing all the time at his schools and clinics. Demonstrations were part of his armoury, and none used them better.

The crowd of a few hundred plainly hadn't expected the treat that followed. Casper led off. 'Don't forget,' says Jacobs, 'Billy had been a great player and was still very good. But he was hitting everything with a pronounced draw. He was a kind of mini-Bobby Locke. He would draw every shot a good fifteen or twenty yards from the right.'

With his sense of fun, Jacobs saw this as a chance to introduce a little mild banter. He had never had any difficulty when demonstrating in flighting the ball all ways. Both men hit a number of shots, each doing a microphone commentary for the other. The British captain saw Casper hit three 'very good shots to the target,' each with this accentuated draw.

The US captain turned to the crowd: 'Now I'm going to hit –' Before he could finish, Jacobs slipped in his dig. 'Don't tell me you're going to hit a straight one.' Another ball followed right on the target – 'a very, very good golf shot,' but still with this exaggerated draw. Chuckles rippled through the crowd.

The British captain at once stepped forward. 'Let me show you, Billy,' he said. 'With all those thousands of dollars you've won I know you'll inspire me to hit it straight.' With that, he invited Casper to move round so he could look the American straight in the eye (instead of at the ball). He then hit three fairway woods straight at the target, no fade, no draw. Euclid could not have drawn a straighter line. The crowd loved it.

'The truth was,' comments Jacobs, 'they never thought I would hit it at all, let alone dead straight . . . Although I say it myself, I did hit those three shots super.'

There was another somewhat bizarre incident involving the two captains. At the end of play on the second day, Jacobs and Casper were each required to place the name of one of their players in a sealed envelope. They had been asked to identify their team member who would be omitted from the singles if, for one reason or another, a player on the opposing side had to withdraw from the concluding series on the final day. The resultant 'pairing' would then be regarded as having 'played' a halved match. It was a convenient way of ordering things in an emergency.

During the evening before the singles, with the match evenly poised and everything still to play for, a US PGA official came to Jacobs with a request. The American captain was said to have misinterpreted the sealed-envelope procedure. Instead of putting in the name of the player he would leave out (i.e., the one who might be a bit off colour), he had mistakenly named his top player. Would the British side, therefore, have any objection if, in view of this very simple misunderstanding, the US captain substituted another name?

It was a little like moving the goalposts in the middle of the match. In cricketing parlance familiar in Yorkshire, it was, for Jacobs, 'the one that ran away with the arm'.

It has never been admitted or confirmed, but word has it that the US captain's original 'reserved' name was that of Lee Trevino, twice US Open champion, twice a British Open winner, three times Canadian Open champion, US PGA winner, and so on – as wily a customer as ever a British and European player could expect to meet on a dark night or may be, in the bright West Virginian sunshine.

There have been one or two British captains who could well have given a 'Harvey Smith', sometimes disguised as a victory salute, in reply. Not so Jacobs. 'A proper gent' (the epithet is John Hopkins's of the *Sunday Times*), he played it straight down the middle. He put it to his team that, if they were going to win the match on the morrow, he did not want to lay the British and Europeans open to any suggestion of meanness, bad sportsmanship or worse.

Magnanimity prevailed. Casper was allowed to substitute the off-colour Gil Morgan for, allegedly, Lee Trevino, who, then playing bottom (!), knocked off Scotland's Sandy Lyle on the seventeenth green.

1981: WALTON HEATH, WALTON-ON-THE-HILL, SURREY

A strange and testing golf course played the second time round sometimes seems more difficult than it did 'blind'. A similar experience awaited Jacobs in his second captaincy of Great Britain and Europe in the Ryder Cup match at Walton Heath, Surrey, in September 1981. He had been over the ground before, but now some fiend had slipped in unseen an extra hazard or two where before there had been none.

The United States had selected 'a corker of a side'. A team which, at the start of the 1980s, opened with Nicklaus, Watson, Floyd, Irwin, Trevino, Nelson and Kite, to say nothing of Miller, Crenshaw and the rest, was clearly going to take some beating. But the European tour managed to shoot itself in the instep before a ball had been struck.

The difficulties for the home side – and for Jacobs in particular – began with the selection. Looking back now, it was a tragic business. There had been one change in the committee from the body which had picked the last two places in 1979: the German Bernhard Langer, leader now of the order of merit, replacing Ballesteros.

At the time, Ballesteros was at odds with the tournament committee over the payment of appearance money on the tour. As a member of this select community, he was expected to toe the line and refuse any inducements to compete in sponsored events. Yet he had already won the British Open once and had triumphed in the US Masters at Augusta in the previous year. He was now in the world league and was well able to command large slices of the sponsors' cash to appear. What irked him – and, as a proud Spaniard, his chagrin was wholly comprehensible – was that his American counterparts at the time, Trevino, Weiskopf and others, were receiving substantial sums to fly over and enter the British tournaments.

Jacobs's position, which he represented in vain to the tournament committee, was unequivocal. 'No appearance money' was acceptable as a rule – provided there were no exceptions. What certainly wasn't right, in his judgement, was to expect a player of Ballesteros's stature to be denied the chance of getting the cash if leading Americans were able to come over and grab it. He was strongly supported in this stance by Tony Jacklin.

When the selection committee met at Fulford, Yorkshire, at the end of the Benson and Hedges tournament in August 1981, to fill the last two places in the British and European team, there was a marked difference from the position which had obtained in 1979. Neil Coles, from the chair, did not say to Jacobs as he had done two years before, 'Come on, John, tell us who you want.' He knew quite well who would be the captain's first choice. Jacobs, therefore, put the obvious question to his two colleagues: 'How do you two feel about Seve?'

Coles's answer was an emphatic negative: the Spaniard was in dispute with the tour, he had played little on it that summer and he should not be considered a starter. Langer, having tested the players' opinions and, in a sense, being their representative on the committee, concurred with Coles. His playing colleagues felt that, because Severiano had stayed away from the tour so much with his dispute going on, he should not be selected. Jacobs had himself talked to them and found similar opposition.

For the British captain, it was a great disappointment. He had only a few weeks earlier telephoned Ballesteros in California. The Spaniard's manager had answered the call. 'Please,' said Jacobs, 'I want to speak with Seve personally, if I may.'

The thrust of the conversation was not, as has been suggested, to encourage Ballesteros to settle his differences with the European tour; psychologically, that would have been a bad move. Rather was it to persuade Severiano to come over and play in two tournaments – Carrolls' Irish Open at Portmarnock and the Benson and Hedges at York. If he would do that, the captain explained, his chances of selection, which Jacobs was so anxious to promote, would at once be enhanced: 'I want you in the team, Seve, but there's little chance of me achieving this unless you are prepared to come over and play in these two events.'

It had been a relatively poor season for Ballesteros. According to his exceptional standards, he hadn't been playing well, and spending so much time in the United States in these circumstances had made him very depressed. Although the Spaniard said he would think about it, Jacobs was not hopeful. In the event, Ballesteros failed to show up for either competition. His exclusion from the team thus became inevitable. For the captain, it was like having to drive a powerful car across a continent without the use of top gear.

Jacobs had sought out Peter Oosterhuis during the 1981 Open at Sandwich, Bill Rogers's year. 'Peter,' he said, 'even with your outstanding Ryder Cup record, you'll have to do something good between now and the selection if you're going to stand any chance of making it again.' Oosterhuis promptly obliged by taking the Canadian Open at Glen Abbey in the face of a starred field. One wondered who else in Europe at that time – other than Ballesteros – could have done it. His place was, therefore, virtually secure. In the end, all three selectors wanted him. That left only the twelfth spot to fill.

Jacklin, who had given the captain such solid team support at the Greenbrier, two years before, was on the borderline. True, the heady days of 1969 at Lytham and 1970 at Chaska, and not forgetting the Jacksonville repeat in 1972, were now a decade away. Despite victories in the meantime, Robert Browning's 'first fine careless rapture' of those glittering times had departed. He was still an excellent, gutsy player, but the inspirational putting streak which had carried him to the heights in the late sixties and early seventies had taken its leave. Although he had been having a goodish season, Jacklin had, the very day on which the committee sat, done himself no good at all. A fine outward half in the closing round of the Benson and Hedges had been followed, when the screw was coming on tight, by a very poor back 9. Had he been able to manage a good solid homeward half that afternoon, he would have played himself into the side. However, it was not to have been and, inevitably, question marks were raised about the durability of his nerve.

It boiled down to a straight choice between Mark James, a deceptively good golfer who was improving all the while, and Jacklin. Jacobs put the question this way to his other two committee colleagues: 'If it was either Tony or Mark to play any member of the US Ryder Cup team this afternoon, who would we put our money on?'

James won the vote – and, straightaway, the press had a field day at the selectors' expense, knocking the decision right, left and centre. In his autobiography,* Jacklin describes how hard his omission from the team hit. In a chapter entitled 'The Captain's Role' – which, in places, is curiously at variance with the circumstances as Jacobs understood them – he opens his heart:

> In 1981 I was passed over . . . because it was argued I was too old at 37! . . . Ballesteros was the best player in Europe [but] he [too] did not make it. He was blackballed out of the side. [When] I didn't make it . . . Mark James got the invitation although Jacobs could easily have vetoed this. [He] clearly considered that what James had done in 1979 at the Greenbrier was of little consequence. [So] James went into the side with Oosterhuis to the exclusion of Ballesteros and myself. I have never discussed the matter with either Neil or John, and neither has ever raised the matter with me . . .
>
> If winning the Open and the US Open were the highlights, being left out in 1981 was one of the great disappointments.

Jacobs, who was staying with friends in Leeds at the time, did, in fact, telephone Jacklin during the evening after the selections had been made. His hosts were, fortuitously, friends of the people with whom Jacklin was staying. The captain was determined not to let the sun go down on the decision without speaking with the principal sufferer. He could appreciate the feelings which were chasing through the former Open champion's mind at that moment.

'Tony,' he said, 'I want to say that I am very sorry you are not in the team . . . I must be honest with you and say that I did not vote for you to be in the side, but that does not alter the fact that I wish you were in the team . . . I remember what a strength you were to me last time.'

Awkward though this episode was, it has made little difference to the relationship between Jacklin and Jacobs. And Tony Jacklin's finest Ryder Cup hour was still to come.

The following week John Jacobs was at Hoylake for the ITV coverage of the European Open. The players were out practising when he got there so he walked over the course to the short thirteenth, where Mark James was just holing out. Two years had passed since the

*Tony Jacklin with Renton Laidlow, *Tony Jacklin: The First Forty Years*, Queen Ann Press, London, 1985.

traumas of the match at the Greenbrier, after which James had been fined £1500 by the European tournament players' division disciplinary committee for misconduct. He had made a big effort in the interim to repair the damage.

'Congratulations, Mark,' said the captain, 'on making the team.' James was clearly thrilled to have been picked, and said so. As they walked across to the fourteenth tee together, Jacobs made his point squarely. 'Look, Mark,' he began, and James probably guessed what was coming, 'I know you have bent over backwards to put things right after the Greenbrier, but I have to say that we are both going to look very, very stupid if you go and upset things again at Walton Health – '

James didn't let him finish. 'You don't have to have any worry about that,' he retorted. 'I won't let you down, I promise.'

As it turned out James's performance in the foursomes and fourballs on the first day at Walton Health was exceptional. The press were eulogizing it at the conference at the end of the day. Jacobs said his piece, but he couldn't resist a dig. 'I might remind you fellows,' he said jocularly, 'that it was barely a month ago at Fulford that you were castigating us and telling us that we had got it all wrong with Mark . . .'

Severiano Ballesteros's absence took much away from the match and from the British and European team. The home side, after leading at the end of the first day, suffered a whitewash in the foursomes on the second – an appalling day, with wind and rain driving across the heath. It was a typically spirited American counterattack, but the European side's performance came in for merciless stick. Jacobs thought that, in the circumstances, much of the criticism was plainly unfair:

'As a matter of fact, it made me very cross indeed. In those awful conditions, all our pairs – and I stress it was *foursomes*, with players hitting alternate shots – were *either par or better* when their matches ended 2 and 1, 3 and 2, 3 and 2, 3 and 2.

'The Americans played quite outstandingly well, and their putting, in the conditions, was out of this world. You expect them to putt well; but all that second day they seemed to hole everything, and that really turned it.'

It is sometimes asked whether the British and European players made use of Jacobs's teaching genius during his two Ryder Cup captaincies. Jacobs had established a clear understanding with the team on this point. He had explained to them that he 'wouldn't dream of offering anyone technical advice', but he was there 'if anyone felt he wanted to ask'. Since most of the players in both the 1979 and 1981 teams had, at one time or another in their careers, been 'seen' by him it would be a matter for them.

The British captain did, however, make one exception – and only one – to his 'non-interventionist' rule, in the Walton Heath contest.

Nick Faldo, for whose golf Jacobs has a high regard, wasn't comfortable with his game during the match and had, in fact, asked to be left out of the second series of foursomes – although the captain wasn't, in any case, going to include him. Sharing a ball with a partner isn't like hitting one's own, particularly for the player who may feel a bit jumpy.

In the second lot of fourballs, things had gone ill for Faldo and his partner, Sam Torrance, and they were beaten far out in the country by Trevino and Jerry Pate. Jacobs saw Faldo before the team left the club in the evening. 'Nick,' he said, 'I'm going to break my rule, with the singles coming up tomorrow. Be on the practice ground, please, at eight o'clock in the morning. I'd particularly like to have a few minutes with you before you go out.'

Faldo and the captain had a good twenty minutes together the next morning. It stands notably to the player's credit – for adjustments, no matter how simple and minor, made on the practice ground during match or tournament are notoriously difficult to reproduce under the whip – that he played very well, beating Johnny Miller, former British and US Open winner, on the seventeenth green, one of only three British and European victories in the singles. Quite apart from the wisdom of the proffered advice, it requires courage and character to produce that kind of recovery in the glare of the searchlights.

What was the brief prescription which the physician wrote out for Faldo at Walton Heath on that autumn morning? Here, it must be said that Jacobs knew the British player's game, as he had been asked to give his advice during the Dunlop Masters at St. Pierre some while before: 'Nick had the clubface very strong (hooded). This meant that he was taking the club back too straight in the backswing and the shoulders, instead of turning, were tilting up and down – rocking and blocking, if you like – in sympathy. He had no view of his backswing, so he was getting too much underneath. And this meant that if he turned on the ball a bit quick from the top, he would hit it left, and if he left the club behind coming down, the ball would go right.

'All Nick had to do was to close the shoulders at the address and put the clubface to the ball in a more neutral, a more open position. This automatically had the effect of putting the right loft on the club and giving him a better view of the backswing path. After that, all he then had to do was to swing the club down on that line, turning through the ball as he hit it.'

Subsequently, when Jacobs was on one of his teaching visits to Florida, and the two men's paths crossed, Faldo asked him for a quick check. The advice on that occasion was direct and positive: 'Don't change anything – it's perfect as it is.' Shortly afterwards, in the spring of 1984, the Ryder Cup player won the Heritage Classic at Sea Pines, in South Carolina.

Jacobs's next close-up of Faldo was on the practice ground at Wentworth in the late spring of 1986, having noted the work which the three-times PGA champion was said to have been doing under David Leadbetter in Florida. He watched him go through the bag – from wedge to fairway wood – in immaculate style, remarking to Faldo that he had never seen him swing better. However, when it came to the driver, this produced a mixed bag of pushes and hooks. It prompted Jacobs later to question the striker about the loft on the clubface. Faldo at once confirmed his suspicion that the driver was, indeed, very straight in the face. Since their meeting in Florida two years before, Jacobs had followed Faldo's lack of form and had been intrigued to hear reports of his attempts to vary his action. Being a perfectionist himself, Jacobs had admired greatly the Hertfordshire man's pursuit of excellence in the face of disappointments. Whatever the doubters may say, the British professor 'firmly believes' that Faldo's 'search for perfection' will be proved 'in the years to come, to have been worthwhile.' The return, he feels, will come 'when once the mind can concentrate on playing the game instead of too much on the action, which must become automatic to be totally beneficial'.*

*John Jacobs gave this opinion in December 1986 when Nick Faldo was still in the doldrums. Eight months later he was Open champion.

10
USA Today

MARKING THE TARGET

John Jacobs's golf schools and teaching activities in the United States, covering almost two decades, have no modern parallel in British golf. Forty years ago, the achievement, given American world supremacy, would have been unthinkable; yet it has gone largely unsung. Golf schools and instruction, important though they may be in personal terms to the game's ordinary players, do not make headlines.

Jacobs's US story has progressed through four stages.

Initially, there was the period of the *Golf Digest* schools, for which Ken Bowden had charted the early course, and which set the pattern for others to follow. For Jacobs, the involvement lasted throughout the first half of the 1970s and embraced the time when, as a member of the magazine's instructional panel, he sat with Snead, Middlecoff, Runyon, Flick, Toski and others and championed his concept of golf as an impact and, therefore, a clubhead game. Everything started from the contact of clubface with ball, and the reaction of ball after impact. Its flight exposed incontrovertibly the truth about a golfer's action.

For the son of Lindrick, golf had become, since the early 1950s, a simple reaction game, not one of complicated and often unattainable 'positions'. At these schools he treated people as individuals. Long before he joined the *Golf Digest* panel, he had recognized that it was useless trying to fasten a Hogan, a Palmer, a square-to-square, a Nicklaus or a Cotton imprint upon a luckless sufferer on the practice tee. He knew what he could do and was utterly confident about doing it: it was to watch a student's impact and the flight of his golf shots and, by instant diagnosis, explanation and correction, improve what was already there. He demonstrated beyond doubt that he wasn't in business to fool an individual by giving him or her a 'new swing' or

176

some high-sounding 'method'.

In his original forays across the Atlantic, Jacobs found that his approach was not accepted on the *Golf Digest* panel or in the schools without quizzical argument and controversy – and, at first, some misgivings. But the United States is nothing if not an open-minded, resilient society. The natural good manners, courtesies and disciplines of its people will always allow a prophet to be heard. It is an environment in which results count; and results were what he got.

After Jacobs left *Golf Digest* in the late 1970s, he took up with *Golf Magazine*. The periodical was resolved, as Cal Brown, its golf schools' director, said to him at the time, to establish its own teaching centres in the face of the strengthening opposition. Brown had himself been *Golf Digest*'s schools' director, but had been lured away to join its competitor. Once there, he immediately set about persuading the British mentor to follow him. From his special vantage point at *Golf Digest*, Brown had seen that of all the schools' instructors it was Jacobs who was getting the most 'returnees'.

Golf Magazine's entry into the schools' business proved to be short-lived. The management of these enterprises, which was not Jacobs's responsibility, required a sophisticated touch. It quickly became clear that the generous budget which had been earmarked for the schools was not going to earn a satisfactory return. The project was summarily abandoned, losses were cut; for Jacobs, it looked like 'curtains' for his US activities. He lost little sleep over the prospect. His work in Europe in the second half of the seventies had escalated, his order book was full for a year to eighteen months ahead, and the teaching visits to America were becoming hard to accommodate.

Jacobs was ready to call it a day. However, his two US associates, Shelby Futch and Jim Hardy, both of whom understood the potential which the golf schools offered, tried to dissuade him.

Hardy had been a tour winner in the States, while Futch had made his mark competing on the Far Eastern and South American circuits. Each had had experience as a club professional, and Futch, with his own retail-store operation in Chicago, knew all about the disciplines required in managing a business and making dollars work. Both recognized their British colleague's teaching ability and the personal qualities which backed it.

They put the thought to him: 'How about taking this business on ourselves and getting financial backing for it?' *Golf Magazine* had lined up a programme of ten or a dozen schools for the following season before it withdrew. Maybe, they said, an organization could be put together to take on a few of these enterprises and run them as a pilot scheme. Jacobs, having seen what could be made of the golf-schools business, was won over.

Investors, including an entrepreneurial character named Stirling Nellis, for whose acumen the British teacher was to form a special regard, were found in the Chicago area. A company, Ball Flight Enterprises, headed by Nellis, was set up and Jacobs flew over from England to attend four spring and summer schools, three in Chicago and one in Boston. But, as with the *Golf Magazine* venture, the Ball Flight project didn't last. Nellis, a successful businessman, with multifarious interests, plainly lacked the time to apply his talents to an operation of such limited size. A manager was put in to direct the business, but it didn't work. So, for a second time in as many years, Jacobs, who in 1979 had captained one Ryder Cup team and had now been reappointed to handle another, decided that he had had his US chips.

'To be honest,' he says, 'I was ready to quit working in America. Taking part in the first golf schools over there in the 1970s had been a marvellous experience. It had been hugely gratifying to have had the chance to develop one's teaching ideas with some of the great names in the intructional business, but I really felt that this was now the end of it. Doing things by fits and starts, under changing auspices, wasn't satisfactory. Besides, there was so much to do at home and in Europe.'

Jacobs has retained links with his former American associates. When he was making, with Ken Bowden's help, his three best-known Practical Golf videos – *The Full Swing, The Short Game* and *Faults and Cures** – *Golf Digest* sought and obtained a 25 per cent stake in their production. The magazine knows its golfing onions and as the success of these filmed sequences has grown so the wisdom of the investment has been proved. Beyond this, he is now in his tenth year as one of *Golf Magazine*'s distinguished teaching editors, periodically contributing instructional copy. Unusually, therefore, the former British Ryder Cup captain has contrived to span the divide separating the two competing sides.

When Ball Flight Enterprises' golf schools folded at the start of the 1980s, Jacobs had one serious misgiving. Certainly, with all his other commitments, he wasn't unhappy about halting the succession of transatlantic visits; he was, however, genuinely saddened to think that

*Produced by the TelEvents company; distributed in the UK by *Golf Digest*'s sister magazine, *Golf World*, Advance House, 37 Mill Harbour, Isle of Dogs, London E14 9TX.

his association with Shelby Futch, Bert Buehler and Jim Hardy, with whom he had worked both in the US and the UK in such easy accord since the early days of the golf-schools business, would now be over.

Then, one day, out of the blue, Futch, who by then had gone back to his own stores operation in Chicago, called him at his Hampshire home. 'John', he said, 'I've been thinking some more about this golf-schools affair. I hate like hell leaving it where it is when I'm sure it has got so much potential. Besides, I'm so goddam interested in it. How about you and I getting together, forming a company and seeing what we can do between us?'

With recent experiences still very much to the front of his mind, Jacobs was not at once enthusiastic. He had more than enough on his plate as it was and he didn't want to get involved in what might well be another abortive start. All the same, he had come to respect Futch, not only as a friend and as someone with whom he could easily work, but also as a thoroughly competent businessman. The American was, moreover, now in the top bracket as a teacher and a dedicated disciple of the *Practical Golf* philosophy.

The two eventually came to an agreement and Futch set about forming a company: John Jacobs and Shelby Futch Practical Golf Schools Inc. Futch took on the presidency and, with it, the executive direction of the business. While the control of it was effectively in Futch's hands, Jacobs undertook to devote whatever time he could to the build-up of the golf schools and, most important, to the recruitment of a personally trained instructional team, which he did not find difficult. Nowadays, Practical Golf School's male and female international teaching staff number thirty-two. They cover the organization's nine resort locations, both in the United States and abroad, and the 156 school or tour sessions which the 1986–87 programme included.

Without the drive and enthusiasm which the company's president has injected into the school's business, however, the enterprise would not have prospered, and none is more aware of this than Jacobs.

Shelby Futch, now forty-six, married with four children, had an early experience which had a substantial bearing on his association with Jacobs. As a schoolboy in Oklahoma and Texas, he had little difficulty in beating most of his contemporaries. Wins in junior tournaments became a commonplace. He played golf by instinct to a standard which singled him out as one of the most promising juniors of his age. Golf meant everything in his young life.

Then it all began to go wrong. 'After three years at Oklahoma State

University,' he recalls, 'I was a worse golfer than I had been as a boy of twelve. I have seen this sort of thing happen so often to good young players. They start out playing the game naturally; then they try to change their swings – maybe to model themselves on one of the great players of the day – or else someone, trying to help them, gives them the wrong advice. They head off along the wrong track and in the end finish up, after having shown so much promise, as ordinary 10- or 12-handicap players.'

Futch's remedy was drastic. He gave up golf, left college before his time was up, did a three-year stint with the US Army and volunteered for the Special Airborne Forces. It was shock treatment, but the discipline he learned in one of the toughest of military echelons got him going. He went back to college, took his master's degree in business studies and played his way into the golf team of which Labron Harris was the respected coach.

After his second spell at Oklahoma, Futch still wanted to play golf. This was what really interested him; he knew that. He went to different pros for lessons and listened to the wisdom of the accepted teachers. He found they all tought the game in their individual ways; a consistent pattern seemed to be missing. Working it out for himself as best he could, and watching the tour leaders, he fashioned his game well enough to feel able to turn professional in 1966.

Soon afterwards, on the Far East tour, he finished fourth in a tournament in Hong Kong which Peter Thomson, the brilliant Australian, took in his stride. Club jobs followed – at Highland Park and Long Grove, Illinois – which gave him the chance to take the Illinois PGA Championship in 1975. But it was the mechanics of the teaching side of the game that gripped his interest.

Then one day *Golf Digest* magazine called him in Chicago. John Jacobs, the teacher from England whose writing had already attracted him, was coming over for one of their schools at the Hamlet, Delray Beach, Florida – Jim Flick's club – and would he care to come along as an observer? 'I told them I'd walk from Chicago to Delray if I had to to get the chance of watching John Jacobs teach.'

That was the start of it: 'I met John one evening at the school and talked with him well into the night. I was struck not only by his warmth and friendliness, but how interested he was in my golf. After all, what did my game matter to the guy? He asked me about everything – where I had learned to play, what my shots were doing, where the ball was going, what my problems were. At the end of it, he told me all about my golf game – the reasons why I was getting this or that reaction and what I would need to do to get back on to the right track . . . And all this, you understand, without ever having seen me hit a shot! I was amazed how simple and logical he made it seem.

'I went to bed that night, but I couldn't sleep for thinking about our talk and the lesson John had promised to give me the next day.'

THE ASSAULT

The growth of John Jacobs's Practical Golf Schools in the United States since 1980 has been fuelled by the emphasis on service and results. Two attributes in particular have underpinned the organization's success. First, the simplicity and effectiveness of John Jacobs's instruction and the speed with which his results are obtained; this is reflected not only in the immediate reaction of the students, but also in the performance and bearing of individual members of his personally chosen and moulded team. Second, the impetus and enthusiasm which Shelby Futch, the company's chief executive, has injected into the business and his flair for exploiting to the full the advantage of Jacobs's instructional talents. Years of managing, with his brother Ron, now its president, one of the substantial, independent, golf-equipment retailing enterprises in the United States has taught him all about the importance of customer relations.

Taking 1980 as the starting point, Shelby Futch describes the development of the schools:

'That year – 1980 – we were based in a very small office in Chicago. We started out modestly to test the ground. We ran one VIP school with ten people and two regular, three-day schools, each with forty pupils, with John Jacobs doing the teaching. That gave us a total of ninety people. It was a beginning.

'A year later, we felt we could extend the business a little to thirteen schools of thirty students apiece – 390 people. In 1982 we became bolder and started looking further afield for fresh locations, in Arizona and Florida. By then, we had gathered a thoroughly competent team of John Jacobs-trained instructors with whom we had worked in one place or another over the previous five or six years. John and I were anxious for these instructors to be given the chance to prove their mettle with the students, working on their own. That year we accommodated 680 people in seventeen schools in Arizona alone.

'In 1983 we ran twenty-four schools in Arizona and thirteen in Florida, taking in 1150 students in all. Twelve months later, we added

Colorado to our established locations. That pushed the total for the year up to 1800 pupils. We felt then that things were really beginning to move our way. There was, moreover, a strong flow of "returnees". The results we were obtaining, and the word-of-mouth publicity this was producing both for John's and the staff's teaching was becoming a big factor.

'In 1985 we expanded again, bringing in Michigan and, across the Atlantic, a visit to Turnberry, in Scotland. With a varied programme of two-day, three-day and six-day schools, the total of students served that year rose to 3500.

'The following year – 1986 – we ran 131 separate schools of varying lengths in six different locations – at Camelback Country Club, Mountain Shadows Resort, Scottsdale, Arizona; Fort Lauderdale, Florida; Skyland Resort and Country Club, Crested Butte, Colorado; Boyne Falls, Michigan; Casa Campo, in the Dominican Republic and, once again, Turnberry, on the west coast of Scotland. More than 4000 people attended during the forty-five weeks we were operating.

'In 1987 we have again extended the schedule of locations, with the new Desert Springs Resort in Palm Springs, California, being brought in along with Waikoloa Resort in Hawaii and, the latest addition of all, Lake Nona Country Club, at Orlando, Florida, a lovely site, where John Jacobs is now doing all his "Red Carpet" VIP schools, each accommodating a maximum of twelve people, all taught individually by him over a three-day period.* This year the intake at all of our separate Practical Golf Schools' sessions will number well over 5000 students – quite a growth since that quiet start in the small Chicago office, seven years ago . . .'

1988 is expected to see the 7000-student barrier breached.

Despite the expansion of the business, the friendly and 'clubable' character of the schools has not been impaired. The team of instructors has been at pains to retain the spirit and intimacy which has been there from the start. A family atmosphere, with so many 'returnees', remains. Jacobs, who responds to a team environment, senses this particularly: 'We have always had a fine spirit in the schools among

*Florida's Lake Nona is an imaginative, up-market real-estate development covering, initially, some 1700 acres out of a total of 7000 acquired by the Lake Nona Corporation, the US offshoot of Britain's Sunley Holdings organization, headed by John Sunley, the group chairman, and John Fryer, the managing director, in London. To supplement the arresting 18-hole course designed by the US architect Tom Fazio (two more 18-hole courses will follow), John Jacobs Practical Golf Schools have created a custom-built practice complex in keeping with the Red Carpet schools it is designed to house.

the students and the staff, who have never lost their sense of fun. From Shelby, right down through the teaching professionals, we have been able to give the impression of genuine interest and enthusiasm. They are, for me, a wonderful lot to work with and we all get on so well. I know that Joanna, my daughter, found this when she was working for a while in Phoenix and certainly Rita has thoroughly enjoyed the visits she has made with me.'

Unlike some of its competitors, it is part of the company's pricing policy to spread the load to suit a comparatively wide range of golfing pockets. Thus, a short commuter (i.e., non-residential) weekend school between October and May at, say, Phoenix, Arizona, to include two days of instruction and one or two 'perks' thrown in, will cost $195 (around £130) per person.

A slap-up, Red Carpet touch at Lake Nona in March, with Jacobs working individually with each of the twelve participants for three days, and including four nights of 'five star' hotel accommodation, will set the student back $1895, or some £1350.

A comforting provision has recently been introduced into the schools' programme. Such is the confidence of the management in the Jacobs message that it is now offering 'guaranteed golf', as Futch puts it: 'If a student comes to one of our schools and does not feel like he has got his money's worth in terms of instruction, and he hasn't improved his golf game, we will give him his money back for the tuition part of the session.' And how many have had the nerve to exercise their 'rights' under this concession? 'We haven't had anyone ask,' claims Futch, 'up to this point.'

A tangible sign of the influence of John Jacobs on golf instruction in the US in the last decades is the success of the Practical Golf video tapes (see page 178), which have generated such respect among many US club professionals that copies are retained in their libraries for showing at their clubs or for their members to rent out.

'The result,' says Futch, 'is that more and more of our students are coming to the schools because their own club pros have recommended them to join a session to help their games.'

It seems at least probable that the modern golfing phenomenon of the well-tutored, residential golf school will outlive the twentieth century and move in strength into the next. The United States and southern Europe, with their sunshine and specially tailored resorts, are plainly better placed than most to prove the belief. What, then, must these establishments provide to ensure their continuing popularity? Shelby Futch, with his Practical Golf Schools' experience behind him, is well placed to speak:

'We have found, beyond doubt, that if you can get hold of a golfer, improve his game quickly through sound instruction and, in the process, give him a good time for a fair outlay, he'll follow you almost any place. I would say, therefore, that, given access to attractive locations, there should be three main aims if a schools' business is to succeed.

1. You must get results. To obtain these, the instruction must be good. We have succeeded with our schools because John Jacobs is an exceptionally clear teacher who gets results quickly which the students can see.
2. You must show the students a good time. The social and entertainment side of a school, the accommodation and the service to the customers must match the standard of the instruction.
3. The instructors must be regular people. They must not set themselves above the student just because they have the ability to hit a golf ball which the other guy doesn't possess. The pupil must feel he can work with an instructor and identify comfortably with him.

'We have tried to keep our instruction as straightforward as possible. But at the end of the day, it's the instruction and the tangible results from it which score. We've tried so hard all the while to keep the integrity of our teaching so sound and simple in terms of John Jacobs's basic philosophy. From the outset of these schools our philosophy has run like this: "You stand to the side of a golf ball which is on the ground. This means that the body must make two turns to give the arms room to swing up and down. Let's not make our basic concept any more complicated than that."'

John Jacobs's view on this point is remembered by Futch from the very first school which the two did together. It is now implanted in the mind of every Practical Golf Schools' instructor: 'If you always explain clearly and slowly to a pupil why something happens, and the logic behind it, he will remember it until he dies. But if you don't spell it out plainly he will always forget.'

To round off Jacobs's remarkable US golf schools' story, it is instructive to look at the related experiences of two long-standing members of his teaching team. One is fellow Yorkshireman Donald Crawley, who, ten years ago in his very early twenties, single and with no ties, hitched his star to Jacobs's wagon to make his way in the United States. Now established as Futch's right-hand man in the organization's headquarters at Scottsdale, Arizona, and as one of the company's two senior head instructors, Crawley currently lives comfortably on an annual salary of some $50,000 plus a share of the profits of those schools he is responsible for.

The other is Bert Buehler, the fifty-seven-year-old Californian from Napa, a highly regarded teacher of the game for thirty-nine years, the last seventeen of which have been played out in harness with Jacobs, first, during the *Golf Digest* period, then, briefly, with *Golf Magazine* and, since, with the Practical Golf Schools enterprise.

Buehler was forty years old when, at his own expense, he first took time off to study Jacobs's teaching method. The initial occasion, at the beginning of the 1970s, was at a school in the beautiful Carmel Valley neighbourhood of California; the second was in Florida. He went to watch and listen four times:

'I had always loved to teach and thought I knew quite a bit about it until I watched John that first time at Carmel. What amazed me – and the impression is still sharp – was the speed of the results he got from those people. Five minutes with each student, and he had given his diagnosis, explanation and correction. What I noticed particularly was John's way with words. He had this ability to express himself shortly and paint a picture which a pupil could not fail to understand. And he went from one student to another, never changing his basic philosophy, starting with impact and its effect on the ball flight, but always, it seemed, picking out a different point with each person. There was no set pattern applied to everyone, no adherence to the manual.

'I noticed he went to the set-up first. That's a static thing. Once it is right, the student can forget it. Then he would go to one, maybe two, corrections – always simple, always graphically explained, always fundamental. And that correction would, of itself, correct other swing faults which were never mentioned. So, after the pupil had got the set-up adjusted, he was left with one, possibly two, thoughts and a picture in his mind . . .'

After that first day at Carmel, Buehler called his wife. He told her he had seen Jacobs. 'Look,' he said, 'why do I have to be forty years old before I can see this fellow teach? It is what I have been searching for for a long, long time. Just think what I've been missing.'

'That's as may be,' came the retort. 'But just remember this. It's still better to have met John Jacobs at forty than never to have met him at all.'

Jacobs fitted in Buehler for ten minutes after the programme was over on the second day:

'That lesson is still right there in my mind, seventeen years later. My action in those days tended to be very in-to-out and shallow. I seldom took much of a divot. John, once he had seen me hit a couple, immediately told me three things.

'The first two – to weaken my grip [i.e., to move the hands more over to the left on the grip] and raise my right shoulder – were related to the set-up. Once made, they could take care of themselves. Then he got me to feel like I was hitting the ball left – left of the fairway, left of the target. So, having got the grip and set-up adjustment right, I just had that one thing to think about – hitting left. That was the trick.

'For the first time since I could remember, I started taking the ball first with an iron club and then the turf.'

Buehler contends that his experience is a good example of the basic strength of Jacobs's teaching: 'John will take a natural swing and adjust it to get the ball flight and impact reaction that he wants. He won't try to change it radically. The more natural and simple you can keep a golf swing, the better it will hold. That was his approach with me and that's why his concept has been so successful with others – and why, I believe, it will live on for a long time to come. What burns me up is that others, having taken up John's ideas, have forgotten to give the credit where it belongs.'

The Californian believes that Jacobs's teaching philosophy – and there is regular evidence of this in the golf schools – has a special application for, as he calls him, the 'ageing student', the fellow who no longer has the physique to spend hours on the practice tee trying to wrestle with some 'system' or 'method':

'John is out on his own with this kind of player because he just takes his natural swing – takes what's already there – and adjusts it. He is an advocate of the arm swing, the full use of the arms to swing the club. This is, of course, one of the speed producers – and, therefore, the distance producers – in the swing. I really believe that, when a person gets past a certain point in his life, golf has few age limitations – provided, that is, the player is using his arms, getting the right angle of attack on the ball and, with it, a good square impact; which is the way John wants it.'

To support his point Buehler cites the instance of an eighty-five-year-old member of his own club at Napa. The two happened to be on the practice ground one morning, each hitting balls:

'I could see at once that this old fellow's shoulders were working too vertically and that his angle of attack on the ball was far too steep. He was tilting instead of turning his shoulders back and forth and letting the arms swing the club. Every ball was going short right.

'I felt like I wanted to help him, so I went over, had him sit up a little more to the ball and square up to it. Then I gave him the feeling of turning his shoulders rather than tilting them, and just swinging the arms. I'm telling you, that guy started hitting the ball with his driver a good twenty-five yards further than he had been hitting it before. And he went on hitting it that way with this small adjustment. His angle of attack, impact and ball flight had at once improved, but he didn't feel he had been asked to make any big swing change.'

Donald Crawley, from a later generation, sees Jacobs's US golf schools business through the eyes of one who, having won the British PGA's trainee of the year award in 1978, and worked under Jacobs at the Delapre Park golf centre at Northampton, had 'to start all over again as a pre-apprentice in America'.

It was a difficult process. But his earlier association with Jacobs and the fact that he had learned to teach under his tutelage, gave him the chance to work for John Cleland, head professional at the Exmoor Country Club, on the north shore of Chicago:

'I didn't know what to expect . . . I hardly knew anyone in the whole country, but John Cleland turned out to be a tremendous person and made me feel very welcome.

'My job was to teach the members and to promote the John Jacobs's golf schools with which I was also connected. John's name was then spreading fast and the golfing public in Chicago were falling over themselves to get a golf lesson from the teaching staff at Exmoor. The pros there in 1980 – John Cleland himself, Hank Haney, who has since made such a name for himself as a teacher and to whom Mark O'Meara gives so much credit for his own advance, and Rick Silverman, who is still teaching part-time at the schools – were all, like me, associated in some way with John Jacobs's schools, as well as running the day-to-day activities of the country club. In the winter, when the weather closed golf down in the Chicago area, we all went off and worked in John's schools until the spring . . .

'The facilities for golf at Exmoor were tremendous. We charged $15 for half an hour's lesson; I kept eighty per cent of that, twenty per cent going to the head pro, while I was also on a monthly retainer. I was living nearby in a one-bedroom flat for $40 a week. The rewards were very good. In two months at Exmoor in 1980, I made as much money as I had done in the whole of 1979 – I think the English accent helped a bit! – but we worked very hard.

My typical day started at the club at 6.30am when the first job was to bring up the electric golf carts and help set up the driving range. Then I had to be available for lessons from 8.00am till 7.00pm. If I wasn't teaching I would help in the golf shop and with the running of the members' tournament (there was one most days) and the various business outings . . .

'The country club life was vastly different from anything I had seen in England. The whole golf business in the States is very service-orientated. Fees are high and members expect first-class treatment a hundred per cent of the time – and that's what, nowadays, we always aim to give the students at the Practical Golf Schools.'

One thing led to another for this go-ahead young Englishman – including a locally sponsored spell competing on the South American circuit – but, as he readily admits, wherever he went it was his association with Jacobs, and the fact that he had learned to teach under him, that opened the doors. Indeed, it was this which first brought him into contact with Shelby Futch at Delapre Park in the late seventies. Futch, Buehler and Jim Hardy had flown over to England to do a golf school there with Jacobs. Crawley, then the senior assistant at the centre, absorbed all the teaching. In particular, it was the short-game tuition, which Futch was himself giving, that caught his interest.

Futch remembers his first meeting with the young Englishman:

'I noticed Donald right off, not because I was aware of John Jacobs's opinion of him, but because he was small of stature and always standing there in the background, behind the students, quiet as a mouse, but obviously keenly interested in how I was teaching the short game. Every time I turned around, there he was watching everything I did, listening to everything I said.

'At the end of the day, he came up to me. "I appreciate you letting me watch," he said. "I found it all quite fascinating. Thank you very much." That was all.'

Four years later, in the United States, Futch offered Crawley a full-time job with the Practical Golf Schools' company in Arizona. By that time – it was 1983 – the Englishman had decided that his future lay in teaching the game rather than playing it, much as he liked competing:

'I enjoyed teaching and I could see the golf schools were then growing fast both in size and in popularity, thanks to Shelby's ability to market John Jacobs's name and his instructional skills. It wasn't a difficult decision for me to take. But little did I think at the time that it would bring so much personal advance.'

Alongside Crawley, there is another character who ranks high in the Practical Golf Schools' executive hierarchy. Craig Bunker ('a good name I suppose for a golf pro'), now thirty-seven, got his introduction to Jacobs's teaching because, like Futch, he took the chance when it was offered of observing the mentor at work. It was at one of the company's golf schools in South Carolina. He made it clear that he was ready to muck in and do the mundane chores which are a necessary part of the daily routine at these establishments. Displaying his willingness to take on the rough load, and his innate enthusiasm for the game – two things which Jacobs, with his own upbringing, will always notice – he got the golf lesson he was after; and more. Soon afterwards, the Illinois PGA's State Championship was in his locker – together with Futch's offer of a permanent job with the company.

Jacobs recalls: 'Shelby and I were confident from the start of Craig's ability to fit in with the business and in no time he had justified that confidence. Now he heads up the company's Fort Lauderdale operation when the schools take place at the Bonaventure Country Club in Florida. With his three growing boys, he adds to the family atmosphere we have been able to cultivate in these schools. He carries responsibility as one of the linchpins of the organization and now, I'm glad to say, his brother, Scott, is working with us.'

In conclusion, Shelby Futch summarizes John Jacobs's contribution to American golf, a contribution which has almost totally escaped British notice:

'When, in 1970, John first started seriously to deploy his teaching principles over here, American golf was about ready for a change. The Ben Hogan era, which had been dominant in the fifties and into the sixties, was at an end. In an article in *Life* magazine in the fifties, Hogan had said that the secret of his golf was that he cupped his left wrist at the top of the golf swing; and there was a photograph of his cupped wrist at the top.

'Hogan was followed almost immediately by Palmer, who won the 1960 US Open at Cherry Hills, Denver. And no one had a more closed wrist at the top of the swing than Arnold Palmer. We were then setting up the conflict which was to follow.

'Then quickly on the heels of Arnold Palmer came Jack Nicklaus with his flying right elbow. So, oh my goodness!, here we had a cupped left wrist, a closed left wrist and a flying right elbow. How, in the world, could all these fellows hit the ball so well! And then into the melting pot was thrown the square-to-square method. People didn't know where they were . . .

'It all came back to what John Jacobs once said soon after he got started on our schools here: "If golf was about the golf swing and "positions", then someone on the tour has to be wrong."

'When John came in, his emphasis was totally different. It was on ball flight and ball control and impact. If you bring it in, he would say, with a closed clubface at the top and then back again from closed to square at impact, so be it. If you bring it in from open at the top to square at impact, and you can do it, so be it.

'John's point was then, still is today, that how you do it is of little importance provided you can do it all the time – do it repetitively. And there have been great players who have done just that. Today, there is hardly anyone who writes a book in the States who doesn't start right in and talk about the ball-flight laws – or about some awful fancy name which means the same thing: ball-flight preferences and so on. John was the originator of the concept, but he took it further and spelled it right out: "If you slice the golf ball you have hit it with an open face. If you hit it with an open clubface that swing path will be out-to-in until they put you in the big box and bury you. And if you swing out-to-in your angle of attack on the ball will be too steep . . ."

'The people who write about the ball-flight laws today describe them, but they don't relate them to reason and logic and explain why these things happen.'

When Jacobs first started out in the United States, and began to get his swift results in the golf schools, his detractors called him a 'Band Aid' teacher – a quack who patched up his pupils with quick, makeshift jobs. It made him very cross. He knew that the principles of ball flight, ball control and impact on which he worked were more fundamental and suitable than any 'system', 'method' or 'faith' that his critics might espouse.

The students in the schools smiled. 'Hell,' they said, 'call Jacobs a "Band Aid" teacher? Why, he gets us hitting 'em good, and keeps us right on hitting 'em that way. Give us another couple of strips of the stuff.'

11
The Particular Genius of John Jacobs

THE PROFESSOR'S BEQUEST

Three or four days before the Walker Cup match at St Andrews in May 1971, John Jacobs, the British coach, went off to look for Michael Bonallack, captain of the home side. He carried good news. He had been watching the United States team working out on the first morning after their arrival. Apart from one or two of the older ones like Bill Hyndman, there was the usual bunch of new faces, refreshingly young players who were either still at, or just out of, college. Several of these would soon be turning pro.

'Michael,' he said, 'I've been having a look at the Americans. I'm convinced we've got a tremendous chance of winning this match. They've got a lot of young, straight-line, up-and-under swingers – rockers and blockers – who are going to find it very very difficult here at St Andrews with these tight lies.' It had been a cold spring in Scotland without much growth and there wasn't a lot of grass on the fairways and around the greens.

Bonallack didn't believe him, and neither did the other members of the British side when they heard what had been said. They thought it was Jacobs's way of hyping up the morale and confidence of the team. But the coach was quite serious. He was adamant about what he had seen. It confirmed what he had found in America the year before when he was at Augusta for the 1970 Masters. It had also been much the same with the United States team in the Ryder Cup match at Birkdale in 1969. This was near the peak of the great Jack Nicklaus era, almost ten years before the marvel from Columbus, Ohio, made the big change in his posture and swing action – and young America was

191

modelling itself, willy-nilly, upon its hero. It was also the period when the square-to-square method was in vogue.

At Augusta, Jacobs had seen, as he put it, 'a lot of these younger players with their straight-line swings and their shoulders tilting in sympathy, the right upwards in the backswing and the left coming up again going through. They were very much "underneath", nearly breaking their backs finishing in that tremendously "inverted C" position at the end of the swing.'

At Birkdale, in 1969, the picture he found had been very similar: 'There were a number of rockers and blockers in the US side, fellows like Ken Still, Tommy Aaron, Dale Douglas, Dan Sykes and others, who were far too steep and getting in their own way when they hit the golf ball. It was almost as if they were saying that Sam Snead, their non-playing captain, and Gene Littler, with their classical, two-plane shoulder and arm swings, were wrong.

'Even Ray Floyd, who, in the last ten years has become such a great player – probably in the first half-dozen in the world – was then very much a straight-line rocker and blocker. That was before he made his huge swing change, taking the club rather flat round his right side – almost clumsily – until about halfway up the backswing from where he pops the club up and puts it into a pretty orthodox position.'

The straight-line, up-and-under approach* was, Jacobs believed, 'the principal reason why we were able to tie the match at Birkdale. The US team that year wasn't of its usual quality.'

So when Jacobs reported to Bonallack at St Andrews, he wasn't at all surprised at what he had found. He was quite certain of his ground: 'Players like Steve Melnyk, Jim Simons, Lanny Wadkins, Tom Kite, Jim Gabrielson and others were very much "up-and-under" rockers and blockers. Lanny, although still relatively steep, is nothing like as much so now as he was in 1971, and Tom Kite, of course, made a big change soon after turning professional and having to face the gruelling competition on the tour. But there was no doubt about the impression the Americans as a whole gave immediately one saw them.'

After the match – which Britain won, for only the second time, by thirteen matches to eleven – Jacobs sat down for a friendly talk with some of the young members of the US side, discussing in his good-humoured way the pitfalls of the straight-line vogue. He explained to

---

*Jack Nicklaus, in his book *Golf My Way* (Simon and Schuster, New York, 1974), which he produced with Ken Bowden, credits Jacobs 'with his tongue in his cheek' with calling it 'the American Disease,' adding with a good-natured dig, 'John's inclined to blame me for it . . . as a model for the whole nation!'

them that the player who rocks in the backswing invariably ends up hitting up on the ball too much: 'That's all right if you're driving the ball off a peg. But with the short irons and pitches it makes it so difficult to get to the bottom of the ball. It's not so bad when there's plenty of grass about, like you have back home, but with these tight lies here it's a different matter ... That's why you fellows were "thinning" those short irons to the eighteenth – and running the risk of taking three putts from the back!'

The British coach had a receptive audience. Tom Kite, in particular, a student of discerning and keenly analytical mind, was quick to make changes for the better. His subsequent swing – exactly what Jacobs works for and recommends – has helped him achieve an enviable and enduring record.

Sixteen years on, there is a wide understanding in the USA, even among the so-called experts, that, while the golf swing is upright, the body action – the shoulder turn – is not. There are two quite separate planes between the shoulders and the arms. The truth had not been understood by the new and rising generation, or by many of their elders, until Jacobs first went to the United States at the beginning of the 1970s and explained it.

His concern then, just as it was with the vanquished young Americans at St Andrews in 1971, was to demonstrate that, paradoxically, the desire to copy Nicklaus, arguably the greatest player the world has ever seen, could, if continued, result in a steady decline in United States golf. His views didn't, of course, stop the knockers (and some others who should have known better) from referring to Jacobs as 'that English guy who makes 'em all swing flat'. He didn't mind very much.

The thrust of Jacobs's approach has now spread across the globe. As he sees it, the best players in the world today are, for the most part, 'across the back, not underneath it, and the club at the top is in an upright, open clubface position from where the ball can be hit with the clubhead. But because the club is across the back at the top, the hit isn't independent of the body. The body turns out of the way to allow the arms to go through and the clubface to square as it releases ... That is a very different thing from an upright swing and an upright body which gets in the way at impact and creates such a change in the clubface.'

SIXTH SENSE

'When I'm teaching people', says Jacobs, 'I genuinely feel, by what they do, that I know what is going on in their mind. I can actually feel what a pupil is sensing. I've had this confirmed so many times that I am quite sure of it. I am fairly quick to let a person know this when I'm teaching because it then makes it easy for me to identify myself with him or her and make my points.'

This is what the Californian, Bert Buehler, one of Jacobs's closest professional observers, calls 'John's sixth sense'. He once put it like that directly to Jacobs. 'Bert,' came the response, 'I suppose it could be. But, truly, I do not know how I do it or why I can do it. All I know is that I just do it.'

Some years ago, Dr David Morley, the eminent American psychiatrist, wrote a book* in which he paid Nicklaus and Jacobs a singular compliment. He singled them out for analysis in their respective roles as player and teacher extraordinary. In his chapter on Jacobs, 'How a Top Teacher Would Like Your Mind to Work', Morley said:

> Jacobs understands the mind of the golfer who is always looking for an Aladdin's lamp that he can rub and thereby turn himself into a scratch golfer; the man who fails to realize that one of the most rewarding experiences in the game is dealing with, and overcoming, the mental and physical blocks that prevent him from realizing his full potential . . . He points out that 'becoming a good golfer is something that happens inside the person himself', realizing that the ultimate responsibility for any achievement lies within the mind and body of the achiever.

A few practical examples illustrate Morley's theory.

There was a time in 1983, during the British Masters tournament at St Pierre, near Chepstow, hard by the mouth of the River Severn, when the former Ryder Cup captain was checking the detail of a story he had been asked to write for *Golf Magazine*. His brief was to comment on the swing thoughts of three of the world's greats whose games he knew well. He was to pick out the points each would have to keep in mind if form was to be maintained.

Greg Norman was one of the players he had selected for comment.

*The Missing Links: Golf and the Mind, Atheneum/SMI, New York, 1976.

194

The Australian had already got one foot on the summit. Being an admirer of Jack Nicklaus, he had, like many others, tended to model himself on the American before he had made his big posture and swing change. As with other contemporary imitators, amateur and professional, Norman had not been without his own problems as his game advanced.

Jacobs explained to Norman what he was about. His purpose was to tell the reading public what the Australian, as one of the game's leading players, was currently working on. He had to be quite sure that he was right. Norman didn't hesitate: 'It's to do with what you told me, when you saw me originally, on this very practice ground – clear the shoulders backwards as opposed to letting them go underneath, and fold the right elbow at the same time.'

Jacobs recalls Greg Norman's Achilles heel when first he saw him: 'Greg's problem then was that he was taking the club back straight and very wide, keeping it swinging as long as he could along the line. He could only do this if he was tilting, rather than turning, the shoulders. He needed to cultivate more of a baseball swing. I feel that, even now, he has to keep it in mind. The very wide backswing made him a poor pitcher and chipper. Now that he folds the right arm as he turns, his angle of attack is so much better.'

Sometimes by contrast, the British teacher qualifies his counsel. There was one such occasion, in the late seventies, when Bernhard Langer, then at the start of his climb, asked Jacobs if he would have a look at him. After the German had hit a few shots, the comment was brief and forthright. 'People will tell you your shoulder turn is too flat, but it is perfect. You need to swing your arms and the club a little higher. The easiest way to achieve this is to put your best girlfriend in the way of a flat arc – but don't change that shoulder action.'

It is sometimes difficult for Jacobs to decide when to be drawn into giving a view and when to say nothing, or very little. There was an instance of this at dinner one evening just before the Ryder Cup match at Walton Heath in 1981. He and his wife were sitting together with Tom Watson and his wife. Watson, who was not then, by his own high standards, playing well, remarked: 'I can't hit my hat. What do you think?'

With the proximity of the match, the timing was tricky. 'Tom,' said Jacobs, 'if I was to tell you what I think and you then played very well, I'd kick myself, but, equally, if you then played badly I wouldn't be pleased either.' Watson smiled. He at once understood – just as Nicklaus had done before the match at Birkdale, ten years before (see page 105).

Two years later, the year the Open was at Birkdale, the two were at Gleneagles – Jacobs giving clinics, and Watson, together with Greg Norman and various celebrities, about to make a television series. Norman and Sean Connery, an old friend and occasional pupil of Jacobs, were finishing a practice round. Watson had a 5-iron under his arm. 'Say,' he said with a twinkle to the former Ryder Cup captain, 'what was that you were good enough not to tell me at Walton Heath that evening?'

Freed from his previous inhibitions, Jacobs first congratulated Watson on his win at Birkdale – his fifth in the championship – with special reference to his 'superbly hit long iron to the 72nd green'. He then made the comment that the American's action varied. There were times when he was the perfect striker – for instance at Turnberry in 1977 and Muirfield in 1980 . . . The Yorkshireman asked Watson what his problem was.

The answer came back pat: 'I rock and block.' He went on to say that, in his opinion, the standard golf shot should be a slight draw – which tied in nicely with Jacobs's own thinking. ('The fact that the ball is to the side of the player leads to an arc which tends to close the club through the ball.') The Englishman wanted to see Watson's set-up. The American then threw a ball down on the turf and lined up with his 5-iron on a distant bush. As he addressed it, he hooded the club – strengthened it – so that the top rather than the bottom of the blade was square to the line. A very strong position, it turned the 5-iron into a 4.

Jacobs gave his view: 'I believe that sometimes you have the clubface too strong. It has the effect of making you push the club back too straight from the ball for too long. This is what causes the shoulders to tilt rather than turn . . .'

Running his finger over the bottom of the blade and then over the top of it to demonstrate, he went on: 'If you square the bottom of the blade to the line and retain the correct loft on the club, the top of the blade will give you a better indication of the correct swing path and so help to turn the shoulders rather than tilt them. You would at first get the feeling that the clubface was more open at the address than you've been accustomed to, but the effect would be to help the rest of the action and let you turn out of the way going through the ball, thus releasing the clubhead and allowing the blade to square up. The golf swing is upright – yes; but straight – no.'

Interestingly, Watson's case was not dissimilar to Ballesteros's problem at Wentworth four years before (see page 139).

When Jacobs offered Watson his congratulations on his fifth Open victory, the champion's rejoinder, spoken honestly without a vestige of conceit, said it all. 'Of course,' he reflected, 'it has become much easier for me to win majors now that I know I do not have to be at my best to do it.'

Advice sought during a tournament, as we have seen, can present the teacher with an unenviable dilemma. Jacobs's inclination is always to help when asked, for he knows from rough experience all about the torments of competition. At the same time none appreciates more keenly the risks inherent in responding to a sufferer's cry at such a moment. Instinct and perception have, however, often enabled him to dispense a single comforting thought or a tiny sensitive adjustment at the height of battle.

One such instance involved Tony Jacklin in 1967, during the Pringle tournament at Lytham, which he eventually won. He and Jacobs, who was there to do a commentary of the event for ITV, were staying in the same hotel. On the Friday evening before the final day (two rounds were played on the Saturday in those days), Jacklin had asked Jacobs whether he would have a look at him first thing the next morning before he went out. He had, in fact, only just made the cut and was displeased with the way he was playing.

Jacobs was glad to respond. He had always regarded Jacklin as a born winner, though he thought that his action at that time had become a bit flat.

The two were on the practice ground soon after seven the next day, as Jacklin was among the earliest starters. The diagnosis was instantaneous: 'Tony had the ball too far forward and his shoulders were very open. He was coming too much inside in the backswing and over the top in the downswing. Everything was hit very much out of the neck.'

The future Open Champion, playing the brave, attacking golf which, with some inspirational putting, characterized his game in those days, broke 70 twice on the last day in difficult conditions. No one could catch him and the tournament was virtually over before the television coverage was timed to begin. To liven up the interest, the producer invited Jacklin up into the commentary box for some cross-talk and comment for which, even in those days, he showed an unmistakable flair. Nothing was said, however, during the broadcast about the early morning lesson. No credit was given and none was sought.

A few weeks later, the Dunlop Masters was played at Sandwich. Jacklin won with a fine, four-round total of 274, holing the 165-yards sixteenth in one on the way. Jacobs was again on hand. He had in his pocket a clipping from a recent issue of *Golf Illustrated*. A story by Jacklin on the theme 'British pros don't help like American pros' had leaped out at him. He showed it to Jacklin and then said what he thought: 'Tony, you are the boy who had that early morning lesson the day you won the Pringle at Lytham? It obviously didn't do you any harm because you shot two great rounds to win. Now I read this. It really does make me very cross.'

To be fair to Jacklin, what he had been intending to convey was that, in the UK, British pros don't walk in and help their fellows unless they're actually asked, whereas, in the States, with their less inhibited customs, they may be more inclined to do so. Jacobs at once accepted the argument. It did not impair their relationship and, in future years, if Britain's most successful player since Cotton ever wanted five minutes (or more) with the professor, he instantly got it.

The immediate correction is often offered by Jacobs in his friendly games, sometimes with unexpected results. Michael Williams, the golf correspondent of the *Daily Telegraph*, and Mark Wilson, for thirty years his counterpart at the *Daily Express*, recount an adventure they had in a match between the Golf Writers and the PGA Tour at the Berkshire, near Ascot. Williams and his partner were playing Jacobs and Wilson. The *Telegraph*'s correspondent was below his best: 'I muttered something to Mark and he said, "Why don't you ask John what you're doing wrong?"'

Wilson admits there was nothing benevolent in his suggestion: 'I thought a word of suitably doctored advice at that moment would finish Williams off for good and we would take the money.' The subterfuge, however, backfired – to Williams's subsequent delight: 'John wasn't a party to Mark's darkest thoughts and really meant what he said. On the eleventh tee, when we were then two down, he said to me, "Michael, all you need to do is to drop your right shoulder at the address and then hit from the top." I at once started hitting the ball far better, and we eventually took the money. As Wilson has said many times since, a classic case of the biter bit.'

But it's not just as the practical analyst, extolling the virtues of ball flight, impact and ball control, that Jacobs offers guidance. He has always been one for encouraging the art, particularly among the young, of getting the golf ball round the course – 'getting it up and down'. Donald Steel had a memorable taste of this as an undergraduate, during the week Jacobs spent with the Cambridge team at Rye: 'I shall always remember that one of John's valuable tips came as a practical demonstration of what can be done from off the green, using a putter rather than a wedge. He challenged us all in turn, he with his putter and we with our wedges, from approaches, dells and hollows which abound round the greens at Rye. We very soon learned which was the mightier weapon and, throughout what I am pleased to call "my career", putting from off the green, particularly on fast, seaside courses, was always my first inclination. I carried that lesson in my mind for years.'

Steel was not alone in picking up a lasting point or two from Jacobs's Rye visit. His team-mate, Peter Cooper, who was to captain the University the following year, recounts another of the professor's thoughts which has stayed with him for thirty years.

> I had always had trouble with rather stiff shoulders. To encourage me to make a proper turn John explained that, for me, all the backswing should consist of was simply thinking of putting the right shoulder behind the left. Just that: Put the right shoulder behind the left going back. Since then I've helped dozens of friends of mine who weren't turning properly by giving them that single thought.

John Jacobs has always been ready to offer succour to the old as well as the young. Leonard Crawley, Michael Williams's predecessor at the *Daily Telegraph*, a fine all-round games player in his day, and for years one of the best strikers in amateur golf, British or American, used to tell of a visit he once paid to Jacobs at Sandy Lodge.

For most of his golfing life, Crawley had played with a weak, one knuckle, left hand grip, the result of four days spent with Henry Cotton in Brussels in 1936. Cotton transformed Crawley – perhaps, in fifty years, the star of all his illustrious pupils – from a good natural hitter of the golf ball into one whose accuracy earned him a place at Britain's top table. For those who remember Crawley's game in those immediate pre-war years, it was a remarkable transition.

Then, as Crawley grew older, an obstinate fade developed which no amount of 'hitting early' or 'going through the rules' would correct. Anxious to improve things, he called one day as was often his custom, on John and Rita Jacobs for breakfast: 'Leonard always seemed to arrive, on his way from Suffolk to some tournament in the south, at the most awkward time – just as Rita and I were trying to get the children off to school.'

But Crawley knew what he wanted. 'Could you just have a look at me for five minutes?' The two slipped out on to the practice ground in front of the Jacobses' house:

'After Leonard had hit two or three balls with a pronounced fade, with the ball moving well to the right away from the target, it was obvious what was happening. As he got older, he hadn't the same strength in his hands and arms still to hit the ball square from such a weak grip. He was leaving the clubface open as he came into the ball. It was this which was producing the fade. All he had to do was strengthen his left hand marginally (i.e., move the left hand a shade to the right on the grip) – half a knuckle, no more – to give him a square impact again.'

Jacobs gave similar treatment to Jack Mellor one winter's evening under the floodlights at Sandown Park. Mellor, a tall, heavily built man, getting on then in years, had been a familiar and popular figure in weekend matches at the Berkshire and Sandwich. He had played golf in his day to a low handicap with much the same kind of untroubled instinct as he would use to sweep driven partridges coming fast down a blustery, November wind, out of the sky. For years, he had hit the ball from a wide and rather old-fashioned open stance.

He confessed to Jacobs that he had been out of sorts with his game for a year or two, making a poor contact with the ball and seldom hitting it in the back. Jacobs watched him hit several shots before he spoke: 'Because we stand to the side of the ball, we have to let the body turn easily both ways to give ourselves room to swing the arms up and down. You are making it difficult to do that with that wide and open stance. At your time in life, you would find it easier if you were to stand more square and aimed to hit the bottom of the ball.'

That was all he said, but it gave Jack Mellor a few more happy years' golf with his friends.

Jacobs has the ability to provide penetrating and original descriptions of a great player's swing movement and game. Take, for example, his sighting of the late and great South African Bobby Locke, a bomber pilot with his country's air force in the Second World War, four times British Open champion (and twice runner-up), possessor of one of the really 'individual' actions in the game, and possibly the best composite putter golf has ever known.

In 1946, Locke played Sam Snead in sixteen challenge matches in South Africa, beating the American in twelve of them, losing two and halving the rest. At the end of the series, he asked Snead whether he thought he would be able to make a living on the US tour. 'With that putter,' retorted Snead, 'you could get rich.'

When Locke did go to the United States in 1947, he took the tour apart, playing thirteen tournaments, winning six and finishing second in two. His phenomenal putting provoked hostile comment from his less successful, frustrated opponents. Even a winner like Lloyd Mangrum couldn't resist a dig: 'That son of a bitch Locke was able to hole a putt over sixty feet of peanut brittle.'*

In April 1982, Jacobs wrote in *Golf Magazine* about Locke's accentuated hook and devastatingly effective putting stroke:

> It was a very particular type of hook; 90 per cent of the time the bad hook is the one when you have the clubhead working purely through the hands and wrists, totally independent of the body. Locke did not do this . . . He aimed a very long way to the right and at the top of the swing the club shaft pointed some 50 degrees right of the target. He had a very weak left-hand grip and at the top the face was very open, wrists under the shaft. *But then he turned into the ball* – he didn't swing as much from the inside as he was at the top. His downswing was outside his backswing, but still inside the target line . . . His turning action in the downswing resulted in his crushing the ball – ball, then turf; and, unlike most hookers who hit up on the ball, his irons stopped quickly.
>
> His putting was very similar. He did not hook his putts by rolling the clubface through the ball with his hands and wrists. Again, he aimed right, the club very much inside on his backswing, but then he turned through, putting *en masse* with the

---

*In his short excursions to the US tour, Locke won a remarkable ten tournaments in all, taking, in one spell, four events in a row. The critics claimed that he had, like Crawley, a weak left-hand grip. 'Fair enough,' he said, 'I take the cheques with the right.'

body, with no independent hand/wrist action. That was why his stroke was so dependable and why he was so good a putter.

BEATING THE COMPUTER

There came to Britain in the mid-1960s, when the big ball—small ball controversy was at its height, an American Anglophile named Dean Cassell. Then fortyish, he was a vice-president of the Acushnet company, makers of the Titleist golf ball, still, after some four decades, widely regarded as one of the most accurate golf balls ever made. Cassell, a good amateur golfer, was a product of the American college system, the United States navy and the Harvard Business School. He had been sent over by his New Bedford-based company for a specific purpose. The Royal and Ancient Golf Club, in an attempt to settle the so-called 'ball controversy', were toying with the idea of introducing a compromise ball of 1.66-inch diameter, halfway between the small British and larger American sizes. The US manufacturers and the US tour players were dead against it and it was part of Cassell's remit to assist quietly in getting the infant strangled at birth. They all knew the existing US 1.68 size, properly made, was the right answer.

One of Cassell's first ports of call on his original mission to London was John Jacobs's office in Baker Street: 'It was kind of romantic finding oneself in the street made famous by Sherlock Holmes. It wasn't long before I found there was something else compelling about it. John Jacobs's mind penetrated to the heart of the golf-ball problem – and the golf game, for that matter – rather, as we read, the great detective probed the cases that were brought to him. Intellectually, he seemed to me to have a broader and deeper vision than I had previously experienced with the run of pros back in the States.'

By the time the ball issue had been settled, Cassell, who had contributed much to its solution, had persuaded Jacobs to join Acushnet from MacGregor. The Yorkshireman had, by then, begun to work for the *Golf Digest* panel and in the magazine's schools. Cassell was fully aware of the impression he was making in the USA with the apparent novelty of his ball-flight doctrine. With his eye for salesmanship, he reckoned there must be scope for exploiting the Jacobs message for the good of the average American golfer. As a low-handicap player himself, he understood Jacobs's approach and had, indeed, benefited from it.

One day, he put an idea to Jacobs: 'We have in our research and development side at Acushnet sophisticated electronic equipment for measuring and recording ball-flight characteristics and swing paths and angles of attack. We believe we could adapt this to your teaching concept and, in time, produce a device which could be used indoors to show a golfer how he was swinging and how the ball was behaving after impact . . .'

For the next two years Acushnet invested substantial resources in advancing and perfecting the system, as Jacobs well recalls: 'With their high-speed cameras, computers and other electronic equipment, they had got to the point where they could actually measure the clubface position, the swing path and the angle of attack at impact. All the information was then fed into a computer and came out, in the printout, as a genuine ball-flight pattern.

'Once I knew which figures represented what, when someone hit a ball in front of me, I found I could beat the computer by calling out in sequence what I saw: "3 – down, out-to-in . . . 2 – clubface open . . . 4 – angle steep . . . etc., etc." Actually to have figures put on them, and to be able to see the ball-flight printout, was fascinating.'

Dick Aultman, who was working at the time with Jacobs at the *Golf Digest* schools, was retained by Acushnet in connection with this development: 'John only wanted to know the impact factors, and Acushnet's highly technical equipment gave them to him. Occasionally, I remember, it would produce readings which didn't correspond with what John's eye had seen. When this happened, and the equipment was tested, *it* was always found to be at fault – not John. The truth was that John's eye was more accurate than the computer. He had the geometry and the ballistics of impact down to a science.'

Acushnet reckoned that the device could be marketed for around $1500. However, well before this point had been reached, the company had been acquired by the US conglomerate American Brands. The project was stopped by the new masters and two years' work and effort was summarily brought to an end.

Dean Cassell quit Acushnet and moved on to the presidency of the Dunlop Sports company, US offshoot of the British parent. Jacobs followed suit, working for the international company both in the United Kingdom and America. This gave him the opportunity to develop what came to be known loosely as his 'anti-slice' clubs. Jacobs and Cassell had given serious thought to them in their time together at Acushnet and the Yorkshireman had written a number of papers for the company on the concept. It rested on the belief that, in the design and production of 'easy' golf clubs, there were 'certain basic variants'.

These could be exploited as an aid for the average golfer in counteracting his weak traits. Jacobs believed there was 'tremendous merit and potential' in their development. He summarizes the principal variants as follows:

The loft: The straighter the face, the greater the tendency for the ball to slice. Loft is the great forgiver. Apply more loft, and weight the clubhead up at the top (instead of in the sole) to counteract the higher trajectory and there, at once, is an 'easier' driver.

The lie: The lie variant is very relevant to the face of the club. A flat lie gives an open face and is therefore anti-hook. An upright lie gives a closed clubface and is anti-slice. The lie can therefore be tailored to suit the player's characteristics.

Grip thickness: A thinner grip encourages fingers, hands and wrists to work, and helps to close what would otherwise be an open clubface. This assists the slicer. A thicker grip promotes the use of the arms and slows down the closure of the clubface – the antidote for the hooker. (Allied to grip thickness is, of course, the type of shaft. A soft shaft tends to make up for a lack of wrist and hand action, and allows the clubhead to catch up quickly – the panacea for the slicer. A very stiff shaft tends to leave the clubhead behind – the answer for the hooker.)

Top edge of club: If the top edge of an iron club is set off – laid off – to a greater angle to the bottom edge of the blade, a more inside swing is encouraged. This helps those whose tendency is to swing too much 'underneath' – too much 'up and under' – and, therefore, to rock and block. Conversely, if the angle is narrowed and brought more into line with the bottom of the blade – a stronger clubface position – this helps to counteract too flat, too shallow a swing, and so assists the player whose tendency is to 'fan it too much open' going back.

When Dunlop marketed the first Jacobs 'anti-slice' clubs in the United States in 1983, and backed them with heavy and extensive television advertising, with Jacobs himself frequently appearing on the small screen, sales were a success. Two further series of 'easy' clubs were introduced – for the better player (who is usually a hooker) and for the ladies with their special needs. The timing was unfortunate, for the move coincided with the introduction of the 'featherlite' clubs – and a resultant 'wait and see' attitude on the part of the public while their popularity (or otherwise) was assessed. This led to a very poor sales period in the US and the clubs flopped.

But Cassell, whose flair for selling was to take him, after Acushnet and Dunlop, to the presidency of Merrill Lynch Realty's mid-Atlantic company in Charlotte, North Carolina, had no doubt that 'actual practical tests with the clubs showed their concept to be proven'. He saw them as a step towards 'giving the ordinary golfer the chance to "buy a game"'.

Today, with the expansion and success of the Practical Golf company in the United States, and the similar success that its president is having with his own club-manufacturing and merchandizing business, the 'easy' clubs are again coming to the US market. With ready-made marketing channels and selling outlets to back Shelby Futch's custom-built operation, it may well be that Jacobs's flair for club design will get the reward it deserves.

12
Past and Future

Wentworth, October 1986. An early autumn day, stolen from summer ... The sun had begun to absorb the morning haze which hung over the celebrated West course, soon to host another Suntory World Match-Play Championship.

Gary Player, fifty-one, give or take a month, had just flown in to Heathrow from America, fresh from another dollar-gathering spell on the US Seniors' tour. He had stopped off on his way home to Johannesburg to make his comments and offer his suggestions on John Jacobs's design for the projected new South course on the famous Surrey estate. He, Jacobs and Bernard Gallacher, the home club's Scottish Ryder Cup player, were nearing the end of their walk over the site. A pause in Great Wood, with its towering Scots firs and contrasting beeches, gave a chance to draw the South African aside.

'It's thirty-one years, this year,' I said, 'since you played that practice round with John Jacobs and Johnny Fallon at St Andrews immediately before the 1955 Open. You were nineteen years old and it was your first visit to Britain. Since then you and John have become friends and played, practised and competed together in various parts of the world. Looking back now, with all the experience you have gathered in the interim, how would you assess the mark that he has made upon the world game?'

Player paused for a moment, those big, round and strikingly brown eyes staring out in front of him. When he spoke he gave the impression that he wanted his answer to seem important and that he was in earnest about it.

'Plenty of us,' he said, measuring his words, 'enjoy playing golf. It's a wonderful game. It brings lifelong friendships and it takes us to beautiful places. All that is for ourselves. But there are very few in the game who can actually say that they give others enjoyment. John is one of the few. He is a contributor to people's golfing enjoyment – through his teaching, his instructional books, by his companionship and humour, by his television work and the interest he takes in others, in their golf and in their lives. His input into the game, over all the years I have known him, has been, frankly, exceptional; and he has said very little about it.

'I have seen John in so many different roles and circumstances. He has beaten me in competition, and I have beaten him. He has helped me at times with my game when I was in need of a fresh view on my action. And I believe that, now and then in his playing days, maybe I lent him a hand with his. But in all this time, it is really as a contributor – putting more in than ever he could take out for himself – that I mainly remember him. And always he has seemed to give the impression of being enthusiastic about it – of *wanting* to do it and not because he had to.'

He paused again, 'I suppose, when you weigh it all up, the thing with John is that he has put the game and people's enjoyment of it first. That way, he has given *them* enjoyment – and earned a lot of success for himself.'

It's close to sixty years now since John Jacobs, as a small child, first started to hit a golf ball about Lindrick Common and went scampering after it. Time enough to look back, but time also to gaze ahead. The Yorkshireman has always been, by habit, a forward thinker, trying to keep ahead of events:

'I see golf swings becoming more similar. Young players will start from a better base, with better grips and set-ups. There will be a better understanding of ball-flight tendencies and what produces them. Occasional geniuses like Nicklaus and Ballesteros will stand out, but there'll be fewer "way-out" players like Hubert Green, Lee Trevino and, for that matter, Bernard Hunt . . .

'The PGA European Tour, resting on a common market of 260 million people, will gradually find parity with its US counterpart as Continental golf expands, prize money escalates and standards improve. No longer will there be extended runs with one side dominating the Walker and Ryder Cups as in the past. The best sides will win at home and put up good shows away. The Australasian and Far Eastern tour will go on gaining strength and challenge the other two . . .

'The scarcity and cost of land in the areas of great population in Britain and Europe – and the necessity to trim the time it takes to play golf to suit family needs – will eventually bring about two separate games. To conventional golf as we know it today will be added a miniature variety requiring less land, less walking, less time, fewer clubs and lower costs to play. Ten clubs – the ideal number – or maybe even eight will be carried, and Jack Nicklaus's idea of a shorter ball for use on shorter courses will come to stay. Eventually, someone will develop a shorter ball with all the same lovely playing properties that the modern ball possesses today. It could be 80 to 100 yards shorter in relation to a 260 or 280 yards hit, with the reduction being scaled down proportionately for a shorter drive. Nine-hole courses, shorter courses and simple, pavilion-type clubhouses will come into their own. . . .

'Virtually the same game could then be played on small acreages in, maybe, less than half the time. The need to meet lower costs and family demands would then be satisfied and an altogether new playing clientele – ladies and men, young and old, girls and boys – would come into the game. Golf would expand again. It would be good for business . . .

'Research is now required into Jack's idea of a first-class – repeat, first-class – shorter ball. The future will demand it . . .'

There is one thing which, in Jacobs's opinion, will not change.

I once asked him whether he thought his teaching concept would survive his demise. 'Do you truthfully think it can last for long, despite the enthusiasm and conviction of your disciples, when the bellwether of the flock has taken his leave?'

The response, vehemently given, was immediate: 'I believe the principles have taken hold and are now generally accepted – certainly in the United States, Britain and Europe. I honestly think they will be handed on and will still be taught, as the basis of all sound instruction, a hundred years from now.'

Then, as if to temper the impression of dogmatism he might have given, Jacobs added, 'You may possibly remember that when I made those three videos with Ken [Bowden] we did not involve anyone else in them – none of the world's great players, as we could well have done. To have done so would have been to include *passing figures* [author's emphasis]. Fifteen or twenty years from now they will have been superseded by others, so that would have dated the films. It would have given them a vintage. We didn't want that because, as I say, I am sure the message will remain fresh and go on for a very long time.'

Index

211